What Is a
Covenant?

GOD'S PLAN FOR OUR BEST LIVES
OUR HOPE FOR OUR FUTURE

MARK JOHNSON, MD

Carpenter's Son Publishing

What is a Covenant?

©2020 by Mark Johnson

Published by Carpenter's Son Publishing, Franklin, Tennessee

Published in association with Larry Carpenter of Christian Book Services, LLC
www.christianbookservices.com

Interior and Cover Design by Suzanne Lawing

Edited by Robert Irvin

Printed in the United States of America

978-1-949572-51-3

TO KAY ARTHUR

Ms. Arthur is founder and head of Precept Ministries International. Her Bible study on Covenant introduced me to the historically correct definition of this relationship. This understanding, now the integrating point of my spiritual life and marriage, is perhaps the single most important thing I have ever learned. In covenant we are not only told how to love, we are motivated and enabled to do what we are told. The sum of God's instruction is to do and be what builds the best, most loving relationships. This is always harder than it sounds, but God's plan of covenant is more powerful and effective toward this end than we realize—until we follow His plan. Covenant is a relationship, and also a development process, producing people capable of loving consistently and deeply.

My wife and I had the privilege of traveling with Kay to Israel in the spring of 2019, and what I saw during that trip only deepened my excitement about conveying this information to each person reading this book series. What I saw in Ms. Arthur on this trip, at 85 years of age, is a woman who had the strength, courage, and wisdom to lead three hundred people through a physically, mentally, and emotionally arduous week of teaching. This was one of the most comprehensive and coherent learning experiences of my life. But beyond leadership, her heart toward each person on the trip was remarkable. She engaged in one or more extended conversations with virtually every person over the course of the week. I have never seen anyone leading a large event be so personally approachable and available. Or so kind and caring and so genuinely interested in the experience of each person in her charge. Her love was powerful, consistent, tireless, even relentless. This is the character and heart formed by faithfulness to covenant.

Contents

Preface

My wife, Holley, and I are living out a decades-long, intense, extremely close, very intimate love affair. We have built many things together; we have grown together in many ways. We have learned much together, and we are far more passionately in love with each other than we were when we each decided that the other was "the one."

I want to share the path to this same quality of enduring and growing relationship, for it is available to every married couple—the *what*, the *why*, and the *how* of a relationship built in the way God intends it to be built. God has a plan for marriage. Holley and I are simply enjoying the benefits of His plan as we follow it. His plan is called the *Covenant of Marriage*.

There is not just one covenant relationship offered to us by God. There are two. My wife and I also have deep and growing covenant relationships with God. As a result, our lives are far from ordinary—in the best way imaginable. Our lives may not look overly impressive to an outsider—and that is not the point, by the way—but our internal experience of living, our personal growth, our growth of understanding of ourselves and of life overall, and most importantly the growth of our intimacy with our Creator, have made our lives truly worth living. Our lives have impacted the lives of many others as God has used us in their lives in ways large and small. I want to share the path to a real relationship with God—a living, active, intimate, growing relationship with a Supreme Being who actually exists; a Being who loves us more than we can imagine. This Creator created a particular form of relationship through which He relates to us, and we relate to Him. Jesus spoke of this relationship, which would be made possible through His death and resurrection, calling it the *New Covenant*.

Covenant is the heart of God's plan to relate to individuals. It is through this very specific kind of relationship that God binds individuals to Himself at a moment in time, for the rest of his or her life on earth, and for all of eternity. It is through the structure and nature of this relationship that God displays His love for us, teaches us to love Him in return, and teaches us to love other people. But covenant is not just a relationship. It is a plan. It is His plan to fashion individuals, to grow and mature them, to motivate and to transform them in specific ways so they become capable of living the lives He intends for them. And not just live these lives, but enjoy the journey.

Covenant is also the heart of God's plan for marriage. This form of relationship fashions romances into marriages, then into families. But the Covenant of Marriage is more than a tie that binds two together; it is God's plan to teach people to love, to mature people and transform them so they are capable of loving well, deeply, and consistently. Then, using mature people who are capable of loving across a broad range of human experience, God's plan is to build loving families and healthy communities. What we are going to see, in the nature of these relationships, is a detailed, intricate, and highly effective plan to lead us to our most blessed and beneficial lives. We will see that everything God tells us to do in relationship—with Him, with other Christians, and in our marriages—is *because* of covenant.

Covenant offers us more than an understanding of **what** to do. It also offers us the **why** and even the **how** of obedience to God and His plan.

Once we see this plan—covenant—in its entirety, I believe you will see what I see: **covenant is the heart of God's plan for every individual on earth.**

This raises an obvious question, doesn't it? What is a covenant relationship? Let's explore this idea together.

ONE

Covenant: An Overview

What is a *covenant*? If we are at all familiar with Christian terminology we have heard this word in at least two places: in reference to marriage, the "Covenant of Marriage"; and in the name Jesus used for the relationship between God—Himself—and individuals, the "New Covenant." But what is the actual meaning of this word? What is a covenant? We tend to brush past this word, assuming we understand it, because we assume we understand these relationships. After all, people in these relationships are all around us. We may be in one or both of these relationships. Don't we understand these relationships if we are *in* one?

In the coming pages we are going to see two things. First, the historic understanding of covenant has gone almost entirely missing in our own culture; therefore, it is highly likely that most of us do not understand the nature of this relationship: what defines a covenant, and what sets it apart from other relationships. Covenant is a specific kind of relationship that has been present in most cultures throughout human history in at least two forms: in marriage, and in something called a blood covenant. Second, understanding the central reality that defines this relationship; the opportunities, privileges, and resources that characterize this relationship, as well as the obligations, responsibilities, and duties it entails; and the vast, far-reaching, and powerful implications of this relationship—all of this will be of enormous help to us if we are trying to actually build one of these relationships either with a spouse or with God.

Would you build a house without a blueprint? What if you started to build something with no clear idea what the finished product was supposed to look like, or how it was supposed to function, or the purposes it was intended to fulfill? You were just in love with the idea of building . . . something. Would you likely end up building the next big thing?

Would it not be better if an expert started with a vision for a particular outcome then designed something that perfectly fulfilled this purpose? If the architect or engineer was really stellar, what was made would not only be functional but beautiful. This product, used as intended, would not just function, it would create a sense of joy and reward. This is why we seek gifted people to design houses, or cellphones, or cars, or public spaces, or our clothing. We want something that is not just OK, but perfect for our purposes, a perfect fit for our individual needs.

How about our marriages? How about our relationship with God? Is there a master plan, a grand design, behind these relationships? A plan that is designed to create something—in this case a relationship—that would have very specific outcomes and fulfill very specific purposes? A plan that is designed to build and form these relationships in very specific ways—and in the process to build and to form *us* in very specific ways—producing over time relationships that would be the most rewarding things we could experience? What if both of these relationships were created with *us* in mind, and we were literally *created with them in mind*?

Unfortunately, not only the world at large, but the Christian community, has shifted from God's original plan for marriage to the idea that a marriage is simply a form of contract—an agreement between two individuals that outlines what each will and will not do. We will examine relationships produced by this kind of agreement, for this misunderstanding explains much of the current confusion surrounding marriage, and most of the dysfunction in marriage. Similar thinking has taken hold regarding a relationship with God. This relationship is ostensibly about things we are *not to do*—"just say 'no' to sin." This view holds that God is responsible for holding up His end of the agreement, which is to do . . . everything else. We will also look at the implications of this thinking versus the actual offer God extends to each of us.

A covenant is not a contract. It is not an agreement. It is not something *between two individuals*. **Covenant is a merger and joining of souls, identities, and natures**. In covenant a very special union is formed; two are joined into a particular form of one-ness. It is from the reality of this joining that every aspect of the relationship flows: everything we are to do and to be in these relationships. People in our world yearn for unity, long for love, hope for harmony. All of these aspirations vaporize, though, in the face of individuals pursuing diverging self-interests at the expense of others, whether in a marriage, in a congregation, or on the street. Covenant is God's answer to this dilemma. It forges an actual unity, and this changes everything in the equation.

If God were to offer a blueprint for these relationships, do you think we could do a better job of building them? Or might the One who created not only us, but the world and universe we inhabit, perhaps know more than we do about what would bring us joy and satisfaction in the end, about how our hearts work, and about how love works? Once we truly understand these relationships and their power to impact us, we can also see how He intends to impact everyone—all of society—through these relationships. This has been his plan throughout history.

This three-book series will do several unique things: it lays out the overall design for these relationships, rather than focusing on an aspect of relationship; it explores the many purposes of these relationships; it explores the potential of these relationships—what *can* be built. If we are to reach this potential, we need to understand our roles in building them according to God's plan, roles which become clear as we examine the nature of these relationships.

In the first volume we will consider the historic definition of Covenant relationships—how this relationship was understood at the time the New Testament and Old Testament Scriptures were written. We will examine the plan for building these relationships and the plan inherent in these relationships for building *us*. We will examine the general implications of these relationships, for they impact every aspect of one's life. What we will see, overall, is that covenant represents a very complex and powerful plan.

Why do we need a relationship so powerful, complex, and multifaceted? We will look at the world into which God introduces this relationship. A relationship and a plan with this power is desperately needed if the issues we confront, in our daily lives and in our world, are to be adequately addressed. We will see that God's plan is adequate to this task—if it is actually applied.

The second volume will apply our new understanding of covenant to the Covenant of Marriage. What is the nature of marriage? How does this relationship work? How is a marriage built to its potential? How are we built to our potential? And what kind of relationship does this plan produce? A relationship that answers our yearning for happily-ever-after, that addresses the deepest needs of our hearts, that builds us to our potential? Yes.

The third volume will examine the New Covenant: the nature of our relationship with God, what we must do to build this relationship, and how we are matured and transformed through this process of building. Then, as in marriage, we will look at the relationship that is produced with God, and the relationship God intends be produced with fellow Christians. We will examine our deepest needs and God's plan to meet those needs. We will see that the New Covenant is God's plan to build the abundant life He promises in Scripture.

Now, to Him who is able to do immeasurably more than all we ask or imagine, according to His power that is at work within us.
Ephesians 3:20

If a working plan from God has existed throughout history, why do our lives and our relationships and our world look as they do? This is an excellent question, one we will examine in detail. The answer has to do with our freedom to choose our own path. But this is not the most important question. The most important questions for our lives are: Do we know God's plan for these relationships, and have we wholeheartedly implemented this plan so far? If not, how can we develop an understanding of His plan? How can we fully implement this plan? And, are there good reasons why we might choose to do so?

God's plan of covenant is designed to do four main things. First, *to teach us how to love,* which includes offering us a comprehensive definition—God's definition—of love. Second, to *give us a working plan for relationship-building.* Third, to the extent that we are not capable of wholeheartedly and comprehensively loving God or our husband or wife, to motivate us to love to the extent we are capable, and to *change us into people capable of loving deeply, broadly, and consistently.* God's plan produces people who are capable of building these relationships to their potential and who learn to fully enjoy them in the process. Fourth, to take these mature, loving people and *use them to parent children* to ensuring the success of the next generation; to *integrate these mature, capable people into society* to produce a more loving, just, and functional society; and in the case of the New Covenant, to *use these spiritually mature people to build the Kingdom of God.* If this is God's plan to develop maturity, what happens if most people do not follow this plan even though they are married? Even thought they are Christians? What would this lead to in many marriages, and in the Christian community? Might this explain what we see all around us in marriages, in the church, and in our society?

God's plan to accomplish all of these things may surprise you even if you have already been exposed to a great deal of Christian teaching. It certainly surprised me when I got my first clear look at it. I thought I understood these relationships as well as anyone because I had been a Christian for several years and was married at the time. It will be interesting to see if you have the same reaction I had to what you are about to learn. Teaching us to really love even one other person, or God Himself, is a much more challenging, difficult, and multifaceted project than any of us would like to believe, especially about ourselves.

We all think we are pretty good at loving other people, and we probably do have real skills and the best of intentions. It shouldn't take *that much* adjustment, should it? But what is really keeping us from loving other people? The answer is obvious: "If all of them would just

. . ." Well . . . we actually know it isn't all about everyone else. Just . . . mostly? Perhaps our estimate of this relative percentage will change as God's plan unfolds before us. And is this not great news? Because so far we have had so little success changing *all of them*. Also, God's plan is not about incremental changes in us. Which is also good news, given our self-help results to date. OK, what is God's plan if not this?

* * * * *

First, let's see what we already know about covenant relationships:

What Is a Covenant Relationship?

Referring either to marriage or to our relationship with God

1) A declaration of our love for our spouse-to-be, or for God

2) A pledge of lifetime commitment to our spouse-to-be, or to God

3) A promise that we will act in certain ways for the rest of our lives toward our spouse-to-be, or toward God

4) Giving ourselves to another person, or to God, just as we are

5) Something different than any of these—and far more powerful

* * * * *

WHY DO WE NEED GOD'S COVENANT PLAN?

How can this one thing, this unique form of relationship, be God's overarching answer to the problems of life? Let's first think about life's central problem and how our world tries to solve this problem apart from God. If we understand the drawbacks of the world's plan—and simply study its outcome on all sides—this will help us appreciate the brilliance of God's plan.

Would it be fair to say that our most serious day-to-day problems have to do with human relationships in one way or another? If so, what is the heart of these relationship problems? We yearn for unity, we long for love. We find either infrequently, if ever. We want happily-ever-after, but ever-after has the odds of a coin toss, and happily might have longer odds. Why are relationships so challenged? We have no unity because we are a fractured, fragmented group of individuals. Each of us has a sense of our own best interests. This understanding may be correct, or we may not really know that is best. We only think we do. Regardless, our personal agendas are built upon our understanding of our best interest. Our world has trained us to think that our best shot at satisfaction comes from getting our way, from successfully pursuing our ideas about the good life—money, education, status, power, stuff, or fill in the blank. If this pursuit is the most important thing in our lives, everything else is less important. Things like other people and relationships. We accept wounding and betraying others. We sacrifice relationships as necessary collateral damage on our various roads to glory.

On the other hand, almost everyone feels a strong need for relationship and for love. Thus we engage in a balancing act. In order to build and sustain key relationships, we are willing to give up some part of our agenda and defer to another to satisfy them . . . to a point. Enough for the relationship to survive . . . we hope. Even if love is felt powerfully, though, our culture trains us to see our perceptions of self-interest as a higher priority. Let's see . . . what is most important . . . that job offer or my future with my fiancé . . . my old friends or my marriage . . . that drug or my marriage . . . that exciting secret offer from my new acquaintance or my old girlfriend/boyfriend, or my marriage? Is this new way to get ahead, or to meet my needs, or to amuse myself more important, or my relationship with God? And this assumes that people actually care. But what if they do not care, which is the case for most of the rest of humanity?

If people do not care, how is this world held together? How do we build anything worth having as we compete, collide, and contend to get what we all think we want and need? Our uncaring pursuit of self-centered desires can easily destroy other people if left unchecked.

Though the ultimate outcome of this plan is still an open question, the world's strongest move to problem-solve is to develop something called a contract. People enter into agreements about what they will do and not do. These may be formal, written, legally binding documents. Or they may be informal, the kind of negotiations we all engage in with others so they will treat us in ways we can accept and vice versa.

This is the way most people build marriages. Who is going to empty the dishwasher or do the laundry; who is going to make it and who is going to decide where we spend it? The most important element in most marriages over time is the negotiated agreement about who-is-going-to-do-what. We are so used to this pattern that we engage in it without conscious awareness on a moment-by-moment basis in a marriage or in any other relationship. "What will they think?" is also a part of the contract system of social expectations, along with everything else we do to build our images in society. In fact, our whole society is held together by something sociologists term a "social contract." We agree to do certain things as a society and refrain from doing other things so we can live together in mutually beneficial ways. Theologians often describe our relationship with God as a contract. "Covenant" is most often defined as "a *contract, only one written by God*" in current Christian teaching.

Why is viewing marriage or a relationship with God as a contract a problem? First, these relationships are not contracts. Covenant relationships are a completely different thing, so this is misleading at best. Second, contracts have an inherent weakness: they are only as strong and binding as the willingness of the parties to obey them. In practice, if you simply have an agreement between two separate individuals or between a few hundred million separate individuals to do certain things that are constructive, and to refrain from doing things that are destructive, what can we reasonably expect? Our world trains people to be most strongly guided by what they feel like doing in the moment, despite any other consideration, commitment, or even common sense. An in-the-moment agreement based on the value one thinks another will add to his or her life over time is not a particularly strong form of glue, especially in the face of predictable marital struggles and disappointments. Loving, good-natured, well-intended people can live together in a contract-model marriage and get by fairly well. These marriages may endure, even thrive to a degree. But what key underlying issue always remains in a contract? The issue of division—nothing in a contract actually unites people. A contract is an attempt to find common ground between two separate entities with different, often conflicting interests. God has designed a different and better approach to marriage, one that solves this fundamental problem.

Is a relationship with God merely a contract? "Make a decision, pray a prayer, and you will go to heaven; don't sin and you will be blessed," would be a fair wording of the supposedly God-authored contract, the updated and revised "New Covenant" as it is portrayed in current Christian culture. In our modern culture we are told that *being told what to do* is bad. And the very things God tells us not to do are marketed heavily as the paths to fulfillment, not to judgement from God. So, in practice we run into the problem noted above: compliance with such a contract is going to be a predictable issue. Most simply will not exactingly follow this contractual plan—to *not sin* in exchange for some not-very-well-defined future benefit from the hands of a being they have never learned to trust in any real way. In the contractual view, if anticipated benefits do not show up in one's life, will one not conclude that God has failed to keep His end of the bargain? If all that binds us to God is anticipation of benefits, mostly in the distant future, this is also very weak glue that easily pulls apart amidst the struggles of life. As a result, "It is not working for me" is often the endpoint of both relationships. I am not sure people should follow this plan, because this is not the real plan for our relationship with God or for our marriage. What could a covenant be if it is not this kind of arrangement?

What we are going to see in the rest of this volume, then in expanded form in the next two volumes, will answer this question. Briefly, we are going to see, within the definition and nature of covenant, an explanation for everything we are told to do in marriage, within the Body of Christ, and in our relationship with God. This includes all the specific ways we are to treat each other, all the attitudes we are to have toward each other, and all the things we are to do for each other. We will find the reason for every ritual of the Christian faith, as well as the purpose of a wedding. We will see a definition of faith that is more than a feeling, more than confidence that God will—we hope—cause things to turn out as we hope they will. Instead, faith is synonymous with faithfulness to our covenant with God—in our attitude toward Him, in how we relate to Him, and in our expectations of Him, which are to align with what He has committed Himself to be toward us in covenant. Further, in order to be faithful to either covenant, we must first *believe*, and *believe* in the Author, for only then will we reasonably submit to His plan. We will see that faithfulness in marriage extends far—very far—beyond physical faithfulness. We will see that this expanded vision of faithfulness, lived out, is the path to building the most loving and rewarding marriage. And all of the above is the path to building the best *us*; to maturing us, to transforming us so that we reach our true potential, not only in marriage and a relationship with God, but in all of life. Our character, it is said, determines our destiny. Faithfulness to covenant is the path to developing the strongest and most virtuous character. From this will flow many new opportunities in the rest of life. It is hard to overestimate the magnitude of the overall change in the direction and quality of one's life if one simply follows God's plan.

What we will see as we commit ourselves to carry out God's plan is that each covenant impacts each of us at every level and in every aspect of life. Simply put, God's plan is the most direct route to building loving relationships—in marriage, with Him, and in the church. But this most-direct route is going to have far more hills, twists, and turns than we could imagine. We will see that God created mechanisms and powers within us which, when properly directed, lead to the growth and transformation needed to carry out His plan. Revising us into beings who can consistently love in mind, heart, and action requires that we be literally rebuilt from the ground up. And this is precisely where we start in covenant: as new beings with new identities, new potential, new resources, and a new, totally committed relationship to draw from. We now have a lifelong partner who, in the case of a spouse, is committed to learn to love us as we learn to love them; in the case of God, we have a Partner who knows more about love than we ever will, and desires that we become like Him in every way our finiteness allows. "Christian," after all, means "little Christ." How this all comes about, what it all means, and the life all of this produces will require three volumes to even begin to cover. Some topics are narrow and defined. This topic touches, and changes, literally every aspect of one's life, in present, future, and eternity. It takes a lifetime to explore these implications even for a single life; yet this same plan is capable of crafting, forming, and directing every unique human life as God desires to produce the individuals and the world that God originally intended. Yet, little of this has come to fruition at this point because so few fully follow God. This is also a topic we will explore, for our decision to follow God, or not, in general and then in each detail, has more power to direct the course of our lives than any other influence.

We will see God's definition of love clearly spelled out, and we will see what love-in-action looks like. We will see what His grace is, and what it is not. We will develop a new understanding of sin, and a new understanding of the impact on our lives of the cumulative rebellion of humanity. Sin is more than an act: it is a direction, a path, an implemented plan. Once we begin to see God's plan clearly, we will also be able to distinguish the alternative plan that is always before us in our world. And we will develop new reasons to resist this alternative, for our lives are at stake, not just in some abstract sense but in real and important ways. We will gain a more clear understanding of the impact of the beliefs we choose and of the choices we make based on our beliefs.

We will see our responsibilities, duties, and obligations in these relationships, which, though clearly spelled out in Scripture, are almost no part of current Christian teaching. The idea that we are supposed to be passive, though grateful, recipients of everything God wants to do in our lives, offering nothing of ourselves in return, could not be further from the truth of covenant. A covenant is an all-in kind of thing, requiring every ounce of strength. Everything of each life must be given into the relationship if two are to build what can be built. This is as true of a relationship with God as it is of a marriage.

Where can we seek a correct understanding of these relationships? The strictly correct answer is, "In the Scriptures, for in them is all the truth we need to build the lives and marriages God has for us." But there is a problem: in order to understand God's plan we must correctly define the words used in the Scriptures. If we mis-define key words, inserting modern concepts instead of defining these terms as Jesus and those who heard His teachings in person understood these terms, might we miss something important? Might we misunderstand the relationship He offers to each of us? If He is offering a very definite, specific kind of relationship with Himself, or if God in the beginning offered a very definite, specific kind of relationship between a man and a woman—marriage—that was intended to produce a very specific set of outcomes in our lives, might we miss out on these blessings if we do not correctly understand the nature, the defining reality, and the principles of this relationship?

TWO

Why This Book?

It is very important how one views one's relationship with God. In particular, what one views as the main point of that relationship is a vital thing. God Himself came to earth and spent three years driving a small group of lessons into the minds and hearts of His core group of disciples. It is significant that this process took several years and required a total revision of these disciples' beliefs, priorities, motivations, goals, and many other things. Why should it take such an extensive process in one's life simply to do what God is actually telling us to do so our lives will have the impact God desires that they have? From our vantage point, we want all the blessings available from the Living God while we go about business as usual. Should any of us, though, view the needed revisions within ourselves as less extensive?

These lessons centered upon the identity of Jesus; the correct nature of one's relationship with God; one's proper response to God and to other people; and the life that flows from these understandings. If a person is one off a correct understanding of the fundamental nature of our relationship with God, or of the central purpose of that relationship, life becomes misdirected. If one is on target about the nature of this relationship, one can develop the life of Billy Graham, or the powerful, godly lives of many lesser known people whom God has used to impact hearts and lives for His purposes and His glory through the ages.

Thus, a proper understanding of the form of relationship God created to relate to us, and within which we are to relate to each other, is vital. If one's view of the nature of this relationship is incorrect, one will pursue an incorrect goal for this relationship, and for life overall. Legalistic people are—they think—pursuing a relationship with God in the purest way possible. They believe this relationship is based primarily on keeping God's rules. Something goes missing, though, in heart and heart development if one grasps one element of this relationship but ignores even more important elements—like cultivating a heart of love for God. We saw how this played out in the lives of the Pharisees in their animus toward the God they thought they were serving through exacting obedience as He stood in front of them and sought to correct them.

In the same way, those who overemphasize another aspect of God's heart toward us—His grace—but ignore the importance of cultivating lives that reflect other aspects of His heart and His plan, like faithfulness and righteousness, mis-build their relationship with God. They devote lives to things that do not build what God desires be built. It is only by grasping the essence of this relationship and devoting our lives to building what God desires us to build—that is, understanding God's plan and being faithful to Him and to His plan—that God truly has His way in our lives. If God does not truly have His way in our lives, whose way are we following? Whose plan are we implementing? Whose reward will we earn in the end? Ask the Pharisees, or myriad others through history who devoted vast energy to misguided purposes. Much less those who made no effort to follow God's path. In stark contrast, Jesus's disciples learned His lessons, implemented His plan, and radically transformed a broken and dying world in their day, exerting an impact felt two thousand years later. We can do the same in our day, but only by following God's way.

If a couple grasps the main point of a marriage relationship and keeps the main thing the main thing, a marriage can reach its potential. But if a couple misunderstands the nature of this relationship, this couple is unlikely to build a relationship that fulfills its potential.

I was first introduced to an accurate historical definition of a covenant relationship in 1983 in a Bible study, aptly named *Covenant*. Though drawn mainly from Scripture, her study also contained many references from a book by H. Clay Trumbull entitled *The Blood*

Covenant, first published in 1885. I was so fascinated by the content of this study that I obtained a copy of Trumbull's book. I retraced his research and conclusions, comparing these at every step with Scripture. This convinced me that his definition of a covenant relationship—backed by an impressive body of scholarship—is correct. It was also clear that this understanding of covenant is far different from anything I had heard, even from some of the best teachers in our day.

I had heard the terms Covenant of Marriage and New Covenant on countless occasions, but for the first time I understood the essence, the actual nature, of these relationships. Initially, this understanding explained for me essentially every aspect of our relationship with God, and every aspect of marriage. Why are these relationships so powerful, so potentially life-changing? Why are we told to conduct ourselves in some ways and not to conduct ourselves in others? Why are we told to take communion, to be baptized, or to go through a wedding ceremony in order to spend our lives together and raise a family? Why are we supposed to treat our spouse in particular ways? Why does the wife's name often change? What is our relationship to other Christians supposed to look like? And, perhaps most importantly, if we are supposed to love God, to love our spouse, and to love our brothers and sisters in Christ, what exactly does this *mean*? How do we know whether we are loving as God desires and commands? Inherent in the definition of covenant is a clear and explicit definition of love in action, attitude, and heart. The functional definition of love, it turns out, is synonymous with faithfulness to our covenants. If we want to live in the middle of God's blessings, to have His power poured out in our lives, obedience to Him and conformity to His plan are the prerequisites. If this is true then it falls to us first to *understand* this plan and what it means to conform to it.

Very early in my Christian life I became fascinated by the spiritual growth and life change that is supposed to be part of a relationship with God. I had the privilege of being mentored by several very mature people and of sitting under some of the best teaching of our generation. I learned much about the processes of personal growth and life change because my own life needed to change. I was out of line with many things I was supposed to be and things I knew I needed to be doing as a Christian. I also soon learned how difficult it is to change even a single habit or viewpoint. Many steps are required to change the simplest things. Life is long. Initially I thought one just chipped away at the mass of needed change over time; with enough time, enough change would occur. Over time, though, it became evident in my own life and in mentoring relationships that some things are so difficult to shift that these changes almost never occur. We run into a wall called "this is just me."

If we think of something as an expression of who we are, unless God changes who we are *in a way we can perceive*—and as Christians we anxiously wait on Him to do this—in the meantime we just continue being "ourselves." However, oddly, God's anticipated direct intervention and transformation seems almost never to occur. The lives of some are radically transformed in a moment, but this is extremely rare, not the rule. I saw no answer to the dilemma of God telling me to do something, or to be something, but believing these not to be within my nature. I could force outward obedience, but the tug-of-war I kept losing showed me that this was not a working strategy. Something deeper, something more powerful was needed. That needed thing is covenant. I thought His grace was the only strategy to cover the mismatch between His desire and my life. But once I understood covenant, I came to realize that in covenant His grace provides *the path, the plan, the tools, and the reasons* to bring my mind, heart, and life into growing conformity to His desire. And I realized that covenant is *the vehicle* through which this happens. Whether these things play out to greatest benefit in our hearts and lives, though, depends on whether we recognize the transformation within ourselves brought about by entering covenant and conform our lives to this new reality.

As I applied this understanding of covenant to my relationship with God and to my marriage over years, then decades, a much deeper and more powerful picture of these relationships emerged. From an understanding of the change of identity came a new approach to growth and change. Everything I am supposed to do and to be in these relationships is actually a logical outcome of something that has *already occurred*; my life had simply not caught up with this change. A profound truth—the heart of God's strategy—became evident: I merely needed to become in practice what I had already become in reality as I entered each covenant. I needed to cease trying to be something I *now was not*, and learn how to *authentically live out my new identity and nature in relationship with another.* God, instead of being seen as a merchant of rules—some of which made sense, some of which seemed out-of-sync not only with my nature, but with reality—could be correctly seen as a loving Father and coach, trying to develop my true potential as He spurs me to maturity. *What is impossible with man is possible with God* (Luke 18:27).

In covenant we find a deeper truth, a new and different reality. But how do we make the most of this truth and this reality? We must recognize these things, and choose to pursue them. God is simply asking me to be who I am and act like who I am. Does it make sense to resist that? As I began to approach obedience and faithfulness in this way, I began to find something wonderful. As my "this is just me" resistance changed into "I'll give this a try if you say so," as I was faithful to do what God said, it felt like I was doing what I had always wanted to do. I just had not realized it until I tried. As I did what God was asking me to do in these relationships, it became evident that I was sowing better things into these relationships, reaping a better relationship in return. There are still struggles related to obedience and faithfulness. I still need God on a moment-by-moment basis to open my eyes to new truths, and to walk with me through the processes of growth and change in accord with these truths. But I now see what God is asking of me as something I can do, should do, and at the deepest level want to do. My job is simply to work through my remaining confusion. What all of this looks like from the outside is the growth and transformation God's plan is intended to produce.

Another issue is met head-on by covenant: loneliness. A marriage is not two people joined by an agreement based on an uncertain set of conditions, subject to change at any moment. We want "happily," but the deeper cry of our hearts is not to be alone in this life. In covenant we can never be alone, because the other is literally within us, and we in them. We have given our lives to each other and received theirs in return. We share something we can never lose except through physical death, which is the other's presence in our lives. We have been accepted into the inner sanctum of another, from which we can never be ejected. If, that is, two are faithful to their covenant. Even a Marriage Covenant can be broken. But this is a vastly different thing from voiding a contract. In breaking a covenant one attacks one's very life, one's own identity.

My covenant relationship with God is based on something very different from me simply trying, and predictably failing, to please Him. Then hoping what happens next turns out OK based on His grace. That plan is not a cure for the loneliness of the human condition, is it? Instead, in covenant, I am fully accepted into Him, and His Spirit is within me. I can never be alone. I am forever loved because He created me and loves me, but also because I have given Him my life, and received back from Him a new life that includes His own nature and identity. We have an inseparable relationship because He will never be unfaithful to His covenant and has assured me that nothing can separate me from His love. Is this the cure for aloneness? In fact, this opens to me the abundance of Heaven and its Creator, and to everything else inherent in God's covenant plan. Is this the good news, the gospel that Jesus came to deliver and to enable? God says we love because He first loved us. What does the fullness of His love really look like, and what would it look like if I really love Him back? As we will see, this changes everything. But we must play our assigned role in all of this, which is…?

Have we ever seen God's plan spelled out in its entirety? Though Mrs. Arthur's study and Trumbull's book are an excellent introduction to this topic, I have not found any work that builds on this foundation, or one that offers a more extensive and comprehensive look at God's plan—how it is implemented and what it produces. If we are to implement this plan, it is also helpful to see why it is so infrequently followed. We need to examine the internal and external obstacles we need to overcome if we are to truly follow God in the way His plan requires.

Perhaps the most important thing I came to understand is my own role in these relationships. We are to be many things to our spouse in marriage. There are many things required of us in a relationship with God. I have not seen the big picture of either relationship—the many roles we are to play, and in each of these roles our specific responsibilities, duties, and obligations—ever laid out in one place. How we fulfill these roles is one question. We have touched on a working strategy to deal with this issue, and will cover this in detail, step by step, in the rest of this series. Here, simply note that *if one's highest priority* is carrying out these roles in relationships, God has provided a way. But how can these relationships become our highest priority, in light of everything else going on in our lives, in light of the various things we think are essential to build the lives we want?

Let's think back to Jesus' task with His disciples. It took Him several years to adjust their views of what leads to a life worth living. It took Him several years to adjust their views of what really matters, and to adjust their priorities accordingly. And it will take Jesus several years to reorient our minds and hearts. This process will not even begin, though, unless we are open to the possibility that our current views would benefit from adjustment. Jesus made this point to His disciples by doing things right in front of them that only God could do. He proved that He was the authority on living because He was the author of life. Even so, this revision process in everyone was just this—a process. Now we do not have the opportunity to walk beside Jesus for several years and hear Him teach us. Or do we? Once He no longer walked physically on earth, He left His Spirit to be within us. His shed blood and His own death and resurrection enabled us to enter a relationship in which we walk with Him, and are in Him, and He in us. God ordained two relationships, two covenants, to be the heart of His plan for each human life. But we must recognize what we are being offered and accept these relationships on His terms—entering them and conducting them according to His plan.

What specifically did Jesus do with His followers that was so effective? He spoke truth with authority to these people. Then He waited for daily life to provide situations in which these truths could be applied. At this point He served as an accurate mirror, reflecting back to each person what was truly in mind and heart, and oozing out into life. He then served as teacher and mentor; encouraging, correcting, and confronting. He also filled another key role: these men were accountable to Him. They had to look in the eyes of God and explain themselves, then listen to His response. How does Jesus replicate this process in covenant? The first thing needed is His truth, which we are offered. Second, in these relationships we walk through daily life, which offers to us the same opportunity to employ these truths in every facet of life and relationship. Then we are issued a mirror: our husband or wife, and/or our fellow believers and Christian leaders. These mirrors do not reflect as flawlessly as Jesus did, but still we have reflected to us an image of ourselves that does much to cut through our self-deception and blind spots. We have spent our lives creating an image for others that looks the way we want to be seen. And we often confuse this carefully crafted image with what we are. God's solution for this is a covenant partner. Defects and struggles *in the hands of a loving partner* are the path to growth, or highlight our need for transformation. What remains is simply to follow God's plan for this growth and transformation.

I have seen the power of this understanding operating at every level in my life and marriage for many years, producing the very things I most wanted in these relationships. I have seen these same truths operating in the lives of others over many years. Marriages continue to grow and love grows deeper over time if His plan is lived out consistently. In relationships with God, including my own, there is growing depth, breadth, intensity, and passion over time, as well as growing satisfaction and compounding reward. God knows how to bless us in the depths of our being in ways that make everything else in life pale by comparison. Covenant is the heart of His plan, the deep well from which unending blessings flow.

At the same time, though these relationships are *potentially* life-changing and powerful, as we look around we see marriages that are struggling and people who are hurting and frustrated. We see Christians with little evidence that God is present and active in their lives, whose walk with God resembles a lifeless and fruitless marriage. There are many who walk away from God because nothing has grown in their lives that offers them sufficient reason to stay in the relationship. We see people who start well—in marriage or in relationship with God—but end poorly. Why does the life-transforming power inherent in these relationships operate fully in some marriages but not in other marriages? Why do some people grow into powerful and amazing examples of godly character—loving, good, and kind—with fruitful ministries of one sort or another, while the lives of other people in relationships with God seem unaffected? Where in these lives is the power of the living God?

The answer in one sense is obvious: Over the decades it has become crystal clear that the ultimate quality of a marriage or a relationship with God has to do with the extent to which people conduct these relationships in *harmony with what these relationships actually are.* To the extent that people live out God's plan, these relationships grow beautifully and end well. To the extent that these relationships deviate from God's plan, they are reduced or even fail. By the end of this three-volume discussion it will become abundantly clear why this is true. People in a marriage may be making no conscious attempt to follow God. But if they conduct themselves and their marriage substantially according to God's pattern, the outcomes can be very good. There are many successful non-Christian marriages. But, as we will see, each detail matters, each decision matters. There is no marriage that could not be made better by consciously following God's plan. Why? Because God created us, our hearts, and our marriages. His directions for marriage represent the path to the relationship most in harmony with the relationship per se, and more importantly most in harmony with our hearts, minds, bodies, spirits, and souls. God designed the process by which He intends that two be knit together and blessed in the most profound ways. Absent the personal growth produced by God's plan, how can relationships grow to their full potential?

LIFE IS A TRAINING PROCESS, BUT TRAINING FOR WHAT?

God's plan is an intense and comprehensive training process. This runs cross-grain with our culture. We do not want to be *trained* to do specific things or to act in certain ways, or to feel certain things. No, we want to express ourselves as we desire in the moment, thinking this is the essence of being ourselves. This will be another part of our discussion, for true self-expression and authenticity are vital in intimate relationships. Our culture misleads us about self-expression in several ways. Training suggests that we do things without thinking, automatically, reflexively in response to certain situations. What God wants to see are people who do good, right, and constructive things—loving things—in every situation as their reflexive response. His plan can produce such people.

According to cultural thinking, this is off-putting for another reason. We want to be free to make our own choices, to do what we think is in our best interest at any point. In fact, we want to be free to make *any* choice we wish to make in a situation, believing that *exercising our own power to choose* is the path to our most fulfilling life. *That* we choose, not *what* we choose, is the important thing. Our culture has trained us to think that having our way, following our desires wherever they lead, is the path to the best life. What we are going to see is that these very thoughts, which lead us directly away from God's plan for our lives, are in fact the result of a training process carried on by our culture that we are not even aware has occurred. Because of this process, we experience certain thoughts and feelings automatically, without thinking, reflexively. Where did these ideas about ourselves, our relationships, and other people come from? And how have we been trained to have these responses without even realizing what was happening?

If we are Christians, we find ourselves caught between competing training processes. These will progressively form us into one thing or another. If we are not Christians, we have been influenced solely by the world's training—with the caveat that many common ideas and values in our culture were actually introduced by Jesus, building upon

God's revelations to the Jews. Concepts like the inherent value of every human life, justice, mercy, fairness, and equality. These are enshrined as cultural virtues, though people are often unaware of their true origin. It is also true that the current cultural definition of many of these virtues—like justice or fairness—may correspond only partially to the way God would define these words; and that lives in general, and certain lives in particular—like those residing in utero or even those recently born—have been devalued progressively in recent decades.

For each of our lives, the key is to choose the process that will train us for success, that will lead to the best outcomes, and thus to the most satisfying lives. We must therefore examine these training processes—who is behind the ideas being advanced, and the outcomes these ideas produce—with unrealistic optimism stripped away. It will be necessary to compare and contrast the training process of the world with God's covenant plan.

WHAT IS THE MAIN POINT OF A COVENANT RELATIONSHIP?

At the beginning of this section, we emphasized the importance of understanding the main point of a relationship. What does covenant teach us about the main point of these two key relationships—with God and with a husband or wife? Covenants are about new life, and covenants are about building and growing. The new life created by entering covenant is intended to grow to maturity, and the relationship one enters is intended to be built to its potential. If the relationship is built according to God's plan, growth, transformation, and maturity are inevitable. As two grow, as they are transformed in mind, heart, and character to increasingly reflect God and His ways, their relationship will inevitably grow deeper and stronger. The relationship will become more meaningful and rewarding. Covenant was created to accomplish all of this, and we are created to need all of this if we are to live our best life.

THREE

Foundational Understanding for God's Plan

THE HIGH POINTS OF OPTIMISM AND HOPE

Optimism and hope are precious things. Three experiences represent pinnacles of optimism and hope: standing before an altar and offering your life to another person in marriage; looking, for the first time, into the eyes of your newborn child; and coming before an altar—figuratively or literally—and accepting Christ's offer of salvation and new life, and in return pledging your life to Him. All of these are turning points in life; our lives are irrevocably changed by them. All speak of new things, new opportunities, new directions. But there is a more fundamental connection among these three experiences that we may not at first fully appreciate: each of these events is a living expression of God's plan through covenant relationships. In all of these experiences *a completely new person is born.* This is the first thing we must understand about covenant. Covenant is about the birth of a new life.

Consider why there is so much hope and optimism in each of these situations. Our wedding day may really be the beginning of our happily-ever-after. Our children may grow into remarkable human beings—loving, good, talented, respected. They may make significant contributions to humanity. One's new life in Christ may result in a radical transformation, with life and character issues overcome, new and godly character built, and many lives impacted by a single individual who loves and follows God. Our hope and optimism are reasonable,

> Our hope and optimism are reasonable, are they not? In the beginning no one knows the outcome of a marriage, a new child, or a life before God.

are they not? In the beginning no one knows the outcome of a marriage, a new child, or a life before God. But we do know that strong marriages have extended from the mists of antiquity all the way to our neighborhoods; many infants have grown to live beautiful and significant lives; and we have heard of, and perhaps know, people living powerful, significant, and abundant lives before the Lord. We innately understand that each of these new creatures is an expression of God's loving will; each is in a real sense God's gift. We also understand something else: each of these best-case outcomes is the result of a massive and sustained building process. We are often not as clear, though, on exactly how this building takes place or why different things are built instead that lead to less desirable outcomes.

WE START WITH POTENTIAL, BUT WHERE DO WE END UP?

New life is filled with God-given potential. The outcome of any life is determined by this potential, plus choices, plus circumstances. But even in our circumstances we have choices; identical circumstances may build maturity in one but leave another devastated. The difference between these two outcomes comes down to choices. Choices flow from ideas, from our reasoning, which is in turn based on beliefs, values, priorities, and motivations. Each of these is in turn based on ideas we decided at one point to embrace. Thus, the most important choices we make in life are about which ideas we choose to believe and to embrace. These choices reflect our desires; we seek one outcome over another and choose what appears to be the most direct path to what we want. The main problem we encounter in choosing is that, from our vantage point, we cannot understand all the outcomes of an idea or a decision. So how do we make the best choices? How do we embrace ideas and make decisions that will be of greatest benefit to us? How do we sort out, among all the voices we hear commending one idea or another, or one approach or another, what is really best? This is another way of asking, "How do we know truth when we see it?" It is essential, if we are to build our best lives, if we are to maximize our potential, if we are to build the best relationships, if we are to find the most satisfaction and gratification in life, that we learn how to identify truth.

God's plan is a definite and detailed thing. God's plan is truth, and God's plan involves communicating truth to us. But there is another variable that is vital to understand: us. At every point we have the option of accepting this truth, or not; of enacting this truth, or not; of fully enacting God's plan, or not. In other words, at every point, in every detail, we have the option of being faithful, or not. We have the option of growing, or not. We have the option of loving, or not. We have the choice to maximize our potential, or not. Overall, we have the option to maximize the outcome of our marriage or our relationship with God, or not. At every point we will be faced with decisions. Each one of these decisions matters. Each decision builds, fails to build, or tears down.

If we are to get a clear look at the task that confronts us in building covenant relationships to their potential, and building ourselves to our potential, we must understand the real challenges we are going to face. God's plan is up to the task. His plan accounts for every complexity, every challenge. But one thing is left to us. Our decisions. Our response to God's gracious offer—on a grand scale, and in every detail.

IF GOD HAS A PLAN, WHAT COULD POSSIBLY GO WRONG?

If God has a plan, what could possibly go wrong? Actually, a lot, as we see all around us. The phrase "newly wed, nearly dead," and many other things we hear people say about their marriages and their spouses come to mind. Or the changing statistics on marriage and divorce over the last sixty years. Or the exodus of college-age people from the ranks of self-professed Christians. If we want to live out the potential God has placed in our lives, we must understand how this potential is reached and also why it is *not* reached. God has fashioned an extremely detailed and comprehensive plan by which we can build a life that exceeds our dreams. A life that represents *God's* dreams, aspirations, and hopes for us. But this all must be built, and we must play our assigned role in the building process.

In addition, God's plan must be seen in the context of the world we live in, a world that is not, for the most part, guided by His plan or headed in a good direction. We need to have a clear sense of the problems this plan must confront and overcome. These problems are the direct result of ideas that are common currency in our world; they reside in the character of people with whom we relate; and they reside within our characters and patterns of living. We must do more than identify these problems; we must understand them well enough to avoid them and undo their effects in our lives. We need to understand their origin. Only if we understand the true source of ideas that oppose God's good plan will we be able to deal successfully with these ideas and the problems they cause.

SEEING THE BIG PICTURE

The underlying assumption of this book is that life based upon truth is more authentic, powerful, and gratifying than life based on anything else.

"Then you will know the truth, and the truth will set you free"
(John 8:32).
—Jesus

"What is truth?" (John 18:38)
—Pontius Pilate, just before endorsing
the plan to execute God.

WILL WE RECOGNIZE THE TRUTH WHEN IT IS RIGHT IN FRONT OF US?

This question is more real and important for each of us than we might realize, just as it has been for every human throughout history. In John 6, a sequence of events is recorded that covers a thirty-six-hour period. First, Jesus fed five thousand people by reaching into the lunch pail of a child that contained pieces of bread and two small fish (vv. 1-15). That evening He walked across a lake to the disciples' boat (vv. 16-21). In other words, that day He did two things that clearly substantiated a claim He continued to make: that He spoke with the authority of God because He was (and is) God, the only Son of the Father.

The next day Jesus was asked by some in the crowd, "What must we do to do the works God requires?" (v. 28). This question reflected the central understanding of the Jews for the basis of a right relationship with God: they must *do* certain, important things that God said to do, and they needed to avoid doing certain other things that He said to not do. Through obedience a good relationship with God would be assured. Jesus was asked what was *most important* because there were hundreds of rules noted in the Old Testament, and one could hardly obey all of them. And beyond those in Scripture, their religious leaders had encrusted an already daunting list of rules with embellishments and additions of their own. So, they were basically asking, "What is the short list of truly important ones? If we focus on these, we will all be in good with God, right?"

Jesus, however, used this opportunity to turn His questioners' thinking in an entirely different direction: away from specific acts and toward the nature of the relationship itself (see vv. 32-59). Jesus answered that they "must believe in the one God has sent." He went on to say that those who *believe* in the Son would have eternal life (v. 40). This is a part of the Christian message we have all heard. If we are Christians, we have agreed with this statement. We have embraced belief in Jesus. But in John 6 Jesus goes further and describes what "believing in Him" really means. This is where the conversation really gets interesting.

If we ask people today what it means to believe in Jesus we get a variety of answers—this phrase means to some degree whatever each of us decides it means. To one person, believing in Jesus may mean devoting every aspect of life to Him. To another it may mean respecting Him as a great moral teacher and incorporating some of the things He said into one's life—or at least a few of them. So, are we actually believing in our own ideas about what it means to believe in Jesus? Might our viewpoints in some ways be in contrast with what Jesus means? As Jesus continued the discussion—revealing His view of what this phrase *actually means*—He shocked those who were listening. "On hearing it, many of his disciples said, 'This is a hard teaching. Who can accept it?'" (v. 60). What did Jesus say that was so far from what His hearers expected that many actually turned away?

> What God offers is not a bad thing, not some pointless rule-based reduction of our lives, not something that will keep us from living our best, most rewarding, and most gratifying lives.

Jesus began to convey to His hearers the heart of God's plan for them: a very specific kind of relationship with God. The ironic thing about most people's response, then and through the ages, is this: what God offers is not a bad thing, not some pointless rule-based reduction of our lives, not something that will keep us from living our best, most rewarding, and most gratifying lives. God's plan is none of these things.

Properly understood, God's plan—which Jesus began to describe in John 6, then further described and detailed in John 17, during the Last Supper, and at other points before and after His resurrection, a plan illustrated and amplified by the entirety of Scripture—is literally the most wonderful thing humans could imagine. In fact, it is beyond human imagination. Once you see this plan clearly, I suspect you will agree that this could only come from the mind and heart of

God Himself. As such, God's plan represents the only true hope for individuals—and for the entire human race.

At times we are confronted with a truth that we do not expect to hear or perhaps do not *want* to hear. In fact, this truth may be the last thing we want to hear because of some bias we have acquired or some distortion of our appetites or priorities. When confronted with *this* truth—that reality conflicts with our own thoughts of how things should be—we face a decision. Do we deal with truth as it is, or do we try harder to pretend that things are the way we want them to be?

> Do we deal with truth as it is, or do we try harder to pretend that things are the way we want them to be?

Have you ever been at this point? Do things turn out better when we acknowledge and deal with truth and reality, or when we resist and avoid truth and reality? Jesus saw those gathered around Him—people who had walked away from their daily lives to follow Him and learn from Him—at this very point of decision, and pressed His point: "The words I have spoken to you, they are full of the Spirit and life" (v. 62). Then He awaited the decision of each person, to see which course they would take. This was a defining moment for each person, for each life. Notice what follows: "From this time many of the disciples turned back and no longer followed Him" (v. 66). He turned to his core group, the twelve specifically chosen by Him, and asked, "You do not want to leave too, do you?"

Peter answered Jesus: "Lord, to whom shall we go? You have the words of eternal life. We have come to believe and to know that you are the Holy One of God" (v. 68). Here is the essence of the issue. Once we realize who is speaking to us, if we trust Him and trust in Him, we can rest assured that whatever He says is true. Further, beyond confidence in His words, we can rest assured that His motive is love for us, that His desire is to lead us to what is truly best for us. If we couple this with the understanding that He possesses the power that created the universe and everything in it, we can safely entrust ourselves to His plan even if we do not understand that plan at the outset. We follow and obey because of our trust in the one who is revealing His plan to us. We understand that He not only foresees all outcomes, He ultimately ordains each outcome. Though at times He allows destructive things authored by His enemy into the lives of those He loves, if one is following Him He redeems these situations, turning them to our ultimate good. We will look more carefully at how God uses adversity, pain, and loss in coming volumes.

And we know that in all things God works for the good of those who love Him, who have been called according to His purposes.
ROMANS 8:28

Please note the contrast of this conversation between Peter and Jesus with the one between Satan and Eve in the Garden of Eden. Is it possible that one person believed in God—entrusting himself to God—while the other, sadly, did not?

This brings us to our second question.

WHAT DOES IT MEAN TO BELIEVE IN SOMEONE?

DID ADAM AND EVE BELIEVE IN GOD? DO WE?

Is it fair to say that Adam and Eve, who were personally created by God, did not believe in Him? They clearly believed that He existed, for He often walked with them and spoke with them. So what is the difference between believing that someone exists and *believing in* that person? We need to go back to the conversation in the Garden in Genesis 3:1-13 and consider something vitally important. Satan offered Eve what? He said that he offered the truth about God: her Creator, he said, was withholding the best option from her because He is the kind of being who withholds the best things (v. 1). Eve leaps to God's defense in verse 2—well, sort of—but we can see that Satan's innuendo about God's character bothered her. In her defense of God she actually misquotes God. In fact, her words created a scenario in which she could appear to discredit God as well by touching "the tree of the knowledge of good and evil" and not dying on the spot. What God actually said was to not eat the fruit. He said nothing about touching the tree. Adam and Eve could build a tree house in that tree if they wished. But they were to refrain from eating the fruit or they would die.

In Genesis 3:3, recognizing that Eve's confidence in God is now shaken, Satan unveils his plan for her—to disobey God—by offering something wonderful if she would merely do as he suggested. Innuendo changed to accusation: God is a liar. "You will surely not die. For God knows that when you eat of it your eyes will be opened, and you will be like God, knowing good and evil." What can this conversation teach us about what it means to believe in someone? Is believing in someone defined by our ideas, our intentions, or our feelings, or is it defined by our actions? Let's see if we can understand this distinction more clearly as this story plays out.

Eve's next step is truly fascinating, not only in light of her story but in light of all of our stories. Eve engages in the first scientific experiment ever recorded—at least science in the sense that it would be defined today. In heavily Christian-influenced countries from the time of Christ until an era oddly termed "The Enlightenment," science was viewed as the attempt to understand the world and universe God had created. The tools in this effort were observation and analysis, and these were placed alongside God's revelation. The core belief was that a rational and orderly God would create a rational and orderly world and universe. The proper role of science was thus to discover and understand this order. This is why scientific advancement over the last thousand years has largely centered in Europe and the United States in self-described Christian countries. The rest of the world—in the absence of belief in a rational Creator producing a rational universe—saw no need to look for such underlying order.

But the scientific community since the Enlightenment has progressively jettisoned belief in such a Creator, shifting from considering His revelation of things we cannot determine on our own to simply studying the creation per se using our own perceptions. Thus, we have forfeited the ability to see beyond our own limited abilities to perceive and understand. We have fashioned, through our own understanding, a world without meaning; lives are stripped of any purpose except those we devise, and, in practice, how we live generally comes down to advancing our perceived self-interests at the expense of others. We have lost the moral direction and guardrails that would lead us safely to our most gratifying and fulfilling lives while respecting and enhancing the lives of those around us. Instead, we are simply instructed to learn from experience, often learning too late that our limited vantage point gives no clear view of the best path or the long-term consequences of our choices. Eve, curiously, chose this approach. But why?

Let's see if Eve's mind-set bears any similarity to such Enlightenment thinking. She also discounted the reality of God's revelation—what would happen if she ate the fruit. What is left? She chose to believe in her own powers of observation. Thus, Eve undertook a scientific examination of the fruit of the tree. "When the woman saw that the fruit of the tree was good for food and pleasing to the eye, and also desirable for gaining wisdom . . . " (3:6).

Now we arrive at the focal point, the same focal point we will be discussing throughout these volumes, the same focal point where each of us will find ourselves innumerable times in our lives: we come to the point of decision. Until this point it is just words. We consider, we ponder, we try to assess the relative merits of different things we hear about a situation, we try to understand our own desires and needs in light of a situation, and we try to weigh the relative credibility of various sources of information. We assign various weights to all of these factors, then try to make the best choice possible. In this process, though, there is one defining moment, the moment when a decision is rendered—the deal is sealed and action results. At this point the consequences of the decision are unleashed—for better or worse. These consequences may follow us, may shape and define us, and possibly even haunt us for the rest of our lives. Ever have buyer's remorse? Ever want something so badly that you ignored objections you knew somewhere down inside were true? We ran over that guardrail on the way off a cliff chasing something that was so important, so desirable—at least we thought it was in the moment. When the reality of the situation becomes apparent, and we are headed toward a painful landing, what do we often say? "If I had only listened to . . . "

One can envision Eve leaning against the tree as she studied the fruit, then reaching up and touching it. Perhaps she even snapped off the stem and held the fruit in her hand, looking closely, smelling, feeling, perhaps squeezing a little. On one level her decision centered on whom she really believed. Would the fruit be dangerous for her or beneficial? If she was having this conversation in her head, she had already gone far down a path toward disbelief in God's words. At a deeper level, though, her decision came down to choosing one of two ways of thinking: whom did she *have the most reason to believe*; or, whom did she *most want to believe*? Did Eve have more reason to believe her Creator? Or should she trust this unfamiliar creature who was coming to her now suggesting that her Creator was not the loving Father she thought He was—and therefore not worthy of her trust? If she had been truly observant and analytical, if she had stopped to think of her life until this point—from the first time her eyes opened beside her husband, lover, and best friend, in a world perfectly suited to her, until the moment this conversation began—could she identify any reason to *not* trust God? The only time she had ever questioned His love was right here, right now, and based only on the words of this unknown being. And what, exactly, had he done to earn her trust? But even this was not the most important issue.

The element in play at this deeper level, beyond what is factual or not, was *desire*. Eve was hearing from a being who was opening her eyes to new possibilities, very desirable possibilities. As a result, she illustrated a truth known to every salesperson, and a closely related truth known to every scientist: the result you get greatly depends on how you frame the question. Eve narrowed her examination of reality to an experiment whose answer reinforced her move away from trusting in God. The fruit simply did not appear to her to be as dangerous as God said it was. In fact, it looked . . . good for her . . . very good, in fact—nutritious, good-tasting, and beneficial. This lined up with the words of her new best friend and confidant. Perhaps he was right when he told her that God really was holding back His best things from her. This is the first recorded occasion of personal bias influencing the design of a scientific study, then influencing the analysis of data. After pondering all of this, Eve exercised her most fundamental human prerogative based on a selective and skewed understanding of reality, a view shaped by how she wanted things to be. She made her decision and raised the fruit to her lips (3:6).

> The problem humans have is we view life from the vantage point called "now." That is, we view everything at a time before the consequences of our decisions and behaviors have fully played out.

She would quickly discover that this newly embraced idea was a lie. Truth and reality are synonyms. Truth is simply a statement of reality, an accurate description of the cause-and-effect universe God created for us to inhabit. It would soon become apparent that everything God said about eating the fruit was true. God's truth, His Word, has been spoken to humanity throughout history. But, since the beginning, there has also been another voice laying out reasons why we should not trust, not believe, in our Creator or His Word. And not follow His directives.

The problem humans have is we view life from the vantage point called "now." That is, we view everything at a time before the consequences of our decisions and behaviors have fully played out. As we face a decision, none of the consequences of the choices are yet evident. All we have to go on are two voices—God and "other." Those voices, heard through the mouths of other people or within our own mind, tell us whether a decision is right or wrong. These two voices always offer conflicting assessments. The other thing we have to draw from is whatever experience of cause-and-effect we've observed from similar situations. We often see people engaging in direct violations of God's laws and principles, yet they seem to be doing very well—prospering in fact—from those very acts of rebellion. For a while. But there is always more to come. In the end the fullness of consequences will perfectly reflect God's revelation about our lives and the world we inhabit. We often do not envision this future, however, preferring instead to affix ourselves to the same hope that Eve embraced, believing that our best interests will be advanced by ignoring the words of a God who, we are told, is more killjoy than benefactor, more rule-monger than lover of our souls.

> We are always capable of being deceived, but we are also always capable of discerning truth.

There were really three lies in play in Eve's encounter with Satan. First, that it was not safe, instead foolish, to believe in her Creator; second, that there were great benefits to not believing in God; and third, that the voice that urges this departure from God is a reliable guide in our search for our best life. An unfortunate truth is highlighted by this encounter. When we begin to strongly desire something, every other consideration—even reality itself—recedes into the background. We want something so badly that we ignore reality and truth. This is a peculiar human weakness we do well to recognize within ourselves, for we all have it. Through this doorway all manner of destructive things enters our lives. We are always capable of being deceived, but we are also always capable of discerning truth. This is the ultimate nature of our capacity to choose—to choose *the basis upon which we will choose*.

WHAT IS THE BIG PICTURE?

To ensure the safety of our own hearts and lives, and to find the best life we are capable of, we need to do what Eve and Adam did not do, which is look at the big picture. You see, we humans did not originally—nor do we now—come up with the agenda of turning from God to rebellious and destructive actions *on our own*. There is another voice in the conversation—always. If we really want to understand the world we inhabit, as well as understand our own life, we must first look clearly at the nature, character, and agenda of the being behind this other voice. To be clear, we are not talking about a literal voice speaking to us directly. But we are talking about all the messages we get from every source in our world about any issue or decision—friends, family, media, school, church, and many more places, including previous influences that form our internal guidance system, our personal frame of reference. We must understand that the enemies of God did not just converse with humanity once, in the Garden of Eden. These beings have been presenting the same message throughout every culture for all of human history that was presented in the Garden: turn from God and follow our ways of living, for it is through our guidance that you will find your best life. We have to realize that this influence is present, and has impacted every life and every culture in history, if we are to make sense of the life outcomes we see around us. And if we understand that Satan's promises of a grand and glorious future in rebellion against our Creator—which is offered to us moment by moment by our culture, our media, our educational system, even our own hearts—are just as much lies and deceptions today as they were when Satan spoke personally with Eve, we are poised to see through the offers he continues to make to us all. Once we see this reality, this pattern, clearly then we need only to search out the specific lies and distortions we have already embraced or are considering embracing.

The other side of the big picture is a clear, evidence-based view of our Creator—one based on God's history-long interaction with humanity, culminating with a personal visit by Jesus Christ. If we look, we can easily see the great blessings and benefits God has poured out on humanity. We can easily see how He loves us and the lengths to which He has gone to display His love. If we satisfy ourselves that God is in fact a being we can reasonably believe, and safely believe in, then it is entirely logical to conclude that the path to our best life will be found listening to and obeying His words to us and, at the same time, identifying, resisting, and rejecting the advice of this other voice.

WE LIVE IN A CAUSE-AND-EFFECT UNIVERSE CREATED BY GOD

Do not be deceived; God cannot be mocked; a man reaps what he sows. Whoever sows to please their flesh, from the flesh will reap destruction; whoever sows to please the Spirit, from the Spirit will reap eternal life. Let us not become weary in doing good, for at the proper time we will reap a harvest if we do not give up.
GALATIANS 6:7-9

Each move we make sets into motion a vast array of consequences. Some of those consequences occur immediately and some in the short-term, while others do not become evident for years. No matter what we think or hope might happen, there are consequences that are going to happen that are not influenced by our expectations or by any other force we can bring to bear. We simply cannot control outcomes in the larger sense—we cannot mitigate or avoid consequences. Another word for these accumulated consequences? *Reality*. This is the exclusive realm of God, for He created this cause-and-effect system for us to inhabit. This system correlates with the moral instructions God has conveyed to us in Scripture. God also has the power to ordain particular outcomes. Thus, this system is not just on autopilot churning out consequences. It is also a function of our individual relationships with a Being who can bless us, chasten us, or return a curse for our curses (see Matthew 12:31, Mark 14:21).

YOU SHALL BE AS GOD . . .

Ordaining specific outcomes is the exclusive realm of God. Which is why Eve was so anxious to become "as God" herself, and why humans ever since, despite all evidence to the contrary, continue to believe that they can rebel against God yet somehow have the outcomes they want—in effect promoting themselves to godhood. As mentioned, there is always a voice in the conversation urging us in this direction: a being whose master plan is to unseat God as the ruler of the universe and install himself on the throne. Humans are simply following his lead on this fool's errand. We can ordain outcomes in our lives to a significant degree, but we can only do this through making decisions that produce the outcomes we want. If we want good long-term outcomes, we must do good and virtuous things, things in harmony with God's moral directives. If we rebel against God and His moral order, we will predictably reap the attendant consequences. Our decisions, in a very real sense, create our lives. Given the number of decisions we make in life, we encounter massive waves of accumulating consequences, for better or worse. The beauty of all this is we get to decide what ideas—or whose voice—we are going to base every decision upon. If there is something you do not like about your life right now, might this line of thinking offer you hope? Perhaps what needs to change is not your luck or the way other people treat you; instead, something else needs to change, something perhaps you've never considered.

If we look within ourselves, we may not at first be able to clearly distinguish things that arise from God's Word and those that arise from that "other voice." It might be best to simply look around and examine the relationship between decisions and consequences in the lives of others. There are things people are, and do, that have strong outcomes in the long term—that build, that grow, that are without question *good* and *right*. Then there are things that people do that blow up in the long run, that tear down, that damage self and others. Sometimes these courses of action might not at first appear to be dangerous. These things might even appear beneficial; the person may receive an enthusiastic endorsement for these things from our culture, and they may seem to work well for a time.

As we try to sort out the things which may prove destructive in the lives of those around us, there are plenty of things for which we cannot see final outcomes. Will these things turn out well or badly? We cannot see this from our vantage point—yet. We must content ourselves with those things that have played out to the point that outcomes can be seen—and there are many of these. First, simply ask yourself whether things termed by God as morally wrong build lives, consequences, and life experiences that are wonderful, desirable, everything life could be; or do lives filled with these things turn out to be something else? Look at the lives of older people who have chosen one course or another for decades. Are these lives filled with blessings or regrets? Are we beginning to draw into focus the problems inherent in the plan of learning from observation and experience? Often we do not think in terms of associating life outcomes with life choices. Even if we attempt to do so it takes a great deal of effort and thought to make such connections. But if one has been alive as long as I have and has looked as carefully as I have at this question, the answer is not in doubt. Choosing good things produce good outcomes; choosing things that are bad, wrong, immoral, unwise, foolish—these things produce poor or destructive outcomes as predictably as the force of gravity will cause something to fall toward the center of the earth when released from your hand. But it often takes years, even decades, for such consequences to become evident. And only when we all stand before the judgment seat of Christ will consequences become fully evident.

Still, if we look carefully now, the patterns are unmistakable.

Due to the length of time involved, it can be easy to miss this cause-and-effect relationship, but an additional layer of confusion is added by our culture. Consequences are redefined as a string of bad luck. Someone always chooses "the wrong people to date." "This is always how people treat me." Our culture trains us to view people who have an accumulation of negative consequences as victims of circumstance, not the *authors* of their circumstances.

But if we examine closely, we begin to see a direct relationship between ways of living and the life that is created. We need to train our eyes to identify this cause-and-effect relationship. If we are to guide our own lives correctly, we must grasp that right actions, attitudes, thoughts, beliefs, values, motivations, and feelings—things also referred to as virtues—move our lives in better directions. Wrong actions, attitudes, thoughts, beliefs, values, motivations, and feelings inevitably create damage and loss in the long run. Unfortunately, bad choices impact not only the life of the person making those choices but ripple outward to impact others. Fortunately, in the same way, virtues that are lived out also have an impact beyond the life of the virtuous individual.

One further challenge we face in assessing final outcomes is that God rules; and this God at times allows apparently good decisions to completely blow up lives—in the short run. Joseph did the right thing when propositioned by his master's wife. The reward for his display of righteousness? He was imprisoned for over a decade. This did not look like a personal win. But the end was not yet in sight. Within a short period of time he became second only to Pharaoh in power over the nation of Egypt. He was able to save his own family from famine— the very brothers who sold him into slavery in the first place—and was reunited with these brothers and with his aged father. At times God uses adversity to build things within us. First and most important, trust in Him and His love; then, in an understanding of His ways. As Joseph was able to eventually say to his brothers, "You intended to harm me, but God intended it for good to accomplish what is now being done, the saving of many lives" (Genesis, chapters 37-50). Even when doing the right thing appears to be the costliest choice, in the end this is never so. If our first priority is to love God and please Him, in the end we will never be disappointed or ashamed.

Not only individuals, but whole groups, generations, and even entire societies can reject God embracing ideas and following courses that end badly, though initially these things might look like cause for optimism. Most Germans who gravitated toward Naziism during the 1930s had no idea where those thoughts would guide them. In stark contrast, but also illustrating the long-term power of ideas, the Godly foundation of our nation has produced benefits, here and abroad, that are unprecedented in history. Though we have our problems—all based on ungodly ideas that mingled with the good ones—things that we take for granted, like representative government, rule of law, due process, and respect for life and liberty still make this a great nation, and continue to offer us the opportunity to solve our problems. The course of our nation, just like the course of an individual, will be decided by the ideas selected for guidance. As we formally turn more and more away from God and from our own foundation, one can only wonder where this will lead. We can, however, confidently predict that such ideas will produce more problems than solutions.

The first group of points to grasp in the big picture: **everything is a decision;** these **decisions create consequences; the accumulation of these consequences produce scenarios** that end well or end badly for self and others; and **the sum of these scenarios defines our lives.**

The next point to grasp: individuals and groups may be very wrong on the front end about the consequences of a course of action. There is not necessarily safety in numbers. The mainstream may be flowing in a good direction or flowing right off a cliff. That any number of people endorse an idea, no matter how learned or intelligent those people might be, in no way ensures that an idea is a good idea. This is not an abstract "spiritual" discussion. Words like "right" and "wrong," "good" and "bad" are not thrown around in a vacuum; these are practical, real-world, real-life concepts with massive impacts on the quality and outcome of each life. Would it not be an excellent thing to have the advice of someone who fully understands the true cause-and-effect nature of things, who could direct us to the best courses of action and warn us of unseen dangers? And to find such a source of truth before each of us learns the hard way? What, or Who, might this source be?

Since there are voices commending every possible bad decision in our world, as well as the good ones, another question emerges: Who is commending good ideas, and who is commending bad ones? Are these just well-guided or misguided people, or is there more to this picture? If so, what is guiding people in one way or another?

OUR LIVES: BATTLEGROUNDS FOR COMPETING IDEAS AND VOICES

In addition to overestimating the reliability of the opinions of other people or groups of people, we may also overestimate the importance of our own perceptions. We have been trained by our culture to value our own perceptions *above all*. This tendency goes all the way back to the beginning of the human race, as noted above, and our individual perceptions do not function any better for us in determining reality than Eve's perceptions did for her. We often do not consider or factor into our equation of decision-making the real limitations of our individual perspectives. We often lose all sense of our own limitations in a social setting when we are trying to have things our way or get others to see things our way. Like Eve, if all we choose to perceive around us is the physical universe while we ignore the moral cause-and-effect universe, if we have no awareness of God and His moral revelations in Scripture that teach us about this realm, if we have no understanding that Satan and those under his influence are feeding us deceptive information, and if we have no concept of the agenda behind that deceptive information, then we find ourselves in the position that Eve and Adam occupied before the consequences of their actions became fully evident to them. And, in the end, we will also find ourselves in their position, when the full weight of the consequences of their actions was meted out to them.

Currently, the viewpoint of our naturalistic, Enlightenment-worshipping society is that all of this "supernatural stuff"—God's revelation via the Scriptures and direct interaction with Him, as well as the presence of supernatural beings with evil intent—represents only myth, superstition, and ignorance. In the end, when each individual is standing before Jesus, looking Him in the eyes and hearing Him speak the eternal destiny of each person, no one will continue to hold the above position. But now, based upon the limited data they have to draw from, our *supposedly* rational thought leaders are quick to tell us that we would be fools to believe in supernatural things. Where do you think these ideas originated? The key, again, is to look behind the human voices to the being instigating these ideas. If we understand the identity and agenda of this being, we can see such pronounce-ments for what they actually are—just another salvo in a spiritual war that has raged from the beginning of human history. Every human who has ever lived is in the crossfire of this war. Further down we are going to look at the nature of ideas promoted by God's enemy, the agenda behind these ideas, and the way these ideas have come to form much of the way of life of every culture in history. For now, just note that there is this war. If you were asked to cite evidence for this war of ideas, could you point to such evidence?

A truly rational person will see that long-term outcomes of lives al-ways reflect, for better or worse, the constellation of values and truths revealed to us by God. One of the truths He revealed is the nature of the spiritual war between Him and the created being who aspires to rule in His place, and the way this conflict impacts every human life. This is that big picture of human life we must understand if we are to understand why covenant is a necessary remedy, and if we are to understand the nature of the war of ideas, and the true impact of ideas on our lives.

The initial question posed in this section is whether or not we would recognize truth if it is right in front of us. We have just con-sidered one important function of truth. Among other things, truth is a statement of reality. Such a statement correctly distinguishes good things from bad things, things that will have good consequences from things that will have bad consequences. As noted, if we are to make the best long-term decisions, we can only be reliably guided by truth revealed to us about a matter, in contrast with our own perceptions, expectations, experiences, and desires, or the guidance of our culture. But where can we look for this kind of truth, and how can we have confidence that we have found it? In this book series, I take the po-sition that God's revelation, as set forth in the Scriptures, is the one and only source of truth. Though these words were written by human hands, this collection of writings represents God speaking directly to all of humanity. This is an objective source of truth against which we may compare any thought or belief of any person, including our own thoughts and beliefs (see 2 Timothy 3:16).

But there are two contenders set forth as the ultimate source of truth in our culture—God's Word and science. Which one is the ultimate, objective source of truth? Because it is so vital that this question be answered correctly—the outcome of our lives literally depends on the answer—let us take a closer look at these two contenders.

PROPOSED SOURCES OF TRUTH

WHAT IS GOD'S WORD?

We possess a several-thousand-year-long continuous written record of God's interaction with humanity. There is very strong evidence that this body of information—the Old and New Testaments, or the Bible—are intact and correct copies of the original documents. Evidence for this includes correlation between current copies and the most ancient manuscripts, such as the Dead Sea Scrolls, which were penned hundreds of years before the time of Jesus. These writings identity God as our creator, then describe His character and detail His interaction with humanity back to the beginning of the human race. God informs us in that same written Word that He created us in His image. We will not cover in detail the considerable evidence for the truthfulness and reliability of the Bible in this book; suffice it to say that compelling evidence is there for anyone who wants to consider this question with an open mind.

I believe it is essential for each of us to reach the point, based upon solid evidence, where we have full confidence that the Scriptures we possess are accurate and true. When I was examining this issue in relation to my own life, one thing most clearly pointed to divine authorship of these writings: fulfilled prophesy. There are around a thousand specific predictions in the Old and New Testaments which have come true precisely as stated, and no outcome that is not as predicted. Most of these can be unequivocally dated prior to the events in question. There is literally nothing remotely resembling this body of fulfilled prophesy in any other writing in history. Only God could do such a thing. These prophesies are laced among proven historical references, or those yet to be proven by archeology, and among writings that set forth the moral nature of our universe. If these writings had been corrupted at any point, the prophesies would have also been corrupted, as well as the historical references. It is as if God placed these three things in juxtaposition as proof texts for each other.

Therefore, we can have reasonable confidence that these writings are accurate, not just about history and the nature of their author, but also about the overall cause-and-effect moral universe we inhabit. The Scriptures contain many descriptions of things morally right and wrong, along with injunctions to do good things and avoid wrong things. If we are to understand the world we inhabit, and the challenges we see on all sides, and in our own lives, we must realize that God's directives to us are not, "Because I said so . . . to ruin your good times." His revelation of His moral universe to us is there to warn us, to guide us, and to encourage us. This is His roadmap to lead us through life, to guide us as we build our lives, our characters, and our relationships.

If we are to *believe* in the God revealed in these Scriptures, we cannot have any misconception or confusion on this point. If we cannot prove to our own satisfaction that the document which reveals God is true and correct, we could logically question anything—or everything—that the entirety of Scripture reveals about Him or anything else. Actually, we should question all of these things, because we have no basis for believing these ideas other than the credible witness of Scripture. If we are not clear about what the Scriptures represent, we cannot be sure who God is, and we will certainly lack confidence in His love for us. Therefore, we cannot have the confidence in Him that would be required for any of us to devote our lives to exactingly following His leadership. In fact,

> If we are not clear about what the Scriptures represent, we cannot be sure who God is, and we will certainly lack confidence in His love for us.

what confidence can we have that He exists at all? If we are not clear on these things, how easy might it be for the "other voice" to lead us away from Him? And we would believe as we walk away from God, and His revelation of His moral universe, that someone has done us a great service, just as Eve thought—for a time.

Throughout history there has been one consistent feature of this spiritual battleground: an ongoing attack on the veracity of God's Word. In the last two hundred years this attack has come mainly through the mouths of philosophers, scientists, and educators. Since the early 1800s some in the scientific community have identified people and events referenced in Scripture for which there was no current archeological evidence. Then these people use the supposed "discrepancy between the scientific record and these scriptures" to assert that the Scriptures are fables. And yet, over the last two hundred years, one archeological find after another has corroborated the Scriptural accounts. An excellent single resource that addresses the issue of the veracity of Scripture is Josh McDowell's *Evidence that Demands a Verdict*. There are many other works exploring this topic. We all should have questions on this point, and each of us should make the effort required to answer each of our own questions, for only this level of certainty will give us the necessary resolve to embrace God's revelation as the definition of truth, then to make correct decisions, and to follow through with these decisions upon this foundation in the face of predictable challenges and opposition.

IS SCIENTIFIC TRUTH DIFFERENT FROM GOD'S TRUTH?

Since the science-faith discussion is creating so much confusion, and since people in the scientific, or "evidence-based," camp are attempting to stridently attack all things of a spiritual nature, I want to take just a few more moments to examine the foundation of their position. This may help us put this discussion in its proper context. First, it should be noted that the most brilliant scientists in past centuries had no issue believing that the physical realm we inhabit, which we can examine with our senses and intellect, was juxtaposed with a spiritual universe which could only be known or examined indirectly. It is this realm, as well as the moral nature of our own realm, for which God's revelation—information that by definition we cannot acquire on our own—is required. Vast amounts of deceptive information about this same spiritual realm, and the moral nature of our own realm, have also been communicated to humanity by the enemies of God.

Only in the last 150 years has the thesis "what we see is all there is" been advanced by more than a few individuals. This position is termed *naturalism*. If one takes this position, many things in life go unexplained, such as why evil exists. Or, why every human makes a distinction between right and wrong, justice and injustice, or deserved and undeserved. The criteria by which one evaluates each of these may vary widely—but why does everyone make these distinctions in the first place? These are in the realm of morality, and morality has no correlate in the physical/electrical/chemical universe. The fact that all people make moral distinctions, even those who claim that this moral universe does not exist, amusingly undercuts this position.

WHAT IF SCIENTIFIC OPINION IS NOT BASED ON GENUINE SCIENCE?

For something to be truly "scientific" it must observed and analyzed in a *reproducible manner*. That is, to scientifically understand gravity or light or quantum mechanics, one must be able to design an experiment which will produce the same observations *every time* in a laboratory or natural setting. This is how we have come to understand all manner of laws and principles of the universe. This is why experiments are designed and carried out, and why well-designed ones provide true and accurate information.

However, when dealing with areas where direct observation cannot occur—say, the origin of life, or of humanity—realms where we have access to only scant pieces of evidence—fossils, and artifacts—to inform us (or no direct evidence at all in the case of the origin of life itself) it is extremely important to contrast the quality of information obtained from reproducible observations versus that obtained from extremely partial evidence plus conjecture. From the former we can deduce truths that are consistent, verifiable, and testable. From the latter, possessing only a few pieces of a very large and complex puzzle, we end up with only opinions—which are inevitably upended by the next fossil find. We have seen this pattern for decades when considering the purported family tree of humans. Thus, it is extremely important not to use the term "scientific" to describe theories informed only by scant and inconclusive evidence. For the "big questions" being considered, like the origin of life, there will never be sufficient physical evidence to have any certainty about what happened. What about hearing the answer to these questions from a credible eyewitness? Perhaps from the One who did the creating?

At the same time, the correlation between Scriptures and the historical and archeological record do need to be addressed. A valid point of inquiry is the Scriptural assertion that God created Adam and Eve, the mother and father of the human race, as immortal beings in a special act of creation at a certain point in time at a particular point on earth. Adam and Eve then joined in rebellion against God, lost their physical immortality, and were ejected from their initial place of residence. One can infer that the Garden of Eden was a point of overlap between earth and the heavenly realm. We do need something beyond merely "God said so" to engage in conversations on this topic.

Archeologists tell us that hominids, or human-like creatures, were the actual progenitors of the human race. These hominids evolved over a several-million-year period into Homo Sapiens, or beings who were anatomically identical with us. There was a continuous increase in brain size through these millennia until this plateaued around 100,000 to 200,000 years ago with Homo Sapiens and Neanderthals. However, though these ancient Homo Sapiens were anatomically like us, they were completely unlike us behaviorally. Even with "modern" human brain capacity, these beings continued to live as other hominids had lived for hundreds of millennia, wandering the landscape in hunter-gatherer groups, employing crude tools, fire, and stone points.

The toys and tools are different today, but the lifestyle in ancient Sumeria grew quickly to be remarkably like our own. This was in stark contrast to everything that had come before.

They did not build cities or cultures.

Then something happened. In an extremely brief period of time on the archeological time scale, at one point in time at one place on the globe, we see beings behaving in a way essentially identical to us. What happened? One archeologist noted that it was "as if a switch was turned on, and Homo Sapiens became us."

If Adam and Eve were specially created, one would expect a significant discontinuity, something new, different, and dramatic accompanying their arrival on the scene. And this is precisely what we see in the historical record. Archeologists date this discontinuity to roughly the same time when the Scriptural chronology asserts it happened. A full treatment of this requires a book, not a paragraph in a book devoted to another topic. Briefly, cities appeared at one point on the globe—in Mesopotamia—and a culture rapidly developed that mirrors every element of modern culture. This occurred roughly 4000 BC (keep in mind that in this time frame the margin of error for dating is measured in centuries). The toys and tools are different today, but the lifestyle in ancient Sumeria grew quickly to be remarkably like our own. This was in stark contrast to everything that had come before. These people were in every sense modern human beings doing the same things we are doing. In the blink of an eye in the archeological time frame this culture had sophisticated textiles, pharmaceuticals, the musical scale (that we still use), the seven-day week, the twenty-four hour day, and a calendar almost identical to our own. They had writing, libraries, and schools. They had a legal system (including medical malpractice laws), contracts, and a penal system.[1]

From where did these entirely new behaviors and capabilities arise? Anthropologists and archeologists have absolutely no idea how this occurred. What turned on this switch, suddenly creating modern-behaving humans? God's revelation, by contrast, offers an explanation in harmony with the archeological facts in evidence. He created Adam and Eve in His image, something—some *ones*—distinct from all that had come before. Beyond these societal changes, another aspect of this most ancient society that begs explanation is the scientific knowledge and engineering capability they possessed, which went far beyond what is possible given the tools they had at hand. Other narratives are advanced to explain these sudden changes, including visitation and genetic engineering by aliens.[1] I mention all of this to illustrate that Scriptural assertions of our origin, and creation in general, are not as far from the facts in evidence as the scientific community continues to assert. Creation and early human history are the areas most frequently employed when attempts are made to discredit God's revelation (Genesis chapters 1-11).

The ultimate reality in play here is that we cannot scientifically prove anything about the origin of life for three very good reasons: first, we did not personally observe it; second, we cannot recreate it in a laboratory environment; and third, physical evidence for this event, we can be confident, will never be found. What remains cannot be called science according to any real definition. Such unverifiable ideas are only opinions. Oddly, people who believe in science as the answer to all questions, who show contempt for people who believe in ideas not discoverable or confirmable by the scientific method—supernatural things, in other words—somehow champion an unending and ever-changing string of opinions about matters which cannot be scientifically tested or confirmed, if those untestable opinions are voiced by people who claim to believe in science.

By the way, what is the first thing Scripture says was created by God, and what is the first thing that scientists say characterized the infant universe? "Let there be light" (Genesis 1:3). Or, as the scientists assert, a blindingly bright, infinitely hot ball of expanding plasma was the first form of our current universe. This plasma ball then went dark when it expanded and cooled to a certain point, producing darkness for roughly 380 million years. This darkness persisted until the first stars ignited. God's first act of creation was to create the first day—light and darkness. Frankly, I fail to see the lack of correlation between these two scenarios. Except that God tells us what predated this act of creation while scientists have absolutely no idea, and no way to find out.

BIASES AND OPINIONS OF SCIENTISTS ARE NOT SCIENCE

In summary, we should not be thrown off-balance by sound bite pseudo-scientific assertions that God's Word is not reliable. God is never bothered by honest questions. He went to considerable trouble to salt history with documented inter-actions with humanity, including vis-iting us in person. If we have ques-tions, fine. We should ask questions. And we should go to the trouble to search out the answer to these ques-tions, for God has gone to significant trouble to leave credible evidence for us to consider.

> God is never bothered by honest questions. He went to considerable trouble to salt history with documented interactions with humanity, including visiting us in person. If we have questions, fine.

Actual scientific reality does not conflict with God's Word. Inappropriate extensions of what is actually known to form "scientific opinions"—what people think or hope they will ultimately find when, or if, sufficient evidence does become available—may certainly diverge from God's truth. As mentioned, these are usually a much better re-flection of the biases of those offering these opinions than they reflect actual evidence or logical thinking. One always-missing element is a clear statement of the degree of uncertainty of these opinions. Instead, these become the "factual basis" upon which "evidence-based think-ers" base their beliefs. Reality is not subject to revision on a daily basis. These opinions are. I would prefer basing my beliefs on a body of truth delivered to humanity in its completed form two thousand years ago that has withstood the harshest of attacks of critics over thousands of years. Truth is unchanging and eternal. So is the Word of God.

Let me mention one other element of true science. Before scientific facts are established, one starts by formulating an hypothesis, or theory. Then, one tests the theory to prove it true or false. Good science requires that one make as much effort to disprove the hypothesis as to prove it. Now, consider the scientific theory that there is "no God and no supernatural realm." Are scientists who advance this idea also making an equal effort (employing good scientific work) to prove He does exist? Are they open to discussing this question, or do they simply state that belief in God and His Word is evidence of defective character and intellect? In the scientific world, documented bias destroys the credibility of the research and the credibility of the researcher.

Which side in this discussion insults and abuses those who disagree? Which side tries to use every possible means of leverage to gain agreement and to silence dissenting views? If you are unsure of the answer, walk onto almost any college campus in the country, find a random group of students, and begin a discussion about the moral universe created by God and our accountability to Him. Then listen to the response. Then, find the faculty lounge and begin this same conversation with whoever you find there. Most college campuses in our day bear more resemblance to mind control cults than to a group of people pursuing truth with open minds.

So what is really going on in this debate between God and the scientific/educational community? Do the voices that dissent from the Scriptures want to establish their opinions as truth, their own views of right and wrong as determinative, their own views of how and why we exist as reality, and do they really not want to bow their knees before the One to whom they are accountable? Could the being who initially rebelled against the Creator also be accurately described in these ways? I would not presume to judge the heart and life of another person, but all of these men and women who are trying so hard to discount and discredit God will one day have to give an account as they look into the eyes of the One they have disdained on "scientific" grounds. Ironic, isn't it, since the very reality they contend they are insightfully studying was in fact fashioned by the Being they will stand before?

Scientists would have us believe that the only path to truth and knowledge is via science, that their offerings are the closest we can get to absolute truth. And if we accept this view without question, will we assign more weight to "scientific opinion" than to God's Word? Of course. But if we understand the larger picture, the credibility of these voices is put in proper perspective. More importantly, if we see the correlation between this question—the actual source of truth upon which we should base our lives—and the one Eve was facing in the Garden of Eden, we will understand the true nature of this debate and its true importance for our lives.

Please note the order of the foundational truths God has revealed to us in Scripture. The first chapter of Genesis—the Bible's "book of beginnings"—describes the creation of our physical universe and the creation of life by God. The second chapter describes the creation of mankind in the image of God and the gift of marriage to the human race. The third chapter introduces us to the war between God and Satan as it plays out in human lives, beginning with the very first humans and the first human family. The remainder of Scripture details the mess that has flowed from humans choosing the wrong master, from lives guided by the wrong voice. But it also offers God's plan for definitively dealing with this mess—if we choose to accept the do-over He offers. We are offered the option of reinstalling Him as Lord of our lives, of affirming Him as our actual Lord in our daily decisions and in a life dedicated to following His path. We must distinguish this from attempting to make Him Lord-in-name-only. This distinction is clearly evidenced by daily choices and the overall path one follows. The opportunity God offers us is to enter the New Covenant with Himself; all else that follows in this relationship, and all that flows from this relationship, is a consequence of the nature of this relationship that rejoins us to God.

Jesus answered, "I am the way, and the truth, and the life.
No one comes to the Father except through Me."
JOHN 14:6

Very truly I tell you, whoever hears my word and believes Him who
sent Me has eternal life, and will not be judged but has passed over
from death to life.
JOHN 5:24

Yet to all who did receive Him, to those who believed in
His name, He gave the right to become children of God—
children born not of natural descent, nor of human decision
or a husband's will, but born of God.
John 1:12, 13

"Whoever has my commands and keeps them is the one who
loves Me. The one who loves Me will be loved by my Father,
and I too will love them and show myself to them."
JOHN 14:21

WHAT IS THE BIG PICTURE
WITH OUR LIVES?

How does the story that begins in Genesis relate to our everyday lives? One thing to note carefully in the Eden story is what all of this was like from Eve's perspective. There is no indication Eve knew who Satan was or what he was up to. Satan did not offer his credentials or explain why he was in a position to "know" the things he was seeking to convince Eve of. He did not even introduce himself! Then, as today, Satan does not correctly identify himself, advertise his presence, or take credit for his influence. He simply continues to sit in the shadows offering information that discredits God (if that information is believed), using myriad human voices under his dominion. He offers enticing opportunities to us, all of which, in one way or another, involve departing from God's will.

As we confront the daily decisions of living, if we make up our minds based only on the things we see around us—things analyzed by minds and hearts filled with biases and "useful information" picked up from our culture (whose authorship and motive we misunderstand)—we will in all likelihood repeat a pattern acted out far too often in human history. We will walk past the one true lover of our souls and reach for some "glorious offering" that will give us the life we deeply desire—the most progressive, powerful, fastest, latest and greatest, most technologic, educated, scientific, famous, impressive, beautiful, liked, enticing . . . whatever. Anything at all, it seems, will do if we can be deceived into believing it is our path to the good life.

"Pleased to meet you; hope you guessed my name"
"Sympathy for the Devil," The Rolling Stones[2]

IDENTIFYING THE REAL SOURCE OF THE MESSAGES

What is the big picture as we try to chart our course through life? The vast majority of people in our world are avidly pursuing things that promise fulfillment, but these are false promises. Nowhere is this reality more true than in our closest and most important relationships. Instead of being the path to ultimate fulfillment, wrong ideas about the nature and conduct of these relationships will create an altogether different experience. Decisions to brush past God and embrace ways of life that oppose the words of our Creator represent acceptance of fundamentally the same offer, made by the same being, to join him in the same opposition to God that he has been effectively selling throughout human history. This is the essence of deception: people making decisions without understanding the true nature of their decisions. What do we need to make the best choices? The truth, which God has graciously given us. But we must grasp this big picture.

DUSTING FOR FINGERPRINTS

We need to be able to identify the sources of the ideas that come before us to accurately determine whose fingerprints are on an idea. What is Satan really up to? The thing Satan offered Eve was the same thing he sought for himself—to be like God. Satan knows the attraction of this offer. Among other things, being a god means one has the power to call the shots in one's life, to have things one's way; to be lord of the consequences of one's actions, to possess the power to ensure that things turn out well in the end regardless of the choices one makes. Isn't this what it means to be "as God"? Are we not all being tempted to become the gods of our own lives as we brush past the real One? After all, it's *my* life—isn't it? I am creating it as I want it to be! "I am the captain of my fate, the master of my soul," as Henley's poem says. Is this true? Did I really create myself? Am I really in control of outcomes in my life? Can I really create reality? Or am I being tempted to embrace deception, to join in the ultimate delusion, to sign on for consequences which, in the end, will be exactly what God has ordained? Satan's rebellion leads to death for all who join it.

Adam and Eve did not die physically immediately after eating from the forbidden tree. They did, however, begin a process of death, for previously they were immortal. Physical death came soon enough, as their first son killed their second son. But the word "death" actually means "separation." This can obviously mean separation of the soul from the physical body, but it also meant a rupture of the connection between these first humans and their God. And, as the rebellious nature of Satan became part of them as they joined in his rebellion, humanity became divided from each other. An incoherence was introduced into human nature as people made in God's image now also contained the nature of God's enemy. All of the internal struggles of individuals, and all of the strife between people flowed directly from

> Isn't this what it means to be "as God"? Are we not all being tempted to become the gods of our own lives as we brush past the real One?

this introduction of death into the human race. How much of life in our current world looks like slow-motion death? It is true that we have vast power to fashion our lives, more power than most believe, in fact (power we will discuss later in detail). But our personal power also has definite limits we need to recognize and respect. We have the power to choose, but we do not have the power to overturn the inherent consequences of our decisions.

As for Satan's role and the role of those who follow him, angelic and human, what agenda are they pursuing? How can we know when things we are hearing in a conversation in our culture, or within our own minds and hearts, actually originate from this source? What do Satan's fingerprints look like? First, know that Satan is trying to upend the proper order of things, to rebel against things that are good, right, and constructive—things commended and commanded by God. Beyond this, he is trying to substitute his own ways for the ways of God, to upend the moral universe God created: a new legal system, a new rendering of right and wrong; a new power structure, with himself at the top and every other being in subjugation; and, in rising to godhood, he aspires to ordain reality itself. That is, he wants to be the one to determine outcomes and consequences. *"You will surely not die."* He wants to become the ultimate ruler and to be worshipped as the universe's preeminent creature. And his followers, mimicking him, vie for power to dominate, to tear down whatever is of God, trying to substitute alternatives to what God has ordained in every detail of life. We see these efforts in our culture in full swing regarding sexuality, marriage, gender, and many other issues.

In Christian culture we acknowledge one major turning point in the moral course of humanity: the Fall of Mankind in the Garden of Eden described in Genesis 3. The Jewish culture at the time of Jesus, and likely throughout their history, saw a second event as even more morally devastating to humanity. The second event occurred after the event in the Garden, when other fallen angels under Satan's dominion began to engage with humanity, eventually corrupting them to the point that God sent the Flood to blot out all but Noah and his family (Genesis 6:1-8). It can be reasonably assumed that this same group of immortal beings continue to engage with humanity, exerting the same corrupting influence.[3]

It is fascinating to see how little creativity is at work in Satan's efforts. His agenda is simply to oppose God, to offer *not-God*. He offers the illusion of better life—things that are supposedly new, progressive, exciting, the product of the forward evolution of humanity—while in reality binding people to himself and leading them toward death. At minimum, if individuals can be seduced into choices that depart from God's path, the consequences inherent in their choices damage those made in God's image. If Satan can successfully corrupt the understanding and practice of covenant relationships, the heart of God's plan to overcome Satan's impact on humanity, at minimum he disrupts the power and blessings God intends these relationships to have. But if Satan can keep individuals from accepting God's life-saving offer of relationship, these individuals follow Satan into eternity, joining him in the final death and judgment he must know, at some level, he cannot avoid.

GOD'S OFFER: AN ISSUE OF LIFE AND DEATH

In the end, the offer God makes is about life and death. God offers us life, new life, abundant life. Most think God's offer to us primarily centers upon forgiveness of sins. We will speak much of this going forward, but note here that Jesus used the words "sin" and "sins" seventeen times in conversations recorded in Scripture. He used the term "life" eighty-one times. Sin, or rebellion against God, is not an unimportant topic for myriad reasons, and it must be dealt with in God's overall plan. This is, after all, one dimension of the original and ongoing problem of humanity. But there is a deeper and more profound dimension: death entered the human race through rebellion, and Satan's nature within each human is a down payment on the fullness of that death. The payment of Jesus for sin by His death on the cross and transient separation from the Father deals with our sentence of eternal death. But this forgiveness will not offer us new life; by it we only escape an eternity in Satan's company. The essence of God's plan is *new life* in light of *our current state of death,* to create a totally new creature in covenant with Himself. This old creature, joined and merged with Satan, literally dies. A new creature, merged and joined with Himself as he or she is indwelled by God's Spirit, is born. In addition to reestablishing the connection lost with God in the Garden, He intends that a proper connection be reestablished between all people who are in covenant with Him. This connection is called a covenant relationship, the New Covenant.

If this is God's offer to us, how does one take God up on this offer? In a pattern that is boringly repetitious, there is not only confusion about the nature of this relationship and its fundamental purpose but also confusion about how one enters this relationship. Once we have a clear understanding of covenant, much of this confusion dissipates. Let us see how Jesus introduces this relationship, this covenant.

BELIEVING IN JESUS

Jesus' answer to the person who asked Him how to be in a right relationship with God—"What must we do to do the works God requires?"—was first to instruct the questioner to believe in Him. Thus, our first step is to consider what it means to actually believe in Jesus. We are addressing this topic at length because we need to become crystal clear about what it means to believe in Jesus. As we will see in the next few pages, our decision to believe in Jesus *in the way He defines it,* versus believing in Jesus as most people would define the concept, may in the end have a greater impact on the course of our lives than any other decision we make. This is the decision that will lead to the full development, or lack of full development, of our relationship with Him. To embrace and fully implement God's plan for marriage also entails believing in God, His Word, and His plan for marriage. Thus, correctly understanding and taking this first step, believing in Jesus, will also determine the quality of our marriages. We want to lay a proper foundation of understanding. So we will begin at precisely the point Jesus began His own revelation of these things.

CAN WE REALLY HAVE EVERYTHING WE WANT?

In our modern world we are used to choosing each element of life—selecting what we like, what we prefer, or what makes sense to us—and passing over the rest, much like going down the line in a cafeteria or shopping in a mall or browsing through online offerings. We take what we want, we leave the rest. This is, after all, our most fundamental right as a human, is it not? To have things *our way*? To exercise *our prerogative*? To get what *we want*? Many in our modern age live as if *believing in* and *following* Jesus consists of seeing the truths, principles, laws, commands, and other things He offers us, and—assuming we are free to select the items we want or agree with—simply pass by the rest. At least the Jews asked Jesus want matters most to God. We content ourselves with the things that matter most to ourselves and assume that God's love and grace will make up the difference. We then think, because we are drawing at least some things from Jesus, we are "believing in Him." Our goal in doing this is to add value to our lives. How does this correspond with what Jesus asks of us?

Jesus does not make believing in Him easy. He has an annoying habit of doing what He did with the people who listened to Him that day in Capernaum, as quoted in John 6—saying something that is far beyond our understanding or that conflicts with our sense of priorities, viewpoints, or beliefs. As He does this He is actually forcing us to confront the issue of what or whom we believe in. He is not content to have people think that they are truly following Him when they merely choose *some* of Him. If some of Him would be better than none of Him, why does this bother Jesus enough that He forces the issue to the point that people must choose all of Him or none of Him? He

> If some of Him would be better than none of Him, why does this bother Jesus enough that He forces the issue to the point that people must choose all of Him or none of Him?

does this because of the origin of the other ideas that people are trying to synthesize with God's ideas. This is the big picture we examined previously. Simply put, there can be no successful synthesis between the words of God and those of Satan, between truth and deception, between reality and false reality, or between a wannabe god and the real God.

Jesus wants to bring us to the point where we define for ourselves whether we are truly following Him. This will be proven not by what we think, feel, or say, but by what we do. We certainly want our thoughts, feelings, values, and more to be in line with God, but, as we will see later in our discussion, the defining moment of our lives and the focal point of our own character development comes when we make a decision about who or what we believe in. Everything else that follows simply carries out and expresses this decision.

For the people who listened to Jesus in John 6, the decision of each person soon became physically evident. Some literally turned and walked away from Him. It is significant to note that He said nothing further to them as they walked away. He allowed them their choices. In doing this Jesus wants to teach us something vitally important: if our plan includes reserving the right to overrule Him, or to edit Him, or to try to get value-add in our lives by applying His wisdom only as we see fit, our plan *is not His plan*. He wants to be Lord of our lives. We want to be lord of our own lives. We must make the most fundamental of choices first, before we address any of our other choices: who is actually going to be our Lord—or lord. Nothing less than actually following God and His plan will produce the life He desires for us, the life He created us to live. If we reserve the right to edit Him as we see fit, who is truly our lord—Jesus, or ourselves? He wants His truth to set us free—from the damage caused by the deception that is inherent in everything but Him. We cannot be freed from the consequences of deception and lies if we continue to embrace those very lies. Do we really trust Him and believe in Him, or when pressed will we turn away to one alternative or another, proving before all humanity that we do not believe in Him in the way He defines it?

Jesus may make following Him hard by leading us in ways that challenge us, but even in this He leads by example. Jesus also followed Someone: His Father. God's path for Jesus led Him at times to question God, and to obedience that was reluctant. Remember Jesus sweating blood in the Garden of Gethsemane? Remember Him asking the Father if there was any other way, and to "take this cup from me"? Crying out to His Father on the cross, "Why have you forsaken me?" He clearly struggled, but then ended up just where He asks us to be as we follow Him: "Not my will, but Thine be done." The pinnacle of believing in God is simply to trust Him when we do not understand where He is leading us, or why our lives are as they are. We can only entrust our lives to Him in these situations because we understand *who* He is, and because we know *how much* He loves us. In fact, it is only in such times of personal uncertainty that we show what or whom we truly believe.

> It is only in such times of personal uncertainty that we show what or whom we truly believe.

If we are looking for God's plan for our lives, what would we expect to see? Would it be something that simply adds value to our lives? Something that gets us closer to having the things the world tells us we need? Or would we expect to see something that surprises us? Something that we might not believe, and may not even want at first glance? Because His plan is far more powerful, more revolutionary, than the modest improvements we seek, or even the most wonderful outcomes we can envision for our lives. What seems possible in our own power and what is actually possible with God's power are quite different.

Would God's plan for our lives likely be radical? Might He want to direct us to lives that are the pinnacle of His creation, the full outpouring of His love for us, the ultimate fullness that He intended for us in the Garden of Eden? Might He even want to erase those things within us that are the millennia-long heritage of the work of His enemy in human civilization and in individual human hearts? And might He want our lives to represent the accumulated blessings that accrue from a lifetime of doing good and right? And beyond this, might He even want a far grander and more glorious future for us, one that rewards our belief in Him in ways beyond our conception for all eternity?

HOW DOES *THIS* DISCUSSION HELP US UNDERSTAND COVENANT?

Why would the above discussion be in a book about covenant relationships? Because covenant relationships are a gift to us from God. To properly appreciate these relationships we must understand why this gift is so important. We must understand the problems God's gift is designed to solve. As we look at these problems on the surface, each appears to be primarily about us making better decisions. However, at a deeper level, there are other issues. There is a fundamental flaw in every person in terms of nature and character that causes us to *want* to make decisions that depart from God's plan at some point. If we take the Scriptures to heart and correlate what God says about each of us—our altered nature, the sentence of death over our lives, our own inner vacuum that can only be filled by an intimate relationship with God—we can see that God is speaking to our deepest personal needs as He offers us new lives in covenant with Himself. If we have exhausted ourselves with fruitless attempts at self-improvement, the words of Jesus take on fresh meaning: *"If you hold to my teaching, you are really my disciples. Then you will know the truth and the truth will set you free"* (John 8:31, 32). Free from what? From bondage—"slavery" is the term He actually uses—or the firm grip that sin (following the wrong path, making wrong decisions, embracing the lies of the enemy about any and every facet of life) has on our lives. We cannot lift ourselves

> There is a fundamental flaw in every person in terms of nature and character that causes us to *want* to make decisions that depart from God's plan.

out of this mess try as we might. We need God. We need a new life, a new nature, in order to be freed from the hold that His enemies have on our lives.

We need marriages that are true exercises in unity, characterized by love. We need to build what marriages are designed to build. We need marriages that are happily-ever-after, not happily-till-it-isn't-working-for-me. Growing grounds and proving grounds, not battle-grounds; sacred space, not a demilitarized zone in a battle of the sexes. But how can this happen if we are following our own misinformed understanding of our best interests, misinformation actually intended to lead our marriages off the cliff? To have a marriage and keep it, must we always be settling for second best? Or, to truly find our best lives, must we sacrifice our wives or husbands? Or is almost everything we think we know about marriage different from God's plan for marriage, the only working plan?

Given the challenges God must address, what we do not need are injunctions to simply be nicer to one another and soundbite answers that have no real power. God's gift to humanity of two covenants is not simply about a way of relating or about rules for relating. What we need is a comprehensive plan for reorienting our lives and revising ourselves at the deepest level. This is a gift that challenges our understanding of human relationships, and challenges much of our understanding of ourselves. It strongly challenges our culture's concepts about what is best for us and about the path to our best lives. It may even challenge our beliefs about who God is and about the nature of the relationship that God offers us. It certainly offered such challenges for most people as Jesus spoke in John 6.

If what God tells us collides with the way we see things or with our current beliefs, we face a decision. This decision is precisely the same as faced by Eve. It is also the same one faced by those who heard Jesus' words in John 6. I would suggest that any voice that dissents from what God clearly says is actually the voice of our enemy. We are unlikely to correctly identify the origin of such ideas unless we have the big picture firmly in mind. If we do not, we will predictably make the same mistake that Eve made, one repeated countless times in countless lives throughout history. The cumulative effects of all the decisions informed by God's enemies throughout history comprise the challenges in our current world, the challenges in our relationships, and the challenges within ourselves that we confront every day. It is this accumulation of consequences that we must endure as we pass through life. This is the true nature of the challenges we all face as we build our marriages and build our relationships with God.

A covenant relationship involves many concepts, principles, duties, and responsibilities that are completely countercultural. This in a culture that increasingly metes out punishment for violating current cultural assumptions and trends. If we follow God's plan, thus departing from the world's plan, we are in for a bumpy ride. Jesus predicted this in the lives of His disciples. His own life certainly evidenced this reality. This is as true today as it has been for millennia. Though covenant is the heart of God's plan for us, it seems that every imaginable force is arrayed against our learning, embracing, and living out these things. The big picture we have painted suggests why this would be so: *to the extent that people live out this plan and build what God desires to build, the lives produced are the strongest imaginable refutation to the lies of God's enemies.*

It is crucial for us to understand these truths as we consider implementing God's plan on a daily basis. We each have a choice at every point as we seek to implement this plan. Our actions will demonstrate whom and what we believe. Do we believe in God, or do we believe in ourselves, our culture, and the one who largely formed our culture, one who is expending every effort to drive that culture as far from God as possible?

In *whom* do you believe?

WHO IS DR. MARK JOHNSON?

Since we are discussing the identity of the voices around us, it would be appropriate that I tell you a little more about myself. I do not have a theological degree; nor do I represent the viewpoint of any denomination or theological thought-system. I am a physician, trained as a surgeon, who attended Emory University on a full National Merit Scholarship. I have a very strong science background. As a surgeon and clinical physician it has been my job to synthesize facts revealed by scientific study—medical research—and the opinions of learned people, along with my own observations, analysis, and experience, to develop an understanding of the problems of individual patients. That understanding in turn is used to craft a treatment plan that ideally will remedy those problems. This is never a certainty in the real world, but if a problem is diagnosed accurately and a treatment is chosen that has demonstrated effectiveness for this condition, good results are obtained in most patients. And when good results are not initially obtained, one must sort through the many variables present in every patient, adapting and adjusting the treatment as one attempts to get the desired result. Having participated in this process of diagnosis and treatment in thousands of patients across several decades, I have an extremely clear view of the way science intersects with reality—both the benefits of science and also the limitations of scientific study and of the opinions of scientists when dealing with the unique set of circumstances in an individual patient.

I applied the same amount of acumen and diligence to question the correlation between another body of truth and reality—the revelation of God in Scriptures with the world we inhabit. Also, the correlation between these Scriptures and my own nature and inner experience. In 1977, during my first year in medical school at the University of Alabama, Josh McDowell did a lecture series on the evidence for certain key Christian beliefs. Those beliefs: that someone called Jesus existed; that this Jesus claimed to be God; that He backed this claim, after being crucified by Romans at the request of the Jewish spiritual leaders, by rising from the dead; that the collection of writings called the Bible have been accurately conveyed to us through history; and that these writings correlate with reality in a way that is unique among all the writings of the ancient or modern world. Further, that the prophetic predictions scattered throughout these Scriptures, each of which has come exactingly true—something not seen in any other secular or spiritual writing in history—strongly argue that the ul-

McDowell also cleared up one other point of contention: people often want a "scientific" proof of the existence of God, yet these same people do not operate on the basis of scientific proof in any other realm of their lives!

timate author of these Scriptures is God. Combining the content of McDowell's lectures with my own study of these topics, it became much more reasonable to believe these assertions: that Jesus lived, died, and was resurrected from the dead as described in the Scriptures; that He was fully human, but also fully God; and that the Scriptures exist in a form that is in every significant detail identical to their original form, preserved as no other document in history for thousands of years. In short, it made much more sense to believe than disbelieve these premises.

McDowell also cleared up one other point of contention: people often want a "scientific" proof of the existence of God, yet these same people do not operate on the basis of scientific proof in any other realm of their lives! Even scientists do not base much of their professional lives on actual scientifically proven facts, much less their political views or personal preferences. Scientific papers present varied and often conflicting results as those papers try to prove or disprove various theories. Scientists take these results and assign more—or less—credibility to one result or another to form their own opinions on scientific questions, which is why the scientific community is filled with debates on almost every topic. If science were the unquestionable road to truth, this ever-shifting world of scientific thought and belief would not be as it is; these debates would not exist. What opinion in any of these scientific debates can one rely upon with 100 percent confidence?

Instead, we all employ a different approach to find our "truths for living," a standard of proof that is *not* scientific, but *judicial*. Judicial proof is about the preponderance of evidence and the credibility of that evidence. Is there more evidence on one side of an issue or the other? Is some evidence more credible than other evidence? What do people around me think, including people whose opinions I value? This is the process everyone engages in to arrive at their *beliefs about what is true and what is not.* People hear the evidence on both sides and render a verdict, which may be correct, or not. We must always remember that deeming something to be true *does not make it true.* Whether something is actually true is a separate question altogether. We will discuss how this process works in great detail, for this is the mechanism that produces a vast array of often-conflicting beliefs that guide the lives of everyone around us, including our own. For now, simply note that when someone disdains belief in God because there is "no scientific proof" of His existence, the statement is not authoritative; in fact, this statement reflects a lack of understanding on the part of the speaker.

> Viewed from a judicial standpoint, when examining the available evidence for the existence of God and the central premises of Christianity, the evidence is overwhelming.

Viewed from a judicial standpoint, when examining the available evidence for the existence of God and the central premises of Christianity, the evidence is overwhelming. Realizing this allowed me to reach a point where I trusted the words of Jesus and the other writers of Scripture as the words of God. "All Scripture is inspired by God" (2 Timothy 3:16). God has laid down a vast written record of His interaction with humanity across many millennia. He went to the trouble to do this for many excellent reasons, not least of which is giving us a credible source of truth—truth not originating in the mind of any human, but conveyed by God Himself, against which we can evaluate any other information, premise, or belief.

I came to view the words of Scripture as true, and to believe the things the Scriptures related about Jesus and other matters. But at this point, did I believe *in Jesus*? No. That is an entirely different question. Soon, I chose to do this as well, to entrust my life and future to Him. This last step was based not only upon the facts of the matter as I came to understand them but was also fueled by seeing the lives of a number of deeply committed Christians in my class at close range under the intense pressures of the first year of medical school. These people as a group exhibited qualities I wanted to see in my life but did not. It became clear to me that these desirable qualities represented the presence of God's Spirit in the lives of my classmates. It also became clear, painfully clear, that I was not in this kind of relationship with God despite the fact that I had grown up attending church and thought I was a Christian. Until I realized that I was not.

I chose to enter a covenant relationship with God as it is described in the Scriptures. Once I was in this relationship, it is an understatement to say that I did not fully understand the nature, scope, impact, or purposes of this relationship. This understanding came gradually over time.

My passion from the beginning was to understand how I could develop the deepest, most fruitful, and most rewarding relationship with God. Thanks to excellent teaching and a mentoring relationship with several mature Christians, I began to grow spiritually. And I soon developed a passion for helping other people grow in their relationship with God. None of us fully understand every aspect of a relationship with God, but I have studied this topic enthusiastically for the forty years since becoming a Christian. This study has not been just an intellectual exercise but one about seeing my own life grow, change, and transform as the Scriptures show is possible, and about addressing real problems, issues, and needs in the lives of other people.

> In each there is a microcosm of the history-long spiritual battle between the Author of all that is good and the prince of darkness.

Over these forty years I have only become more convinced that God actually exists, loves me more than I can imagine, and is in a real-time, intimate relationship with me guiding every detail of my life. Thus, I was right to believe in Him and to give myself to Him in the way He desires and directs. And I have gone far enough down this road, and seen other people far enough down their own roads, to see vast numbers of consequences play out in my own life and in the lives of others. This is the ultimate reality test. All of this is to say that my belief in God is not based upon ignorance, lack of acumen, or some bias against scientifically attested reality. It is based upon reality in every sense of the word. And one reality that becomes even more clear over time is the battle that is being waged in the minds and hearts of every human—in each there is a microcosm of the history-long spiritual battle between the Author of all that is good and the prince of darkness.

This is the world we inhabit, and this is who we are as we inhabit this world.

* * * * *

We have looked at the big picture, a world caught in a spiritual war, a crossfire of competing ideas and agendas for each individual. Much of the reality of this spiritual war is out of our sight. We only see glimpses and occasionally have a clear view of consequences. Our only clear and comprehensive source of information about ourselves and our world is the Bible. The overall quality of life and relationships in our world and the problems of our world certainly line up perfectly with the big picture presented in Scripture, which we just discussed. If all of this is true, it is imperative that we take all of these things into account as we confront our own life decisions. The most important life decision is whether we choose to enter a covenant relationship with God.

The second most important decision we will ever make is about how faithful we intend to be to God's plan for our lives. The more we understand about the big picture we have painted thus far, the less drawn we will be to the competing plan of the world, and the more we will desire to be wholly faithful to our loving heavenly Father and His plan. His plan, as noted, is centered around two relationships, two covenants. Here, we want to lay a conceptual foundation that will help us put God's plan for these relationships in proper context in our lives, and our lives and God's truth in proper context in the world we inhabit.

Next, let us look at our lives, hearts, and relationships. How do our hearts work? What do we really need? Do we simply fall into the relationship of our dreams, or must the best relationships be carefully built? If so, how are they built? Does the institution of marriage actually help us do this, or not?

FOUR

Do We Know How to Build the Best Relationships?

God wants relationships that are constructive, cooperative, productive, stable, and gratifying. He wants relationships to create an environment that promotes personal growth and transformation. He wants us to grow into the people He created us to be, people who love well and deeply. Growth of those in relationship and growth of the relationship happen in tandem. People who learn how to grow together, grow together.

How do we get there from here?

We next want to look at how the enemy's deceptions have impacted the way we conduct relationships, and the impact on our hearts and minds. We are certainly doing some things right in relationships. At the same time, we may have some misconceptions about ourselves, about other people, about how relationships are built and sustained, and about what needs to change in ourselves for best results. And even if we see a need for change in ourselves, we may have no idea how these changes can occur. Frankly, if we simply take what our culture tells us about all of these things at face value, when we see God's plan it may be difficult to understand this plan or its benefits, much less its power.

Based on the world's way of thinking, God's plan makes little or no sense. In other words, if we accept the world's ideas about what our best lives look like, God's plan is definitely *not* the way to get there. The thing we must carefully consider is whether the promised benefits of the world's way of living are actual—or an illusion. Does this path lead to true love and deep fulfillment? In order to see the true potential of God's plan, we first need to understand some things about how we are constructed—how our hearts and minds work. We need to better understand what is, and is not, changeable within ourselves. Deep relationships are about love. What do we really understand about love? What do we know about building the best love relationship over a lifetime?

For most of this chapter we will look at our relationship IQs in relation to marriage, but exactly the same issues are in play in other re-

> Based on the world's way of thinking, God's plan makes little or no sense. In other words, if we accept the world's ideas about what our best lives look like, God's plan is definitely *not* the way to get there.

lationships, including our relationship with God. We are already in many relationships, and many of them we would consider successful. But the more we understand about relationships, and about ourselves, the more possibilities we will see for improvement. This is the goal we are pursuing: the best relationships. Part of God's plan is to teach us how to improve all of our relationships.

ALL ARE EQUALLY MARRIED, BUT ALL MARRIAGES ARE NOT EQUAL

Two couples are standing at the altar in different churches on the same day. All four have just looked in the eyes of their beloved, spoke vows to each other, and said "I do." Their hearts are filled with delightful feelings, and they are filled with optimism for their future. They long for and are determined to find their happily-ever-after. But somewhere, way in the back of each mind, is a nagging question. All four people have had friends who had marriages go terribly wrong, yet all of those couples started out just like this. Those friends also vowed that their love would never fail. So how can these couples, who have just made their vows to each other, who have such high hopes for their lives together, really know how things will turn out? What does it mean to keep a vow that involves loving each other for a lifetime if that love is something they just "fell into"? What if their love doesn't last? How do they know, even now, that their love is true love, even though everything inside them tells them it is? How do they know this is the right person, their true soul mate, even though they believe this to be true? What do they do *now* to make these relationships really work? And is the relationship working—in the long run—really up to them? These are merely fleeting thoughts, though. They are all madly in love with their chosen other. Surely love will conquer all.

Three years later, one wife is telling her closest friends that her guy is an insensitive idiot with a golf addiction who would never dream of helping her around the house, or with his child. Meanwhile, he is telling the guys in the golf clubhouse that his wife's nagging and control issues are driving him nuts to the point that he is staying later at work and playing even more golf. They haven't slept together for three months. How's it going in this paradise?

The other couple is sitting on the porch of their home, sixty-three years later, reminiscing. Their marriage has been a lifelong love affair. They have four children, nine grandchildren, and eighteen great-grandchildren. They have been many places, done many things, and learned many lessons since the day their covenant journey began. Their most profound lesson has been how to build and sustain their love for one another and for the Maker who led them together. Upon this foundation everything else in life was built. One will be leaving soon. Their journey together now includes an incurable disease that will soon end one life. But there are no regrets, only the joy and satisfaction of a life well-lived, and an understanding that life here is not forever, though life itself is eternal. Theirs will be a temporary separation, and with that sadness and pain, but also a coming reunion for both with the God each will follow to their final home.

So let's ask ourselves: what is the most important difference between these two stories?

What is the secret of enduring love in a marriage?

1. Finding the right person, a true soul mate.

2. Being deeply in love with each other.

3. Finding true love.

4. Being true to each other.

5. Not falling out of love.

6. Forces beyond one's control.

7. To a substantial degree, living out God's plan for marriage.

If you are in love and contemplating marriage, or if you are recently married, you likely believe that you do not need much advice about how to build and sustain a loving relationship. After all, you are doing this right now. But anyone considering marriage, or already married in our culture, must have a question in the back of his or her mind. That is, how does one ensure a successful marriage "until death do us part"? How can we build a lifetime love affair? How can we reach the potential that marriage offers us?

> But anyone considering marriage, or already married in our culture, must have a question in the back of his or her mind. That is, how does one ensure a successful marriage "until death do us part"?

We all know married couples who have great marriages, so-so marriages, struggling marriages, cold marriages. We know people who are unlikely to remain married for long, and we know many people who are already divorced. We know people who had awful marriages who put things back together and are now happily married, and we know people who were madly in love who are now struggling. Yet, do not all of these relationships—every single one—have the same potential? What causes these marriages to turn out so differently? I suspect that almost every couple standing at the altar sees much that is very right in each other. They have deep, loving feelings toward each other. Virtually everyone, at this point, would describe themselves as "in love." So virtually everyone starts well, and more or less at the same point.

But let's think for a moment about what builds a successful marriage in the long run. Every choice in the boxed question on the previous page, or some combination of those items, is believed to be *the answer* by a substantial number of people in our culture—except, ironically, the last choice. Of course, there is an element of truth in each of those seven points. We need to choose a mate carefully, we need to enjoy being with that person, we need a depth of feeling toward each other we would describe as "being in love." But we will see that the last item is the key to building a relationship that progresses, a relationship in which love grows over time, versus two people looking back longingly to the time when they were so much in love. So, what is God's plan? It is a comprehensive path to building hearts and lives around each other and around one's marriage so that, through the years, a relationship is built that is strongest, deepest, and most satisfying.

But if we are truly, deeply, madly in love, if we have found the right person—our true soul mate—why do we need a plan?

WHAT DOES A HAPPILY-EVER-AFTER RELATIONSHIP LOOK LIKE?

What do you think about when you hear the words "great marriage"? Given that marriage is the most deep and broad relationship we can have, one that impacts literally every part of our being, our thoughts might go in many directions. We can think of what it feels like to be with each other, of our hearts lighting up each time we see each other. We can think of romance, passion, being swept away in someone's arms for the rest of our lives. We can think of being consistently treated in ways we deeply appreciate. We can think of someone who is true to us consistently and for a lifetime. We can think of creating a safe haven for one another. We can think of the many ways two people can support each other and display care and concern for each other. We can think of protecting and being protected. We can think of provision, of being nourished and blessed. We can think of things we would enjoy doing with the other person, things we would like to introduce them to, new things we could explore together. Still more: shared interests, common vision, co-laboring to build lasting and important things. We can think of joining another person on a journey through life that is far more delightful and rewarding because we are sharing that journey and growing toward a common goal. We can think of the things that grow out of marriage and family that offer more satisfaction and gratification than any other human experience, blessings like children, grandchildren, and extended family. We think of growing old together.

Most do not yearn for all of these things at the outset, but God in His wisdom has blessings in mind that we do not see as we begin our journey.

> How would you define "true love"? How would a person find one's true love once he or she knows what they are looking for?
>
> Please consider your thoughts on this before reading further.

WHAT IS TRUE LOVE?

There are many opinions about authentic, heartfelt love. What is it? Does it really exist? How do we know it when we see it? Is there something about another person that can make me happy for a lifetime? Is it something someone else sees *in me* that makes them think I can make them happy for a lifetime? Is it someone who completes me? Someone who deeply needs me or whom I deeply need? Someone who advances my life goals, who is definitely value-added to my life? One thing is obvious: intense romantic attractions defy explanation beyond a certain point. Another thing is obvious. The intense feelings that characterize "falling in love" are not a permanent feature in relationships. Not that strong and intense feelings cannot persist and grow over a lifetime—they can. I have experienced this, as have many others. But they do not necessarily do so no matter how strong those feelings were initially. And the reasons that they do grow stronger, or do not, are some of the most important things to understand about marriage.

While two people are getting to know each other, intense feelings can develop well before these two people really know each other—which we often term "love at first sight." While we may be able to discern some things about another person this quickly, can anyone fully understand another person at this point? Or are our feelings early in a relationship more about who we *think* the other person is, and the role we *imagine* the other person is going to play in our lives, versus things we know with certainty are true from experience? We see cues and hints that indicate to us that this person will be this way or that way, or that they will do this thing or that thing, or play this role—or that—in our lives. We imagine how wonderful our lives will be together.

But in reality the first few months of a relationship are about comparing what we *hope will be* with what we actually *find the person to be* as we get to know them. It takes months to begin replacing a hoped-for view with an accurate view of a person based on experience. At this point of transition, often about six months into a relationship, most romances end as reality overcomes the optimism.

Also, this is about the time that people begin to shift from *trying-to-win-you* behavior to their more typical ways of treating people.

> Also, this is about the time that people begin to shift from *trying-to-win-you* behavior to more typical ways of treating people.

THE GOD WHO IS LOVE CREATED US TO LOVE

In relationships where no obvious deal-killer comes to light and two people are finding more and more common ground, where feelings for each other continue to grow, there is a logical progression. There is a drive to be more connected, fully connected, permanently connected, to the other person. This is the drive to be married that is wired within us by our Creator. People expend vast effort and resources toward winning the agreement of the other person, then toward staging the huge party that is a wedding. God has also built within us the sense that marriage is something so special that such effort and expenditures make perfect sense. Everyone is reaching to grasp their happily-ever-after. Through the profound emotion we call *love*, God gives us the desire and energy to build something intended to be one of the most broad, deep, and meaningful of human experiences—a marriage and family. Our feelings motivate us to treat the other person in ways we have never treated anyone else, offering example after example of our love through our actions.

God's plan is that we rest in each other, savor each other's presence, experience the depths of the other, and enjoy giving and receiving loving attention. He intends that we revel in the security and strength, in the softness and tenderness, of each other. God is the ultimate romantic. He *designed* romance for us. The vows and expectations of marriage sum up our deepest desire: love until death do us part.

These things are all well known. What is less well known is that God actually offers us a *plan* to fulfill this desire. There are two major facets to His plan. One is the formal relationship of marriage. Second is the quality of the relationship, our heart experience and the experience we create for the other person. God's plan for the formal relationship involves the key to developing the best long-term heart relationship. Both facets are necessary for God's plan to produce best results if two people are trying to join together for life. Some think that the formality and commitment of marriage stand in the way of the best heart experience. This could not be further from the truth if we truly understand marriage. None of us want a lifeless or troubled heart relationship within the strong confines of marriage. We want a lifelong, passionate love affair, don't we? This is also what God intends.

THE TRUTH ABOUT TRUE LOVE

If we think that true love is some kind of inherent quality that another person has toward us, if we think true love is something we fall into in some random and mysterious fashion, will we be more focused on building the relationship or just enjoying the relationship we have somehow fallen into? Most people, when the initial rush of loving feelings rocks their world, just want this state to continue. And they think that if their feelings are true love, that it will. This is the central premise of Hallmark movies: path to true love is simply to realize we have found the *right person.* When we reach the point that we want to give our life to another person, everyone thinks their love is strong enough, true enough, and the other person is right enough for this state of love to continue forever happily. Here is the truth, though, about love. True love is not something that anyone has at the outset. We may have a great beginning to a relationship, but this is only a great beginning. Predictably, the initial rush of attraction, the feelings that draw people together, do not last indefinitely. What will determine how we feel toward each other in five or ten or forty years?

HOW WE ARE TREATED = HOW WE FEEL ABOUT A PERSON OVER TIME

Think of two people you have known for a long time—one with whom you have a close and healthy relationship, the other with whom you do not have a healthy or close relationship. What is the primary difference in these two relationships? Is it not the ways these two people have treated you? And are the different ways they treat you determined by the very different ways they view you? One sees you as a friend, an ally, and acts accordingly. This person respects you, trusts you, and values you highly. The other sees you as something else and acts accordingly. Have you been around someone you thought would be your friend, but over time your relationship went in a different direction . . . because of the way they treated you? The simple equation heading this paragraph is as certain a thing as gravity.

WHY DO PEOPLE TREAT OTHERS IN WAYS THAT DAMAGE RELATIONSHIPS?

If the way relationships turn out in the long run depends on how people treat each other, why do people act toward one another in ways that damage relationships? First, is it always about you? Or do people often treat others in ways that have more to do with what is going on within themselves? People may not be trying to hurt you, they do not intend to offend you—but they do. Why? Is it because this is the way they have learned to treat people? And what of the person who is trying to hurt you? Is this because they view you in a certain way, as someone it is OK to hurt? If your husband or wife views you as someone it is OK to hurt, how might this impact your heart toward them? If they have true love toward you, though, would they ever do something to hurt you? Why do people predictably do things that hurt each other, even with the deepest feelings toward each other? This is because our feelings for another are only one of the reasons we act in the ways we act. It is important to understand the other reasons why we act as we do.

THOSE IN LOVE EXPECT TO TREAT EACH OTHER WELL FOREVER

Now I want to think about what happens over time when two people are in the closeness and intimacy of a deep, heartfelt marriage. As we are falling in love, things are awakening within, new and wonderful feelings toward each other. These feelings lead to the very special ways people who are in love treat each other. People are better than they have ever been toward another—attentive, kind, understanding, generous, protective, and much more. This in turn produces an experience truly worth having, and to ever-deepening feelings in our hearts. As we are falling in love, we actually think we will always be at our best toward each other, don't we? And we expect the same of the other person, the one who truly loves us. These are the hearts God created in us functioning in the way He intended. And our expectation that this goodness of heart will be a lifelong state is a reasonable expectation if

. . . what? What would it take to continue this kind of relationship for a lifetime?

BUT HOW DO WE END UP TREATING EACH OTHER?

Over time, though, what happens? Eventually, we begin to treat each other according to how we have always treated other people. Our habits emerge. Will we not treat our spouse as we have learned to treat everyone else? Will we not view our spouse as we view other people? What happens next in the relationship is determined by how constructive our habits and patterns are. These habits and patterns come to us by lessons learned from our family of origin, our friends, and our culture. At times our habits and patterns are misformed by traumatic experiences, or they may be misinformed by wrong ideas or wrong values. What happens next can also be guided by God's plan for building an intimate lifelong relationship with another human being. Ideally these two are one and the same, but often they are not.

AREN'T WE JUST BEING OURSELVES?

If the ways we treat each other have to do with our attitudes, values, habits, viewpoints, and priorities, where do these things come from? Are these things that simply flow up from the core of our being? Are these the characteristics that define us as us? Is this what being ourselves looks like? Isn't expressing these things the essence of being authentic? Or do these things represent something else entirely? Certainly our authentic being is somewhere in the midst of the ways we express ourselves, and at times we are expressing the very core of our being.

But how do we separate our deepest self—the parts of us that must be loved, accepted, embraced, and affirmed if we are to be truly loved—from those things that are not indispensable parts of us? How can we identify the things it would be beneficial to change, if we knew we could change them? This is a vital question to answer. Why? Because all of us do things in relationships that cause damage. The question for each of us is whether these are things *we can and should change*, and then to learn to conduct ourselves differently. Or are these things that, if we are truly loved, the other person must figure out how to adapt to successfully? Whose responsibility is it to adapt and adjust in these situations? God has an extremely specific answer to this question. This understanding—what needs to change, who needs to change, and how this change occurs—is the key that unlocks the door to the best relationships.

THE WORLD'S CONFUSION ABOUT LOVE

The world, on the other hand, wants us to view things in a different way. It trains people to think that love comes and goes in random and mysterious ways. Attractions merely fall upon us, or we fall into them. It is true that we are built—hardwired—for such attractions to occur, and strong attractions often seem surprising, random, even at times highly improbable. As these attractions occur, however, the world's viewpoint quickly becomes reality-challenged. Our world teaches us to continue pursuing our old priorities, to continue "being ourselves," just as the world has trained us to be up to this point. Isn't true love, after all, about someone loving us deeply and forever for who we are? But "being ourselves," in the sense that most people understand this phrase, often leads to actions, attitudes, and values that damage hearts, lives, and relationships. Once a critical mass of such destruction occurs, what change happens in our hearts toward each other? People stop trusting each other as friends; they start wanting to avoid each other; they lose respect for each other. Rather than viewing the other person as the path to a wonderful life, the other person comes to be viewed as the path to unsolvable and unending problems. The relationship grows distant; hearts grow cool. Then it "isn't working anymore," and people walk away. What just happened? Did two people just fall out of love? Did they not really have true love? Did they not find the right person after all?

Is this cooling of hearts a random change, or is this the predictable consequence of actions and attitudes? And this is not just about the effects of another's behavior toward us. We bring our own set of issues to the table. How do our minds and hearts handle difficult situations? What are our expectations, and how do we deal with people when they do not meet them? A vast array of events and interactions can cause feelings to change over time. Is any of this really under our control? We will soon see the extent to which all of this is directly under our control. Is there any way we can negotiate through the issues of life and actually grow closer? Yes! God saw all of this coming, and He laid out the plan for us. The key to enduring love is for two people to build the relationship in ways that will create this experience; and at a deeper level, for two people to adjust the things in themselves it is necessary to adjust if they are to build the best relationship. Of course, we cannot singlehandedly make a relationship grow if the other person does not want to build a relationship. But there are far more variables within our control than most realize, and these are vital to understand if two people are seriously trying to hold things together and build something worth having.

Our world, by contrast, teaches us that no one is responsible, that damaged or destroyed relationships are not the predictable consequence of wrong actions and displays of bad character qualities. Instead, we simply fell out of love or find that we found the wrong person. Or we remain in an uneasy alliance between separate kingdoms, living out the sum of negotiations and agreements in some kind of cold war. Many relationships are about settling for something—not building for a lifetime. How often do we hear about the "can't live with them, can't live without them" plan? These are people who genuinely want to figure out how to love each other. But what is missing here? Why isn't "being ourselves" working?

Perhaps these struggling relationships reflect a fundamental misunderstanding of marriage, or love, or of one's deepest needs, or of simply how to treat another person. Perhaps there are key character issues that need to be resolved or key growth that needs to happen. But for many people, the idea that a successful relationship requires growth and change is not in view. People begin in love, and want to keep their love alive. We all want to love perfectly, and even expect that we will. Though we often do many good things that build relationships, we have also been trained extensively to treat people in ways that damage relationships. Where did all this training come from? From the accumulation of voices in our world. And what is the origin of all our world teaches us regarding relationships? Here is one simple test: If something differs from or contradicts God's plan for human behavior, if it is impressed upon us that this is a better way to conduct a relationship than God's way, does such a pattern reflect something we have already examined?

Does it not resemble the conversation between Eve and Satan? We know how hers turned out. Might we reasonably become a bit uncomfortable as we consider how things might turn out as we carry out directives from this same source? How important is it, after all, that we win every argument or always come out on top? Why do we think we need to?

> Jesus would not allow people the delusion that His way could be synthesized successfully with the ways of His enemy and our enemy.

I want to ask you to consider a new way of looking at the cumulative advice of the world in which we have grown up. Is it possible that, not merely some, but pretty much all the advice floating around in our world about how to live—that differs from God's plan—originated from the original deceiver and seducer of the human race? I understand that is a remarkably strong statement, that few people in our world view reality in this way. I also understand that a fair amount of our common cultural understanding about how to live our best lives did originate from God and is reflected in Scripture. But what about the rest? Where did this come from? Are these just exercises in human creativity and diversity, or is something remarkably powerful happening just out of sight that has influenced humanity throughout history? Could humans really get *this much* wrong all by themselves? I don't expect you to draw a conclusion about this question here and now, or to agree with me at this moment. But I do want to raise this question, because we will speak to this point many times in the remainder of these volumes. As noted earlier, Jesus would not allow people the delusion that His way could be synthesized successfully with the ways of His enemy and our enemy. The reason Jesus would not allow this synthesis is because of the ultimate origin of the "other" ideas and the destructive role these ideas were ultimately designed to play in our lives—though by embracing these ideas we believe we are on the right track (see the definition of "deception" for details). Thus, we want to blend these "great ideas" for living in with Jesus' ideas. Jesus flatly rejected this synthesis. Why? It is extremely helpful to carefully consider the differences between the world's plan of relationship and God's plan. It is vital that we are able to tell one from the other, to spot the fingerprints of the respective authors.

Even if we have a solid foundation of character and relationship skills, we still have a lot to learn about day-to-day intimate relationships with another person. With all due respect, even if your relationship skills are considerable—and I am sure yours are—your skill set does not begin to approach the wisdom of God's plan when it comes to building an intimate relationship. He wrote the Book. We would all do well to read it. The most underappreciated aspect of true love is *learning*. A happily-ever-after relationship is one that continues to grow and deepen over time. It is one in which people's hearts toward each other grow more loving over time. It is one where the feelings, the sense of pleasure in the relationship, and the sense of reward from the relationship all continue to grow. But this requires that *we* continue to grow over time in very specific ways. In some relationships people continue to grow together, while in other relationships—most relationships, sadly—people do not grow at all in the way God intends, and therefore grow apart. In these relationships people are simply not engaging in the process of learning how to conduct themselves constructively; they are not in the process of growing as individuals, and so they do not know how to grow as a couple.

Why would people not devote themselves to growing in these ways? Because our society, in addition to teaching people that it is not about growth, but about expressing oneself, teaches other ideas that challenge the growth of relationships. We are not taught that we have responsibilities, duties, and obligations in relationship. Instead, we are taught that we have many *rights*. We have every right to treat each other in ways that damage hearts and relationships. Oddly, we have the right to do wrong, and our whole society is gravitating in this direction. Behaviors are commended and reinforced in our society that are far from God's ways of treating people, ways that do not wear well over time in intimate relationships.

WHAT IS AUTHENTIC SELF-EXPRESSION?

Our culture's highest ideal—self-expression—poses a huge problem. Why? For two reasons: one, the word *self*; and two, the word *expression*. First, we are taught that true love is unconditional love. What this roughly translates into in practice is believing that, if someone truly loves them, they will be accepted just as they are. This is true to a point. But if this belief extends to the idea that the other will, therefore, receive all that they do and say, and experience all of their attitudes, and be disrespected and dishonored by their priorities, and not only tolerate these things, but affirm and even celebrate the other person in the process . . . well, do you see the problem? The question is, whose responsibility is it to adjust and to change in the face of destructive behavior? Our world relieves the guilty party of this responsibility. Further, is the expression of these things not our most fundamental right as a human being? Don't I have the right to be myself?

But are these behavioral choices really the essence of *self*, or are they something else altogether? People who come from a Christian background fall into this thought process just as easily, convinced that true love—God's kind of love—means loving someone as *they are* without any further expectation, or even comment. As with all the best deceptions, this is partly true, but only partly. The consequence of this viewpoint is that people continue to inflict things on each other in relationship that can only damage the relationship and each other. These are destructive forces which God intends that we remove from the relationship, not tolerate.

The world's premise is that finding true love means finding a person who will endure any and every treatment one displays, yet the love will be so strong, so true, that the relationship continues to grow and deepen in spite of these things. This simply cannot happen. This concept misdefines our true natures, denies the true nature of love, and completely misunderstands how our hearts work. It leads to irresponsibility about something for which God has assigned us full responsibility—how we conduct ourselves, and all the pieces and parts within us that lead to that conduct. Relationships only grow when one consciously (or even unknowingly) treats another person in the ways God instructs us to treat other people in intimate relationships. If we do this, relationships grow. If we treat people in ways that are the opposite of how God says to treat people, regardless of the motive, reason, rationale, or expectation, what will happen is that relationship will be reduced and damaged in the long run. We sign up for less-than-happily-ever-after as we embrace these misconceptions.

> We all start with rough edges—we do things, and are things, that create problems in relationships.

We all start with rough edges—we do things, and are things, that create problems in relationships. And it is true that God wants us to be loved and accepted as we are in this moment. But it is also true, since every counterproductive move in a relationship has a price tag, that *it is our responsibility to take responsibility for our own rough edges and deal with them.* We give each other grace, forgiveness, and mercy, but at the same time we do not affirm and celebrate things that are destructive. Instead, we identify these things truthfully and teach, admonish, encourage, or confront these destructive things as they occur, both for our own sake and for the best interest of the other party. Our culture teaches us that such a lack of total acceptance is *judgmental*, and judgmental is a terrible thing to be. The argument for full and total acceptance of the other person is that an authentic relationship can only occur when two people are authentically expressing who and what they truly are. This is true in one sense, but raises again the question of what is truly and authentically us. God's plan clearly answers this question, but goes much further. Covenant, as we remember, alters identity.

Could God's plan be aimed at correcting issues by revising who we are at the deepest level?

> *"'You' is a very fluid concept right now."*
> —Will Smith's character Hitch talking
> to Albert Brenneman in the movie Hitch,
> Columbia Pictures, 2005[1]

WHAT IS TRULY 'SELF'?

The first problem with the world's view of self-expression is the word *self*. What, exactly, is one's real self—assuming that one wants to express it? The best relationships, authentic relationships, are ones in which two people are relating to each other from the core of their being. These are transparent relationships with no pretense, in whihc honest interactions express to each other the essence of the other person. For two people to conduct such a relationship they must have a correct understanding of who and what they actually are. What is one's true identity and true nature? About these questions there is much confusion; here, God's plan of covenant cuts through all the confusion. It's important to spend time talking about our true identity—what we are expressing that is, or is not, a valid and true expression of ourselves. Oone of the greatest journeys in life is discovering the fullness of who we are.

We will see that we have been misinformed, perhaps grievously, about who we are by our world, and we have been sold the idea that counterproductive attitudes, thoughts, values, feelings, priorities, and

Could God's plan be aimed at correcting issues by revising who we are at the deepest level?

the like represent us at the deepest level of our being, when in fact this is not the case. People with incorrect views of themselves may be so afraid to fail that they are afraid to try, or view themselves as so likely to be rejected that they sabotage relationships or avoid getting too close to anyone. We will see that gaining clarity about who we truly are, and who we have become as we enter a covenant with our spouse, is the key to living an authentic life. This understanding is also the key to developing our true potential. The only path to the greatest satisfaction in life and in relationship is to live out our true identity via His plan of covenant. God cares even more about authenticity than we do.

Building a relationship also requires that we see the other person clearly. Have you ever had someone make an effort to be nice to you, but the things they did just did not connect with you? Why? Simply put, they did not understand you. One cannot have a close relationship, much less build the intimacy of a good marriage, unless both people can see the other clearly to a significant degree. We must grow past the assumption that what we want and need must also be what the other person wants and needs. We are individuals, even within covenant, and while loving actions are universal in one sense, it is not one-size-fits-all. Our love must recognize the uniqueness of our partner and be individually tailored to their uniqueness. A principle of life is that we cannot know another person more deeply than we know ourselves. If this is true, can you see how getting to know ourselves more deeply, seeing ourselves more clearly, will allow us to see our lover and friend more clearly in marriage? Thus, God's plan for our relationship entails personal discovery and personal growth, in addition to focusing on our partner.

TRUE LOVE MEANS LIFELONG LEARNING, CHANGING, AND GROWING

True love means learning the depths of ourselves and our beloved. If we are fortunate enough we will have the privilege of getting to know another human being across the breadth and depth of his or her being over a lifetime. True love means learning how to relate—

successfully, constructively—with another person across the scope of human experience. True love means learning to integrate ourselves with another person, to join with them, to believe in them, to invest our life and our future in the life and heart of another. True love means supporting the other person as they become the fullness of what God created them to be. The reason we must learn is that no one knows how to do any of this well at the outset. The reason that our understanding of our own responsibility for doing damage to our relationships is so important is because this provides the motivation to do what is necessary to grow. We are the only one who can grow ourselves up in a relationship. This is God's plan. We must move from having profound feelings toward another person toward developing a lifestyle of loving them in attitude and action. This requires taking the corrective action needed to allow these things to happen. God's plan is that this be a mutual pursuit: two people growing and growing together. The goal is to learn to build a relationship that is worth having for both people. This is but a glimpse of true love.

> The goal is to learn to build a relationship that is worth having for both people. This is but a glimpse of true love.

In the second volume in this series we will see a detailed list of the ways God tells us to treat each other in marriage. We will see the array of attitudes, viewpoints, values, priorities, and approaches that create the best marriage. As you consider this list, first consider how you would feel about someone if they treated you in these ways for a decade, or two, or five. Then look around at couples you know. Think how you would feel after a decade if you were on the receiving end of the ways they treat each other. Hopefully you see good things; these couples are in the process of building great relationships, and you would deeply appreciate being treated as they treat each other. But is this the kind of relationship we see most often? I am amazed that some couples treat each other as they do. Why do they not see what they are doing to the other person and to their marriage? Why do people treat people in the ways they do? The short answer is that they usually feel their mistreatment of the other is a deserved response to the other's mistreatment of them. What is keeping one from being the perfect lover is, of course, the other person. But is there more to the picture than this?

WHY DO WE TREAT PEOPLE AS WE DO?

If God wants us to treat each other in the most constructive ways, building the best things for ourselves and our true love and life partner, why is this such a hard sell? Why the shift between "in love" treatment and the things that often follow? Why is it such a struggle at certain points when we try to continue loving with our actions? If we are going to change how we act, it is crucial that we first understand why we act as we do, and why we resist change.

We have all drawn from many sources—our parents, friends, media, school, church, and more—about how to treat people and how to be the person that we are. We have tried things and found things that work. Or we simply fall into line with other people who behave in certain ways. We blend in with our friends. Part of how we act is determined by the expectations of people whose opinions matter to us and part by people we are trying to emulate. We want to be that person living *that* life.

Every way we treat people reflects a choice we first made at a point in time for a specific reason in a specific situation. Some choices build relationships. Other choices are ways we have found to get our way, or to advance our cause, while others create an image we want to create. While each choice may serve our interests in a certain moment, our behavior choices can also create problems. We may stop noticing, if we ever noticed, the damage these things also do. We tend to repeat behaviors that work for us—at least in our perception. Over time these approaches to other people come to feel natural for us, comfortable for us. We use an oddly apt term for these things: second nature. That is, things to be distinguished from our *first* (true) nature.

Such behaviors, simply repeated over time, become habits, something we do without thinking. And over time these habits come to feel like "us," as if they are some intrinsic part of who we are as a person. This type of habit pattern includes more than how we act or what we say. These patterns extend to our expressions, gestures, and the ways we carry ourselves. They include our choice of words and our typical reactions to various circumstances. They include our viewpoints toward certain types of people, or toward people in general. They include how we view ourselves in relation to other people. Even emotional responses can be habits instead of intrinsic reactions from the core of our being. The sum of our habits is the sum of things we have drawn from others, tried, found beneficial (at least to some degree), then repeated until we do them without thinking. Then we forgot how those things came to be. In our experience, they just are. In sum, these things form an important part of our being, for overall this is the way we relate to others and how we experience the world from inside ourselves.

OUR IDENTITY VERSUS OUR HABITS

This sum of our patterns and habits we would term a *persona*, or personality, or a person's character. These patterns become the things that other people expect of us and that we expect of ourselves, for better or worse. The key understanding here, despite our perception that these things are deeply ingrained parts of our being, is that these things instead reflect decisions we have made at some point. Therefore, these are also things we can *un*-decide and *re*-decide if we have sufficient reason to do so.

Another interesting thing is how resistant people are to changing these patterns. People often seem blind to the impact of their behaviors on other people, even to the impact on their own lives. And when someone does realize the extent to which a behavior is causing damage, what do we often hear? "Yeah, but this is just me." People often mistake these patterns for *their* essence as a human. When these embraced things are challenged, how do people generally respond? As if his or her very life was being threatened? As if a fundamental right was being violated?

Do you think it would help us, especially in our close relationships, to have a more clear read on what is *actually us*—that core of our being that needs to be loved and wants to love—in contrast to the things about ourselves that are actually optional add-ons, things that our world teaches us to misidentify as genuine expressions of self? Things we think are so much a part of us that we (mistakenly) think removing them would be like cutting off an arm? In reality, however, losing these things would be like having an infection cured or a cancer removed. What if one realizes that one's best move is not holding on to and expressing such things, but *identifying* and *ridding oneself* of such things? What if one realizes that this is one's true path to happiness and relationship fulfillment?

THE CUMULATIVE EFFECT OF CULTURAL DECEPTION

In light of these questions, let's consider the massive amount of relationship dysfunction around us. Let's consider how much pressure is exerted on each of us by our culture to see things in certain ways and to adopt certain beliefs, especially about other people ("masculinity is so toxic"; or, "all women are so____"). Our culture has been extremely comprehensive and persuasive, showing us how to stand up for our rights, how to get our way, how to fit in, how to stand out, how to get the attention we want, and much more. Though we may not be aware of its impact, or even its existence, our society has a massive and powerful training process in place that puts these ideas before us via many sources day after day. This barrage of ideas influences how we see ourselves and other people. This process strongly directs us toward certain behaviors, viewpoints, values, attitudes, and more. How many of these ideas cause damage to hearts and relationships? Once this picture snaps into focus and we realize why people act as they do, we can now see why our cultural training process exerts such an impact on the quality of our lives and our relationships. And, if we realize who is behind the progressive ideas sweeping through our culture, as well as many ideas brought forward from past generations, and the agenda of this source, the rapid progression of discord, strife, and dysfunction in our culture begins to make sense. The rapid disintegration of the family makes sense. The exodus of youth away from Christianity makes sense. The key insight is applying a correct understanding of these forces to one's own decision-making. How do we avoid being drawn into damaging patterns and ways of living? Fortunately, God has a plan to counteract this destructive influence.

WHAT IS ONE'S TRUE IDENTITY?

Let's further consider the nature of *self*. If we are going to relate authentically, we need to know ourselves. How do we separate things that are the essence of ourselves from the habits that have formed around this core of our being? Here is the difference. We are created with a unique set of capacities and abilities that exist initially as our *potential*. We are also created with a unique set of deep emotional needs—time, touch, attention, service, affirmation, and more. And we are created with certain basic orientations—extroverted or introverted, auditory learner or visual learner, and so forth. People will also relate to others in characteristic ways—some prefer leading, others prefer following. We all have a particular level of intelligence, a particular aptitude for music, art, or sports; a particular capacity for creativity, and a certain degree of physical coordination. All of these represent attributes or characteristics we can develop to full potential. Our potential in every realm of life is a fixed part of our identity. This is an inherent part of who we are.

We also have a relational identity. We are connected and related to certain other people via this identity—our family—and this connection forms part of our sense of self. Not only do we have certain capacities, we have certain inclinations. We are created to develop and use our gifts to fulfill certain purposes. In doing so we find the purpose for our lives and much of the meaning of our lives. One person is an explorer, trailblazer, or entrepreneur; another an accountant, manager, or caretaker of things already built. We are created for relationships,

> We are made in God's image, and to varying degrees we will reflect God's image and attributes.

and though we have various needs and capacities in those relationships, we are all created to love and with the need to be loved. Within relationships, various actions or words that people use may either meet our emotional needs or not according to the particular set of deepest needs with which we are endowed. This set of particular needs is also an inherent part of who we are.

We are made in God's image, thus to varying degrees we will reflect God's image and attributes. It is because of this that we have the capacity to love and the need to love; we are creative and value beauty; we are compassionate and capable of kindness; we have an innate sense of justice and are capable of defending those who cannot defend themselves; we have an innate sense that there are moral laws, a conscience that feels pain when we violate moral law, and we have a sense of judgment when others violate such laws. We have an inborn capacity to recognize truth and detect falsehood and deception. We have the capacity for generosity. This is but a sampling of the attributes of God which are mirrored in us. All the virtues God requires of us have been deposited within us and are waiting to be cultivated and developed. These are the things at our core, but they may be buried beneath conflicting and confusing ideas we have embraced; our sense of justice may not be completely in sync with God's or our moral compass may point in wrong directions. But we all have a moral compass that will function properly if correct information is loaded into it.

These are some aspects of who we are created to be as individuals. One of the most profound journeys in life is discovering who we are, for many things within us are not immediately apparent. What we note over time is that things in accord with our identity are the most gratifying; these are things for which we have the most energy and enthusiasm. The drive to do these things wells up from deep within us, for such things are a true expression of who we are at the deepest level. This is the place from which our passions arise.

Our awareness of the capacities and inclinations that make up our true identity emerge as we go through the circumstances of life. It would seem fairly straightforward, then, to simply observe ourselves over time and take note of what we see and experience, and by this to determine an accurate understanding of who we are at the deepest level. However, as we have said, we can also be deceived about who we are. And it is almost certain that we have been if we have lived in this world. Our true nature can be misunderstood; what we actually are may be missed and we may become convinced we are something that we are not. Any way you would describe yourself by completing the following two sentences involves your sense of your identity: "I am a _____"; and "I am _____." This could be a developed capability—say, a football player or a singer. Or, it may be filled with a system of thought that's been embraced—say, a liberal, a conservative, a communist, a five-point Calvinist, or a feminist. Or, it may be filled with one's perceived place in the hierarchy of humanity—a loser, say, or one who deserves bad things in life, or one who deserves everything, even if it belongs to someone else.

How did we arrive at our view of ourselves? In addition to our own perceptions, there is another source of information we often mine. The people around us are holding up a mirror reflecting us to us. We get to look in the mirror of the reactions of people on all sides. But how clearly do we see our real selves in these mirrors? We see how the people around us regard us—the esteem in which they hold us (or do not), the quality of relationship we have with them. We read the reactions of people close to us and read into those reactions their opinion of us. But how much of this is about us and how much is about them? How much is true and how much is badly distorted? Has incorrect information about who we are been conveyed to us and we have simply taken it at face value? Have we drawn incorrect conclusions about ourselves from unfortunate experiences? To what extent are we wrong about ourselves?

The question, then, is how we correctly identify our identity. First, how do we know when we are not being ourselves? We've all had the experience of being forced into doing something or trying to be something that was simply not us. We are faking it; someone is trying to make us be something we are not. Such things never feel like us, never connect deeply with something within us; they always feel foreign to us. We may learn to play the role and even to do something successfully, but it never truly satisfies. In fact, at some level we resent being forced to do or be whatever is not us. Thus, we all seem capable of perceiving when something is, or is not, consistent with our identity—at least to a point.

At the same time, in areas where we have undeveloped potential, trying something new may feel awkward at first. At the outset, we may not be sure this is us. But at a point something within us will start to connect with, then start to enjoy, then start to desire whatever it is we are doing. We find our passions for living in this way—by trying things and noting what happens within ourselves over time. The perception of "me/not me" is something that grows and solidifies, something we glean from our inner experience. Our identity and our deepest and most precious experiences of living are deeply connected. Wouldn't it be nice if our Creator offered us significant information about who we really are? Wouldn't it be nice if we came with an owner's manual? What if this were a big part of God's plan?

Really getting to know ourselves is a lifetime process. The closeness of a relationship that leads to marriage, then the increased intimacy and transparency of a marriage relationship, are huge factors in getting to know ourselves. The mirror that will be held up for us, reflecting us in the eyes of our marriage partner, will be up-close-and-personal and extremely comprehensive. One thing we want to see in a marriage is that these mirrors are increasingly accurate, that the distortions in the mirrors we hold up to the other person caused by our own self-misconceptions are progressively stripped away. Can you see the benefit of this?

Two aspects of our identities play the most significant roles directing the course of our lives: our actual identity, and what we believe about our identity. Can you see how a discrepancy between these two would pose a problem as we confront decisions that will direct the course of our lives? There are two foundations for such a decision: first, our true identity; second, who we believe we are, but actually are not. If you were God's enemy, trying to sabotage God's creation—us— as powerfully as possible, what opportunity might this reality present to you? Wouldn't you focus on misinforming individuals about their identities? What impact might this be capable of producing in people's lives, relationships, and societies?

Covenant alters identity. We are detailing the issues surrounding identity so we can understand the many ways the identity change inherent in covenant can, and should, impact our lives. And so we can understand how dramatically a correct understanding, or an incorrect understanding, of our new identity in covenant will impact us.

Speaking as one who has more decades behind me than most who will read this, I will tell you there will always be new things to discover about yourself. Quite often we are not exactly who we think. I did not think of myself as a ballroom dancer, and that view was reinforced when I tried it the first few times. I distinctly remember at one point looking straight ahead and seeing the ceiling instead of my partner, which does not reflect proper dance form! Still, I picked myself up off the floor and continued. Somewhere along the way dancing began to feel like "me" as I continued attempting to dance with the person who is now my wife. (The words of Antonio Banderas in the film *Zorro* come to mind: "She's dancing, you're trying."[2]) Now we can pretty much light up a dance floor, and we thoroughly enjoy doing so. There have been many things I never thought I could do

> I did not think of myself as a ballroom dancer, and that view was reinforced when I tried it the first few times. I distinctly remember at one point looking straight ahead and seeing the ceiling instead of my partner. This is not proper dance form!

or would ever enjoy doing. Many of these are now prominent parts of who I am, things I am passionate about. And my viewpoints and perspectives continue to shift and mature over the years. My priorities now are far from where they were even fifteen years ago, for I have a much more broad view of God's plan for myself, my family, and my sphere of influence. All these changes seem to have grown outward from a growing relationship with my wife and with God. In other words, I have learned much more about myself in the context of my close relationships than in any other way. And I have learned how to learn, and how vital it is to continue to learn and explore the inner reaches of myself. God's plan truly is about learning, growing, and changing.

Can you begin to see how our understanding of how we are put together—the component parts—can impact our relationships? First, what actually *is* self, then figuring out what we need to devote ourselves to developing, amending, changing, discarding, or strengthening to build the best and most rewarding lives. And along the way, identifying and developing those things upon which strong relationships are built, things we will cover all of these things in detail in the second volume in this series.

RECONSIDERING THE WAYS WE VIEW, AND TREAT, OTHER PEOPLE

Once we have a better understanding of our actual identity, versus optional add-ons, let us extend this understanding to dealing with another person. If we view a relationship as two people who are sharing themselves and sharing life, and if we assume that *what we are* that the other person is interacting with, and *what they are* that we are interacting with are pretty much fixed things, then likely such a relationship becomes an increasingly painful series of compromises, of putting up with destructive things. But the real price tag is far higher. If we are not aware of the things about us that can change, and at points should change, and if the only things about the other person we think should change are that they should love us more unconditionally, gratify us

111

more completely, and serve our interests more enthusiastically, this is a great prescription for not growing as an individual or as a couple. The problem then is not just what we will experience, but what we *will not* experience because we did not fully develop the opportunity that is right in front of us.

Or I can view myself and the other person as most definitely a work in progress, and we can work together to make the relationship work using God's blueprint. Careful partner selection is important—we certainly need someone who shares a deep love and connection with us—but we also need to find someone we can work with, who embraces a path of growth as opposed to a path of simply expressing who they insist on continuing to be. The key to the success of God's plan is how far we are able to grow, and what we are able to grow into, instead of what we are at the outset. This is good news, is it not?

THE STARTING POINT FOR GOD'S PLAN

At long last we are going to begin examining God's plan for each individual life—covenant. Covenant is a form of relationship, but also a development process; and it is a plan to harness the potential of both. As we have seen, we are not exactly blank slates when we come to God's plan. We have all been deeply impacted, extensively trained, and our perceptions of self and others have been distorted by the world. We have seen the source of the ideas that oppose a loving, trusting relationship with God and that oppose following His plan at every point. And we have briefly examined ways we have been misinformed about our true best interests, about how to build the best and most loving relationships, about the nature of love itself and how our hearts grow in love for others. Our image of ourselves may be badly distorted, and to the extent that this is true our view of others will be distorted. Our concept of what represents the core of our being may be incorrect, prompting us to hang on to dysfunctional patterns and destructive character elements as if these things were our left ventricle. And, if we are talking about a change of identity in covenant, we will encounter the same issues correctly identifying our new identity that we faced trying to correctly identify the old one—if we base our understanding on our own perceptions. Fortunately, we have God's revelation, which will clear up the confusion.

We have touched on an even more significant problem that impacts every person: the nature of Satan that has infiltrated every person's character as a result of the parents of our race joining themselves to Satan via joining his rebellion against God. We have all joined in this rebellion in one way or another, even if we can think of few actions that would evidence this. We are nevertheless under a sentence of death from God because the very nature of God's rebellious enemy is within us—juxtaposed with elements of our Creator, since we are also made in His image.

In brief, God's plan is to address the issue of division between two individuals who desire to join in marriage by transforming them as they enter this relationship, welding them together at the level of identity and nature via covenant. God's plan for a relationship with Himself, which erases the sentence of death and qualifies us to live with Him eternally, is for us to be made completely new in identity and nature, to literally have our old nature and identity put to death and be raised up from this death as a new creature, a new creation. But entry into these two relationships does not address the issue of *building new and different lives* based on these new realities. In fact, the job of building new lives in accord with these new realities is anything but a certainty because this relies on our understanding these changes, understanding that will determine the choices we make going forward. God offers us opportunities; He gives us new potential. He gives us every resource we need to make the most of these opportunities. But He continually to offer us a choice: *will we make the most* of these opportunities?

Therefore, if we are to enter these relationships and make the most of them, we must discuss not only the relationships but the choices we will face going forward that determine how these relationships are built, and how we are built in the process. We can live out these new identities, grow, be transformed, and build according to His plan. Or we can choose to continue in our old habits and old ways. These are no longer a true reflection of who and what we are, but they are comfortable and familiar. The forces urging us to continue in these ways are strong—both from within and without. God's plan is fully capable of producing everything He wants in us, and everything we want to see in our lives and marriages. But we must choose this outcome day by day, moment by moment, or the fullness of these things will not grow as they might. Which way do you think most people approach marriage? Would you choose the majority approach for your marriage?

We make choices for reasons. God offers us sufficient reasons at every point for every decision. However, there is always another voice in this discussion, also offering us reasons and attempting to lead us away from God's plan. This is the dilemma we all face every day in every decision. This will be the underlying topic of the remainder of this volume and the two that follow in this series—cutting through the confusion to make the best choices day by day, hour by hour, for the rest of our lives.

If covenant is God's plan, our next task is to define a covenant. To do this, we will draw from the scholarly work of H. Clay Trumbull and his 1885 book *The Blood Covenant*[3]. .

THE CONCEPTS WE ARE GOING TO DISCUSS ARE NOT INNOVATIONS

Before we examine Trumbull's work I want to emphasize one more thing. We are going to discuss the definition of a covenant relationship. This definition may be new to you, and may not be common currency in our Christian communities today. But the view we are going to discuss is not new, not some recent innovation. We are searching out what I believe to be a correct understanding of the terms *Marriage Covenant* (Malachi 2:14) and *New Covenant* (Luke 22:20). We are attempting to define these terms in the way those who heard Jesus' words, or who wrote or read the letters that were later compiled as the New Testament, would have understood these things.

Words and phrases are often not extensively or exhaustively defined within the Scriptures themselves, especially if these definitions were common knowledge at the time they were delivered. For instance, when Jesus used the term "eye of a needle" (Matthew 19:24), if we do not know what He was referring to in the common vernacular we lose something of what He was saying. The eye of a needle in biblical times was a low and narrow gate. For a camel to get through one, it had to be unloaded, and it had to go through on its knees. When Jesus compared this to a rich person getting into Heaven, rather than the idea of "impossible"—which would be evoked by visualizing a camel trying to get through the hole in a sewing needle—"difficult" would be a more correct understanding from the metaphor if we have the correct picture. A more rich meaning can be seen in the camel actually needing to be unloaded, then adopting the posture of humility—on its knees—to enter. If I am writing about a baseball game and I mention a "foul ball," I would be unlikely to add to the text a section on the rules of baseball and explain why this particular ball was "foul." Everyone today understands this term, but a reader a few centuries from now in another culture might reasonably assume from this terminology that the ball . . . smelled bad?

> In fact they are ancient meanings whose understandings have been obscured by the mists of time, or perhaps even intentionally, by the influence of God's enemies.

What we are emphatically not going to do is introduce definitions that are not completely consistent with the Scriptures as they were written. I believe you will see, as I have, that an accurate understanding of covenant opens new worlds of understanding within the Scriptures, but again, these are not new things. In fact they are ancient meanings whose understandings have been obscured by the mists of time, or perhaps even intentionally, by the influence of God's enemies. We will show that people whose stories are told in the Scriptures understood these same things in these same ways, from David and Jonathan in

115

the Old Testament to the early New Testament believers in the book of Acts. This understanding allows these stories to come alive in new ways, and it allows Scriptural stories to be directly applied to our lives in new ways if we are in these same relationships.

As we go forward we will cite numerous Scripture verses that illustrate, or are illuminated by, our growing understanding of covenant. Please assure yourselves as you read these things that I am not in any way taking improper liberties with the truth of God! Instead, it is intended that we understand, for instance, exactly why Jesus' words in John 6 had such a powerful effect on His listeners. What was the reality that His words forced them to confront? If we understand this we will understand the true nature of the opportunity He was offering His followers that day—and offers each of us today. As we go through the rest of this book, examining these two covenants, I want you to consider *why* sober and thoughtful people, people who were trying to follow Jesus, trying to be in a right relationship with God, had these reactions as God began to reveal the true nature of His plan to them.

> We can be offended that God challenges our right to see things the way we choose to see them, to make our own decisions, and to build the lives we want to build. This is the majority position.

I believe people have these reactions because they thought marriage and a relationship with God were *supposed to be* one thing—and they had made peace with *their* ideas of how a relationship with God and marriage were supposed to be. Part of the reason they thought things were supposed to be this way is because *this is the way they wanted them to be.* Another reason is that their own views were commonly held in their culture, and surely "everyone cannot be wrong about something like this!" But now God is standing right in front of them challenging these deeply held views in much the same way as when

He stood before the religious leadership of the Jews questioning their traditions in contrast to God's intentions. As God confronts our own preconceptions, we have two choices for response. One: we can be offended that God challenges our right to see things the way we choose to see them, to make our own decisions, and to build the lives we want to build. This is the majority position. Two: we can understand that God created us, our hearts, and our world. We can begin to grasp the reality that He wants to build something new and better than we could ever possibly engineer in our own lives by our own efforts. We can ponder more deeply the reality that He truly loves us. And we can begin to understand that what He offers us is far more beautiful and powerful than life as we thought it should be lived. Ultimately, He invites us to trust Him to lead us on a journey, the end of which we cannot see from the starting point. But He tells us that this is the path of true blessing, power, and peace. We have only to trust Him and to set out with Him on His path. Will we?

With this question before us, let's begin our study of the heart of God's plan, covenant relationships.

FIVE

One Man's Journey of Discovery

REDISCOVERING AN UNDERSTANDING OF THE DEFINITION OF COVENANT

Jesus said to them, "Very truly I tell you, unless you eat the flesh of the Son of Man and drink his blood, you have no life in you. Whoever eats my flesh and drinks my blood has eternal life, and I will raise them up at the last day. . . . Whoever eats my flesh and drinks my blood remains in me, and I in them." . . . On hearing it, many of his disciples said, "This is a hard teaching. Who can accept it?" . . . From this time many of his disciples turned back and no longer followed Him.
JOHN 6:53-66 (EXCERPTS)

I suspect when you read this passage for the first time you had the same reaction I had: I was puzzled and disconcerted. We are not sure quite what to make of what Jesus is saying, although as Christians we now know that this must have something to do with the ritual of communion. But these statements are not something we fully understand to say the least. Then we look at the reaction of His followers, who were obviously disturbed by these words. We assume that they were having the same reaction we are, for the same reason. We assume they also were baffled by what Jesus is saying. But this could not be further from the truth. Jesus' followers. They were disturbed to the point that many turned and walked away because they understood

119

exactly what He was saying! Their problem was that these were the most mind-bending words they could imagine coming from someone who claimed to be God Himself, and powerfully substantiating this claim two different times in the previous twenty-four hours. So what did Jesus' hearers that day understand that we do not?

To best answer this question, allow me to introduce you to H. Clay Trumbull (1830-1903) and his story of discovery. Like any good detective story, this one started with what looked like an unexplainable coincidence. Before we tell his story, though, let me first introduce you to the man. He was termed a world-famous author by Wikipedia (fifteen books), editor, and pioneer of the American Sunday school movement. He has been called the "father of Sunday school" and was president of the American Sunday School Society. He was a good friend of the noted evangelist D.L. Moody and also grandfather of the internationally known missionary Elisabeth Elliott, whose story was recounted in the 2005 movie *End of the Spear*. This is a man of immense credibility, a man with a deep and abundantly fruitful relationship with God, someone who impacted many lives in his generation.

> Like any good detective story, this one started with what looked like an unexplainable.

At one point Trumbull lived in a location frequented by missionaries on furlough (temporarily returning from the mission field). He heard one of these missionaries tell of a strange ritual in the tribe they lived among, one in which two people would take each other's blood into their own bodies. This was accompanied by a ceremony that included vows of deepest commitment publicly spoken before each other and their gods. Then a wound was produced on each person's body that would cause scarring as a permanent and visible reminder of this joining. Gifts were exchanged—clothing, weapons, and food—then there was a feast for the participants and assembled witnesses. The two people were now joined by the deepest and most sacred bond. In this bond they became part of each other's families. They shared friends, enemies, debts, obligations, and resources. They were to come to each other's aid at the risk of their own lives, and they were to regard the interests of the other party equal to, or even more important than, their own. It became their most sacred duty to uphold the honor of the other party. This bond was indissoluble except by death. The missionary had not been allowed to witness this rite until he had gained the trust of the tribe, as this ritual represented one of their oldest and most sacred traditions.

Soon after Trumbull was speaking with another missionary from a very different part of the world who also worked among a primitive tribe in a remote area. This missionary recounted witnessing a ceremony that was nearly identical to the one described by the first. Intrigued by the fact that two isolated tribes, separated by thousands of miles, from totally different cultures, would have such an unusual custom in common, Trumbull began asking missionaries from other areas if they had seen such a custom in the cultures they lived among. One missionary after another recounted local rites that, though varied to some degree, were intended to accomplish this same joining of two people in an indissoluble bond of mutual benefit and mutual responsibility. Though bearing some similarities to marriage—in terms of bonding, sharing, and permanence—the bond of blood-covenanting in most places was counted of even more weight, and there was no "out clause" akin to divorce. If a male and female were so united, later marriage between them was deemed incestuous and was forbidden.

The means of obtaining and offering blood between the parties varied, including being drawn from one and then inserted directly into the other's veins; or blood from each party was poured in a glass of beer or wine that was then ingested; or two hands with bleeding cuts were clasped together in a handshake. Regardless, a physical exchange of blood was the hallmark of this rite. This was always accompanied by vows of mutual commitment and an appeal to the local deity for enforcement of any breach of the arrangement. Beyond this there were variants of feasting, gift exchange, and other customs.

As Trumbull continued collecting these stories and began to realize the geographic and cultural scope of the practice, his interest increased. How could such a thing be so widespread across the earth, yet, at the same time, be (for the most part) hidden from the eyes of his "modern" nineteenth century Western world? And what was the underlying understanding upon which these rites rested?

As he investigated further, Trumbull found that blood covenanting had been present in earlier centuries in Europe, but in more recent centuries the practice had largely disappeared. In the Americas of his time blood brotherhood was still a known practice among Native Americans, though not among "civilized" European emigrants. As the symbolism of the rites became more clear, though, he began to see vestiges of it enduring in many places in Western society, in customs such as a handshake or drinking a toast to the health of another—watered-down pledges of friendship and goodwill, yet clear vestiges of a covenant ceremony. What Trumbull ultimately discovered was a practice that was literally worldwide in scope and present on every inhabited continent—from the Asian interior to the islands of the Pacific, from Norse lands to the tip of Africa, throughout the Americas, the Far East, India, and Australia. In short, this practice has essentially the same universality in the human race as does marriage.

Trumbull then turned to history books to look for evidence of this practice in ancient civilizations. Classical Roman and Greek literature referenced this rite among Scythians, Persians, and Iberians. Ancient Norse literature mentioned this rite between humans, and also between humans and their gods, as does the literature of other ancient cultures. He found references to such rites in Palestine in Jesus' day. The more he looked, the more widespread Trumbull found the rite to be in ancient writings, even in the earliest then available. An Egyptian depiction of a blood covenant was noted in stoneworks attributed to Ramses IV, circa 1200 B.C., and in the most ancient Egyptian writing of all, the Book of the Dead.

How, he wondered, did this practice arise, and how did it become so widespread?

His observations and research led to a book first published in 1885, *The Blood Covenant*. In his book Trumbull analyzed the rite and offered a sampling of his collected examples from around the world and from the historical record. His work established the rite as something with almost universal penetration in the human race from deepest antiquity. While there are variations across time and geography, the basic elements of the rite are quite consistent.

From Trumbull's cited examples, the following list of common elements is drawn.

COMMON ELEMENTS, PRINCIPLES, AND PRACTICES OF BLOOD COVENANTS

- Two parties desire to enter a lifelong bond of mutual benefit and mutual responsibility and agree to do so.

- A public ceremony is arranged.

- The two make vows of commitment to each other and to deity, vows to honor, protect, defend, provide for, and generally promote the best interests of the other party in any way possible. The lives and futures of the two are henceforth inextricably joined. They vow to pay any price and make any sacrifice to fulfill their vows to each other.

- A mark is generally made on the body as a visible, permanent token of these vows. Alternately, an amulet or other ornament becomes the symbol of this joining and is to be worn continuously.

- Clothing is exchanged to signify the exchange of identity.

- Armor and weapons are exchanged to signify the obligation of mutual defense.

- A meal is eaten by the parties and the assembled witnesses to signify the obligation of mutual provision, and generous gifts are given between the two to exemplify the obligation to mutually bless one another.

- The result of identity being altered and joined is that relatives are now shared. Full familial obligations are in force toward each other's extended family.

- Friends and enemies become mutual, as do obligations of friendship or vengeance.

- Debts, assets, obligations, and resources are shared.

- Basically, any asset, resource, capability, or potential of one is at the other's disposal as needed.

- The honor of each is at stake in fulfilling these vows, and the highest honor is found in upholding the character and integrity of the other party.

- There are counted both temporal and supernatural consequences for unfaithfulness. These bonds and vows were taken so seriously in ancient and modern times that, even in the case of otherwise untrustworthy people—thieves, etc.—these bonds are held most sacred and almost never violated. It is counted the height of foolishness to incur a divine enemy in such a way. A more modern example is the Triad society, the Chinese organized crime syndicate, entry into which requires a blood covenant with other members.

While details of covenant ceremonies are of interest, they are not the thing of true importance when examining this relationship. You may have noted the phrase in one of the above items: "identity being altered and joined." The thing we must understand about covenant is the underlying principle: *the changing and joining of identity through the exchange of blood*. This change and joining of identity is universally believed to occur by cultures practicing this rite. Pledges to the other party and vows to treat the other in certain ways do not actually bind the two together in covenant—the vows, in essence, simply state the parties' *intentions* to live out the natural consequences of a new reality which is about to come into being. What binds them together is mutually offering, then receiving into their own body, something that contains the identity of the other person—their blood. Once one's blood enters the other party, some of what makes person A "themselves" now enters and remains within person B and vice versa. Thus, each person from this point forward has a new and altered identity and nature, which incorporates the nature and identity of both parties. The vows and pledges to the other party simply recognize that the other party will henceforth be treated as *what they have become.* If I enter covenant with another person, I will treat this other person as well as I would treat myself, because this other person is *now a part of myself,* and I am a part of them in a most real and practical sense. The identity, the very life, of the other has entered me—and my life and identity have entered the other person. Everything that flows out of this relationship in terms of behavior and attitude is a consequence of the nature of "self" changing and being conjoined between two formerly separate individuals.

> The identity, the very life, of the other has entered me—and my life and identity have entered the other person.

Understanding this core concept was the inestimable contribution of Trumbull's book. Four passages from *The Blood Covenant* that convey this understanding will be reproduced here, again with permission.

- It would seem . . . that no one of the modern students of myth and folklore, of primitive ideas and customs, and of man's origin and history, has brought into their true prominence . . . the universally dominating primitive convictions: that the blood is the life; that the heart, as the blood-fountain, is the very soul of every personality; that blood-transfer is soul-transfer; that blood sharing, human or divine-human, secures an inter-union of natures; and that a union of the human nature with the divine is the highest ultimate attainment reached out after by the most primitive, as well as by the most enlightened, mind of humanity (p. v.).

- Here is evidenced that the same view of the absolute oneness of nature through a oneness of blood, which shows itself among the Semites of Syria, among the Malays of Timor, and among the Indians of America. And so this close and sacred covenant relation, this rite of blood-friendship, this inter-oneness of life by an inter-oneness of blood, shows itself in the primitive East, and in the wild and prehistoric West; in the frozen North, as in the torrid South. Its traces are everywhere. It is of old, and it is of today; as universal and full of meaning as life itself (pp. 57, 58).

- It was a primeval idea, of universal sway, that the taking in of another's blood was the acquiring of another's life, with all that was best in that other's nature (p. 126).

- All my thought is, to ascertain what new meaning, if any, is found in the Bible teaching concerning the uses and the symbolism of blood, through our better understanding of the prevailing idea, among the peoples of the ancient world, that blood represents life; that the giving of blood represents that giving of life; that the receiving of blood represents the receiving of life; that the inter-commingling of blood represents the inter-commingling of natures; and that a divine-human inter-union through blood is the basis of a divine-human inter-communion in the sharing of the flesh of the sacrificial offering as sacred food (p. 209).

Trumbull recognized as he studied this topic that the core principle and reality of covenant is what drives everything else in this relationship. All the rules, principles, responsibilities, duties, and obligations, as well as the benefits and opportunities inherent in these relationships, are logical extensions of this core principle, or, better put, this new reality. If nature is changed at the most fundamental level to incorporate the identity of the other party, there is no more "me and mine, you and yours," but only "us and ours."

> In a very real sense these die and are replaced by a new nature and identity jointly held between the two parties.

What other implications flow from this joining? Covenant involves potentially massive sacrifice by one or both parties. And on a more down-to-earth level, there is a sharing of material goods and relationships that involves every facet of each party's existence. Why would people regard their covenant partner in this way? Because, as they look at the other party, they are not doing these things "for someone else." Their former separate identity and nature literally cease to exist; in a very real sense these die and are replaced by a new nature and identity jointly held between the two parties. Individuality is maintained in one sense, but identity and nature are shared to the very core of their respective beings. What would it look like to fully reflect and live out this reality? We get some sense of this from the vows and practices of the ancient and more recent world.

However, there is one other place where there are extensive details of the implications of this kind of shared nature and identity: the Scriptures. With Trumbull's mature relationship with God and his deep understanding of Scripture, he clearly realized this. One can easily see where he would next focus attention: on correlating the understanding that came from his study of blood covenants with his understanding of the New Covenant and its corollary, the Covenant of Marriage.

THE NEW COVENANT IS A BLOOD COVENANT

Might Jesus' words about taking His blood into ourselves be related to the ancient practice of blood covenanting? Might His talk about people becoming one with Him and with each other (John 17) be related to this covenant concept? To our being "in Him," and already "seated with Him" in the heavenly places (Ephesians 2:6)? What about being indwelled by the Holy Spirit? What about the imagery of our own death—"buried with Him through baptism into death"—as we enter the New Covenant, and our being raised to new life as a "new creature" (2 Corinthians 5:17): "as Christ was raised from the dead to the glory of the Father" (Romans 6:4)? What about the thing Jesus said we must do in John 6:56 to be in eternal relationship with Him? "Whoever eats my flesh and drinks my blood remains in me, and I in them." In fact, the more one looks for the correspondence between the New Covenant and the historic practice of blood covenanting, which, again, was widely known and practiced in Palestine in Jesus' day, the more corresponding elements are noted. Beginning even with the name Jesus offers for this relationship, the *New Covenant*. (We will explore the correspondence between blood covenant and New Covenant in the third volume of this series. Simply note for now that this correlation is remarkably strong.)

THE COVENANT OF MARRIAGE AND BLOOD COVENANTS

How does the core concept of blood covenanting shed light on the Covenant of Marriage? If identity-containing physical material is shared in a blood covenant, and identity and nature are joined and altered, might this be the reality that is reflected in the term "one flesh"? A marriage is not fully entered until it is consummated via sexual intercourse. In the historical view of marriage, the union has not occurred until this point. If intercourse does not occur the marriage can be annulled, or deemed null and void, even if a wedding occurred, vows were spoken, and rings were exchanged. Does this correlate in any way with the sharing of blood as one enters a blood covenant? Might married people be instructed to treat each other in certain ways for the same reason because of this change of identity and nature in addition to these ways of treating people producing better relationships? Does the term "one flesh," describing those in a marriage covenant, speak to this question? (Genesis 2:24)

My earlier assertion was that covenant is the heart of God's plan for living—specifically the Covenant of Marriage and the New Covenant. Both of which share many elements with a blood covenant. So, did the concept of the blood covenant come from God? In Trumbull's book we see nothing mentioned as he recounts these practices that specifically ties them to the God of the Bible. The Bible itself does not identify the author of the blood covenant as God in the same way that it does for the Covenant of Marriage. This rite is certainly not confined to Israel or the Middle East, though it was practiced there from antiquity. Instead, this rite is worldwide (as is marriage, the author of which is clearly God). How can we determine if the original author of the blood covenant is God Himself? Let's think about that for a few more moments.

WERE BLOOD COVENANTS ALSO AUTHORED BY GOD?

We mentioned that this is a detective story. Sometimes, when trying to reconstruct an event, there is a confession or eyewitness testimony of a fact. We have the confession of God regarding His authorship of the Covenant of Marriage in Genesis chapter 2. Then there is ongoing instruction throughout the Scriptures about how marriage is to be conducted. But the origin of the blood covenant is out of sight, at least to a point. We are left with what I freely concede is, for the most part, circumstantial evidence that this covenant comes from the hand of God. However, I believe this circumstantial evidence is considerable. What is needed for police and the court system to tie a person to a crime? (Though this is not a crime, but the giving of a gift to humanity.) Establishing a connection here involves the same three elements: opportunity, means, and motive. Did God have the opportunity to give this practice to the human race? Yes, in the same way that He gave us marriage, and perhaps at around the same time. Perhaps this is something we can see between the lines as God instituted things such as shedding the blood of an animal to clothe Adam and Eve after they sinned against Him, and in blood sacrifices to Himself by Adam and Eve's children (a lesson taken to heart by Abel but not Cain). God not only had opportunity but the means. Genesis recounts God speaking directly with these people. And they had every reason to take Him seriously, to assign massive importance to His words, particularly once the consequences of failing to do so became evident. But what about motive?

Why would God want to make sure that this particular understanding resides in human minds and hearts, essentially worldwide and throughout history? And if this concept was important enough that God went to this much trouble to maintain it in human consciousness worldwide, how is it that in industrialized Western culture we rarely see this relationship? Why did this disappear, except in vestige, from our modern world?

At the risk of stating the obvious, in order for the practice of blood covenanting to have such worldwide distribution through history, this must have been a concept conveyed to the earliest humans—created in God's image at one point in time, at one point on the globe—in the same way and at the same time that marriage was so conveyed. Humans simply took this relationship with them as they populated the earth. Or, less likely, for those who believe that civilization and humanity arose spontaneously at several distant sites across the planet from hunter-gatherer ancestors, there must have been some form of worldwide cross-cultural travel at a very early time in human history. Somehow there was communication worldwide that was compelling enough to insert this practice into a vast number of indigenous cultures scattered across the planet. Or did people all over the planet simply spontaneously innovate precisely the same arrangement, based on identical understanding, at some point in time? If so, informed and motivated by what? Which scenario best fits the available facts and is most logical? Again, since the origin of this rite is not mentioned in Scripture, we have only conjecture as to its time and point of origin as well as its authorship. But we will see further down why I am so sure of the authorship of this rite—because we will see this rite again, with all its elements, right in the heart of the most important Scriptural account of all: God's offer to individuals of a relationship with Himself.

Why is the concept of blood covenanting important enough for God to engineer this kind of preservation among humans? I think there are at least two reasons. First, we have already discussed the challenges people face in properly understanding what God desires of them. This is a realm more characterized by confusion than clarity even for those like the Pharisees, who devoted themselves to studying God's written revelation to the point that each could recite the entire body of Scripture from memory. While these concepts are simple and straightforward in one sense, we often have trouble wrapping our heads and hearts around these things. Jesus spent three years with His disciples doing what? Mostly correcting their misconceptions about things He had already told them. But there was one thing God obviously wanted people to get right—the heart of His plan for a relationship that would literally save individuals from an eternity separated from Him. What if God could preview the essential nature of this relationship to humanity via blood covenants in their own cultures? Then people could simply translate their working knowledge of a relationship between individuals to a relationship between individuals and God. There is evidence that God has done such a thing with even more specific understanding pertaining to particular tribes.

A wonderful book by Don Richardson, *Eternity in Their Hearts*[1], details specific cultural knowledge possessed by certain primitive tribes from their distant past that correlated perfectly with the arrival of a missionary. When the tribespeople saw the missionary and noted the correlation with their cultural story—for instance, a white-skinned person wearing white clothing arriving and holding a black book that would show them the way to a relationship with God—they viewed this situation as remarkably significant. This person must have been sent to them from God with a message of paramount importance. People listened and responded accordingly, often with thousands or tens of thousands of rapid converts. There are many such stories. It seems that God may have done the same thing using blood covenants on a much broader scale. Often indigenous peoples have a better understanding of what wholehearted commitment—giving one's life to God—really means than the missionaries from our "developed" world who are presenting God's offer of relationship.

The second reason flows from something uniquely accomplished by covenant. Look again at the list of principles and behaviors inherent in blood covenanting—honoring, protecting, providing, defending, and much more. If you sum these up as an approach to another human being, what do you see? Would this not be an excellent functional definition of what it means to truly love another person? What is God's most important requirement of us? In fact, do the enumerated duties of covenant (as presented earlier in this chapter) not correspond amazingly well with God's instructions about how we are to treat one another? Are these ways of treating each other not the practical application of His command that we love each other? If God wanted to keep before humanity an example of how we are to love one another, how might He do this?

Might the bond and connection between two people inherent in covenant teach people around the world something important about working, productive, and beneficial relationships? Might God have been trying to keep these things before all of us, even among people who did not have the benefit of Scripture or anything resembling true worship of Himself? In fact, it seems likely that God wanted to brand into souls and into each culture a vision of what treating another human well actually looks like, and what faithfulness to another person, and to our own commitments, looks like. He wants to demonstrate the benefits that occur for people when love and faithfulness are lived out. It seems likely He wanted to leave this example before us in light of what was coming for the human race: the twisting of our sense of self-interest under the tutelage of Satan, which would in-

> He wants to demonstrate the benefits that occur for people when love and faithfulness are lived out.

evitably lead to division, discord, hatred, betrayal, separation, abuse, brutality, and the many other fingerprints Satan has left on the human race. God's offer of life to humanity is made via relationship. So, also, Satan's offer of theft, destruction, and death comes through the agency of other humans. Thus we are left with two distinct sets of fingerprints on the ideas and practices of individual humans and on human culture: those of God and those of Satan.

Through one human of Jewish stock, who was also God, God offers a covenant relationship to each of us. When Jesus declared that the way to have a new life, eternally joined to Him, was to eat His flesh and drink His blood, He clearly wanted not only those in one nation in one corner of the globe to grasp the fundamental essence of His offer, He wanted all of us to understand it. When He offered new life, the death of the "old person," the indwelling of His Spirit, a new family relationship with God and other people already in such a family relationship with Him, eternal and indestructible life, forgiveness of sins (via a debt paid on our behalf in a covenant exchange— our debts are held in common in covenant), and the many other facets of this relationship, He clearly wanted there to be a cultural context for such understanding worldwide. It appears reasonable—to me at least—that He ensured the worldwide distribution of the concept of the blood covenant to accomplish this.

> Thus we are left with two distinct sets of fingerprints on the ideas and practices of individual humans and on human culture: those of God and those of Satan.

There is no acceptable alternate path to God's offer of a covenant relationship with His Son, Jeshua (or Jesus), because there is no other pathway than entering a blood covenant with God, the New Covenant, for the life of God to literally enter our very selves. There is no other way for our old nature, corrupted as it is by the incorporated nature of Satan, to die, and no other way for a new nature to be born that qualifies us to be in an intimate relationship with God, our lives fully intertwined with His, not only now during our earthly lives, but for all eternity.

In John 6, then, it is clear that *this is what Jesus was offering* to the people who were listening. The people who heard Him clearly understood what He was offering—God's plan worked, it seems. They were simply at a loss to understand why He would make sure an offer in light of everything they thought they knew about God—beliefs that had been corrupted courtesy of their religious teachers and leaders. What about what we think we know about God? Do we want to join the larger crowd and walk away to find someone who will teach us what we want to hear? Or will we go sit next to Peter and James and John and those whose lives were radically transformed by God, who literally turned the world upside down over the next few decades, who took Jesus' words at face value and put them into practice?

> Do we want to join the larger crowd and walk away to find someone who will teach us what we want to hear?

ONE EXAMPLE OF A BLOOD COVENANT IN SCRIPTURE

We have seen blood covenants defined and seen the scope of this rite. It has been asserted that this understanding was common at the time the Scriptures were written. If so, the concept and practice of a blood covenant would be seen in Scripture. Is it?

We will see that the Scriptures have many references to the practice and principles of this covenant both in terms of blood covenants in general and of a specific example, the New Covenant with Jesus. But at no place in Scripture is this practice clearly and extensively defined and described. Why? Because, as mentioned, there was no need to do so for most people through history. Once we know the principles, underlying realities, and implications of covenant, we see these things referenced on almost every page of Scripture. (In fact, I initially intended to provide an appendix with the Scriptures referencing some aspect of covenant. But this, I soon discovered, would be longer than any of these volumes!) Once the concepts presented in these volumes are understood, simply read through the Scriptures from beginning to end and see if you do not find reference to one aspect or another of covenant on virtually every page in the New and Old Testaments.

Much of the imagery of the Old Covenant with the nation of Israel resonates with and prefigures the New Covenant as well—initiated by and commemorated by the shedding of blood through animal sacrifice. The Old Covenant was not the fullness of God's plan because the shed animal blood only illustrated what was to come. It was not the real thing, which was the blood of God Himself shed for us, which we may receive and gain new life (2 Corinthians 3:6; Jeremiah 31:32; Hebrews 8:13). The blood of an animal could never substitute for the blood of Christ. Much is made of the blood of Christ in relation to forgiveness of sins. But unless one understands the role of blood in ushering in new life for those entering covenant, one misses the even more important reality that His blood was also the vehicle through which we become new creatures with a new life, a new identity, indwelled by the Holy Spirit. He did, after all, invite us to drink His blood. Now do you see why? Though poured out for us and offered up to us, at the same time there is no physical way we can actually take Jesus' literal blood into each of our bodies. Thus, this is done in a symbolic sense. Nor do we physically offer Him our own. We simply trust that, as we follow the pattern He laid down for us, approaching Him with a wholehearted desire to give Him our lives and to accept His offer of covenant on His terms, He will create within us this new life, akin to the way He created our lives initially.

In Scripture we see aspects of covenant in abbreviated accounts of people's lives, in the unusual level of commitment people display toward each other on occasion. If we do not understand covenant, we will not understand that a covenant relationship is the guiding force producing certain behaviors. If we do understand covenant, we can infer, probably correctly, that behaviors consistent with covenant obligations occurred because there was a blood covenant in place.

This type of shorthand inference was common among Jews versed in the Scriptures in Jesus' day. If one wanted to make a point referenced in one of the Psalms, for instance, that person needed only mention the first line of the psalm. This would evoke the entirety of the psalm in the minds of the hearers and make the intended point.

Let us look at one example, the story of Jonathan and David, and see if our new understanding of covenant sheds light on this biblical account. And let us see if, in light of this understanding, we can now reasonably assume that certain other things transpired between David and Jonathan beyond what was recorded in the 1 Samuel account. Even in a story recorded in as much detail as this, including such things as Jonathan giving David his armor—something clearly consistent with a blood covenant ceremony—there is still no specific mention of a blood covenant or of blood being shared between the two. The text does note that a covenant was entered, but the wording of the text, in the absence of this understanding, leaves an open door for the belief that this arrangement consisted only of a vow or agreement between Jonathan and David, a construction that is consistent with the beliefs of current theologians about covenants in general. As we read this account, though, note the extraordinary behaviors that occurred between these two men. Consider whether anything beside a blood covenant, and a proper understanding of its implications, would produce the following behaviors.

Now it came about when he had finished speaking to Saul that the soul of Jonathan was knit to the soul of David, and Jonathan loved him as himself. Then Jonathan made a covenant with David because he loved him as himself. Jonathan stripped himself of the robe that was on him and gave it to David, with his armor, including his sword and his bow and his belt.
1 SAMUEL 18:1, 3, 4

Might we reasonably infer that this abbreviated account simply failed to mention an exchange of blood? Or that this account, the details of which are completely consistent with a blood covenant ceremony, was in fact a blood covenant ceremony? Since modern readers, even in academic circles, are mostly unaware of the existence of blood covenants, much less the role this relationship has played throughout history, can we see how modern readers and commentators would almost certainly misconstrue this situation? Recently I heard a prominent Christian teacher on the radio restate a view I've heard for decades, the position that "a covenant is a contract, but one authored by God."

As to the question of whether Old Testament-era blood covenant relationships were viewed as a gift of God, akin to marriage, we have the words of David.

Therefore, deal kindly with your servant, for you have brought your servant into a covenant of the Lord with you.
1 Samuel 20:8 (emphasis mine)

Therefore, while we do not have a clear statement from God Himself as to if, when, where, and how He instituted blood covenants, we do have the testimony of one called "a man after God's own heart," a man used by God to pen a significant portion of Scripture, who attests that the covenant entered with Jonathan was something "of the Lord."

If a blood covenant was entered between these two, what behavior would attest to this? What is the relative strength of this bond versus family relationships? Whose interests and honor are we to uphold first in a blood covenant? Whose life are we prefer even before our own? What price are we called to pay, if necessary, to protect the other party?

The bond between these two young men was about to be tested in the most graphic and extreme way. It can be a challenging thing to assume the enemy of a covenant partner. More so if this enemy happens to be your own father, and the situation is yet more overwhelming when your father is the king of Israel, one who literally holds your life in his hands. If Saul was trying to harm David, would Jonathan put his own life on the line by protecting David from his own father and king? Here we should note another price Jonathan was willing to pay to honor this covenant. Saul correctly pointed out to Jonathan that his support of David would help David's ultimate claim to the throne of Israel, to which Jonathan was current heir. Would Jonathan be willing to give up his relationship with his father, his home, his family relationships, his future throne, and, if necessary, his life—all to satisfy a commitment made by a king's son to a young shepherd boy in covenant? Let us see.

Please read the entire account in 1 Samuel 18-20. Here are four pertinent excerpts.

> . . . *then Saul was even more afraid of David. Thus Saul was David's enemy continually.*
> 1 SAMUEL 18:29

> *If it please my father to do you harm, may the Lord do also to Jonathan and more also, if I do not make it known to you and send you away, that you may go in safety.*
> 1 SAMUEL 20:13

> *Then Saul's anger burned against Jonathan and he said to him, "You son of a perverse, rebellious woman! Do I not know that you are choosing the son of Jesse to your own shame?"*
> 1 SAMUEL 20:30

> *Then Saul hurled his spear at him [Jonathan] to strike him down; so Jonathan knew that his father had decided to put David to death. Then Jonathan arose from the table in fierce anger, and did not eat food on the second day of the new moon, for he was grieved over David because his father had <u>dishonored</u> him.*
> 1 SAMUEL 20:33, 34 (EMPHASIS ADDED)

Do the excerpts cited here, and everything in the entirety of Jonathan and David's relationship following the initiation of their covenant, correlate perfectly with what would be seen if two men were faithfully living out a blood covenant? I do not think there is any question that this is the case. Jonathan and David made faithfulness to their covenant relationship a priority exceeded only by their relationships with God. Their relationship overruled blood family relationships, self-interest, even self-preservation. This is the necessary place these relationships must hold if God's plan is to be carried out. Why is this so important? Because placing a higher priority on anything else will necessarily change our priorities and redirect our decisions. We will no longer faithfully live out our covenant. In fact, we cannot do so. Covenant is first and foremost about priorities. Covenant is an all-in kind of thing.

> Covenant is first and foremost about priorities. Covenant is an all-in kind of thing.

Covenant, though a simple concept, has myriad implications, effects, and consequences, as we might expect if God were behind it. Here is a fascinating implication: Jonathan appeared to be giving up his right to the throne and acknowledging David's anointing as the future king by entering covenant with David. But Jonathan was also *ensuring* that he would sit on the throne, either personally or in the form of his covenant partner. Jonathan also included in the vows of covenant (perhaps looking forward to his own premature death) that David would deal kindly—read: "covenantally"—with Jonathan's relatives. This was an interesting—and highly risky—commitment on David's part as well. Jonathan's relatives might well decide to assert a claim to the throne upon which David was sitting, a claim which would have merit based on the rules of succession as they were commonly understood in the ancient world. David took this risk and proved faithful to this vow as well, taking the last remaining male relative of Jonathan to live in his household and eat at his table (2 Samuel 9).

There are many reasons I feel safe in asserting that blood covenant is part of God's plan for humanity. David's own words attribute this arrangement to God. This arrangement was certainly a part of God's plan for David and was literally used to keep him from death. David's life prefigured One who was coming, who would eventually take His seat on the Throne of David, eternally ruling all Israel and all of humanity. But Jesus was also prefigured in the life of Jonathan. We see Jesus, only Son of the King of all, prior to being seated on His own throne offering a blood covenant with Himself to those He loves—prior to His own death. In this death He leads the way into covenant, for to enter this relationship one's current self must die, then arise from this death as a new person joined at the deepest level with one's covenant partner(s).

SIMILARITIES OF BLOOD COVENANT, THE NEW COVENANT, AND MARRIAGE

We enter blood covenants as humans via a physical exchange. In terms of the New Covenant, God, not being confined by time as we are, first became fully human yet remained fully God in His incarnation. That is, by becoming fully human He engaged in the first half of the exchange of natures in a general sense. Next, He offers up His blood for us as He died for any who will receive Him (John 1:12). Might there be something in addition to "paying for our sins" involved in Jesus' shed blood based upon our foundational understanding of covenant? By embracing Jesus, and receiving in a spiritual sense His blood shed on our behalf two thousand years ago, and by offering ourselves up to Him in a death-for-death and life-for-life exchange, the Spirit of God enters and becomes a part of those who have entered covenant with God. The Bible says that those who are in covenant with Christ are "in Him." This extends the exchange of identities to an extremely personal and individual level for all who are in covenant with Him. Thus, the exchange of life and natures is complete. There are other exchanges which we will detail in the third volume. There are new relationships and shared identities beyond those with Christ; we are also in covenant with all who are in covenant with Him. All of the responsibilities, duties, and obligations that are part of a blood covenant translate exactly into the requirements placed on us as we enter this relationship with Jesus, and these same obligations also define Jesus' relationship with us. In fact, we can use this correlation to much more clearly understand what we are to do as Christians. Are you beginning to understand why I believe covenant is not just part of God's plan but the very *heart* of God's plan for us? And can you see how the concept and practice of blood covenants plays a central, foundational role in this plan?

Further, since God used the term "covenant" in the context of marriage (Malachi 2:14), and since a change of identity and nature ("one flesh") characterizes this relationship, I believe we can reasonably infer that marriage is created, offered, received, and executed with an identity change that is analogous to the one noted in blood covenants. The Covenant of Marriage is entered in a way that is completely parallel to the way a blood covenant is entered—via sharing identity-containing body fluid. It would follow that a similar set of duties, responsibilities, obligations, and opportunities attends this relationship and that the reason for these is identical to the reason for these behaviors in a blood covenant—the newly conjoined identity between the parties that was created by entering the covenant. If we examine the Scriptures, both Old and New Testaments, regarding marriage and its obligations, and if we examine the larger topic in Scripture of what it means to love one another—which we are told to do in marriage—we will see that these injunctions regarding love correspond beautifully to the duties, responsibilities, obligations, and opportunities of covenant in general. As we have said, those aspects, in sum, are a wonderful functional definition of love in action.

We can assume that carrying out this plan will produce the heart experience of love in those who live these things out. This heart was specifically mentioned between David and Jonathan—not love in a romantic sense as has been suggested by some in recent years—but love in the broader sense, in the way that God commands us to love other people. It is noted that Jonathan loved David as *himself.* Curious language indeed in light of our understanding of covenant. Note the convergence between the structure of the relationship and the heart that is intended in the relationship.

God's command to love one another certainly involves behavior (beginning with obedience), but it also involves cultivating certain things in our mind and heart toward others—certain viewpoints, values, and priorities which will in turn alter our feelings in predictable ways. For instance, if we make someone else our highest priority and devote ourselves to their well-being, our hearts will warm toward this person. Could it be that faithfully living out the principles of covenant is the key to developing our hearts in this direction? Might this be the key to building the very inner experience that we all want to enjoy—a life characterized by love? If this is true, when it comes to marriage can we also reasonably infer that faithfully living out our covenant obligations in marriage plays a huge role in forming this same heart experience—growing and deepening love? Is this God's path to happily-ever-after?

It is noted that Jonathan loved David as *himself.* Curious language indeed in light of our understanding of covenant. Note the convergence between the structure of the relationship and the heart that is intended in the relationship.

Can you see how gaining clarity and understanding regarding any of the variations of covenant—Blood, Marriage, or New Covenant—informs our understanding of all three? What we will see is that a full, functional definition of loving another person synchronizes completely, in every way, with the things that would occur if we are faithful to fully live out our covenant duties, responsibilities, and obligations in any of these three relationships. These things also correlate completely with how we want to treat someone we love with all our heart. It not only coincides with, but also creates and builds our hearts and inner experience in a way that leads to the deepest fulfillment and gratification, in addition to leading to the best possible relationships. Therefore, it certainly appears that covenant is God's bid, in addition to specific Scriptures regarding specific behaviors, to teach us what it means to love one another. The more we understand the gravity—and the Authorship—of these relationships, the more we are motivated to conduct them as they are meant to be.

This will lead to myriad benefits in our lives and in the lives of others. In fact, is faithfully living out our covenants synonymous with fulfilling God's most important commandments: to love Him and to love other people as we love ourselves?

Though these are magnificent and important goals, this is not the end of God's plan. In fact, every purpose for the family, every purpose for the church in its full definition as the collection of those in covenant with God, and every purpose that God has for individuals flows from the beings *we are grown and transformed to become* as we faithfully live out these two covenants. This, again, is why I believe covenant is the heart of God's plan for everything in our lives and our world.

If this is true, how do we faithfully live out our covenants?

Covenant: How God Does Relationships

H. Clay Trumbull identified the core principle and defining reality of covenant: a transformation of identity and nature brought about by a sharing of identity and nature as this relationship is entered with another person. Here we will summarize the key elements gleaned from his descriptions of this rite.

Though two are joined in a covenant, individuality is maintained. The best model to understand this individual/unity phenomenon is found in the Author of covenant, the Trinity—three personalities, all of which are God, sharing one nature and identity. The fullness of Godhood is seen in the three taken together, or in any one of the three (John 14:9, 17:21).

WHY A CORRECT UNDERSTANDING OF COVENANT IS IMPORTANT

We all know that marriage is special. But if a sampling of people in our church or community were asked exactly what is so special about marriage, we would get a wide range of answers, wouldn't we? After reading this far about covenant, is your answer beginning to change? And if we were asked *why* we're supposed to do the things we are told to do in our marriages in Scripture, do we now have a reason beyond "God says so?" Some of these things could be tied to loving each other, but other things God says about marriage seem to threaten our sense of self-interest, and they certainly threaten our culture's sense of what this relationship is supposed to look like. So, what is marriage supposed to look like?

The first implication of understanding covenant is that marriage is an extremely specific thing. Marriage was defined by God when He created it; and all that marriage is flows from what God created marriage to be—a merger and transformation of the identities of the participants. But God did not just create something and say, "Here it is."

God created marriage in the context of us: our minds, our hearts, our needs, our lives, and our futures. We are going to see in the next volume that this relationship does a number of things simultaneously, all of which address our deepest needs and strongest desires. Through covenant God teaches us to love, then offers strong motivation to refrain from unloving words and actions. God's plan for how two people in a marriage are to approach and treat each other is completely in sync with how loving feelings are built, sustained, and strengthened. His plan is simply that we express the deepest love of which we are capable. But this plan is not just about a better now, about two people being the nicest they can be toward each other. He intends to grow and transform us into people who can face the rigors and challenges of marriage and family life. The challenges of life can crush people, leave them broken and bitter, and destroy relationships. Or these same challenges can refine and mature people and build deeper and stronger relationships. God's plan for covenant is strongly focused on growth and change—things at the outset we are usually not aware we need.

All of God's plan must be seen in light of the merger of identity and nature. Through this lens everything about marriage makes perfect sense. More importantly, through this doorway leads the path to our happily-ever-after. This opportunity is available to every married couple. Sadly, though, most do not experience this life because most do not know what marriage is, much less how to build the relationship into what it can become.

> Most are not aware that by entering this relationship they are *already transformed.*

Most know that marriage is something special, unique, and supposedly powerful. But most do not know how or why. Most are not aware that by entering this relationship they are *already transformed*. Almost all problems in marriage can be traced back to people trying to live as if this joining and transformation had not occurred.

WHAT IS OUR REAL SELF-INTEREST IN MARRIAGE?

Here is one example: if two people are in love, and want to do loving things for each other, what limits the loving things they do? Pulling on the other end of this rope is one's sense of his or her self-interest. One will do loving things . . . to a point. One will give up one's way . . . to a point. But one will not give up something he or she thinks will too strongly threaten his or her self-interest. But this begs a question: what is our real self-interest? If our self has changed, if our nature has changed, if in fact everything about our lives has changed, what about our self-interest? And least the way we defined this when we were single. Has our real self-interest changed? Absolutely. The tug of war just noted is one of the principle sources of conflict in marriage. Yet this source is not even real. People are fighting to protect things that, in their estimation, will benefit a life that no longer exists. We will work through this issue in detail in the second volume; suffice to say that our real self-interest in covenant incorporates three things: 1) our true best interest; 2) the true best interest of our partner; and 3) the true best interest of the marriage/family. To chart the proper course, we must take all three vantage points into account and craft a course that best protects the interests of all three. What is our primary consideration in covenant? To look after the interests of our covenant partner, to treat them as well as we treat ourselves because *they are ourselves.* Can you see how this upends every previous pattern intended to get one's way? Can you see how this removes a major impediment to love? Can you also see that this does not mean we give up all of our legitimate interests for the sake of another? Our interests are important—just as important as our partner's. But rather than approaching issues as adversaries in a winner-take-all conflict, we approach every situation, every decision, as allies and friends. Conflicts in covenant should focus not on being right, or on winning, but on *getting it right*.

CORRECTLY UNDERSTANDING THE NEW COVENANT

Our fundamental problem as humans is separation—which, as we noted, is the actual definition of the word translated "death." We are separated from God. We are separated from each other. We devour each other pursuing individual and divergent self-interests. This is the rough neighborhood in which love tries to live. This separation cannot be addressed by cultural injunctions, or even laws to the effect that we should love each other—because what definition would lawmakers write for love? We can agree as a culture to treat each other well, and will do so on a good day. When we feel like it and think it best for ourselves to do so. When people say we cannot "legislate morality" they are usually referring to sexual behavior; but the inability to legislate the constellation of behaviors and attitudes that would constitute love is a much larger and more important issue. Even within the church love seems lacking—not completely, but often more than one would expect. For the same reason, people are not cognizant of the actual connection among them created by the New Covenant, and they often reduce the nature of the relationship between themselves and God to a rule-based contract. So what does God intend all of this look like?

First, we are united with God at the level of nature and identity. His Spirit has come into us; we are in Him. While we have not been elevated to Godhood by this joining—the Trinity is still an exclusive club to which we do not belong—God does intend that we live new lives and fulfill new roles in His kingdom that would be impossible in an un-joined state. He offers us an inheritance in eternity with Him, fulfilling roles not clearly revealed, but involving administration and ruling. He intends a relationship with Himself that is intimate, deeply connected, and obedient. This obedience is purely intended to produce in our lives what God wants to see and to enable us to function in His kingdom as He desires. We may be useful to others and love others in myriad ways in the Body of Christ; we may fulfill many roles in the lives of others. But only if the necessary groundwork is laid within us—which is also a function of our obedience. He equates our love for Him with our obedience to Him.

A less well known aspect of the body of believers in Christ is that they are also joined in a bond of covenant. This is a corollary joining that occurs when we enter covenant with Christ. If "A" enters covenant with "B," and "A" also enters covenant with "C," what is the relationship between "B" and "C"? Their identity has now become joined within "A," and they are joined by both containing the identity and nature of "A." So, if three, or three billion are joined to Christ in covenant, what is the relationship among them? Was this concept understood by early believers in Christ? If one reads Acts 2:42-47 in light of the understanding of covenant gained so far, the relationship among these people is certainly consistent with a covenant relationship. In verses 45 and 46 behavior is described which could only be explained by covenant: "All believers were together and had everything in common. They sold property and possessions to give to anyone who had need."

If this is God's plan for the body of Christ, in light of all the other aspects of covenant we have learned so far, how close is our current Christian community to living in accord with this relationship that exists among believers? If the true power and impact of an individual or of a group of individuals, or of the entire body of believers on earth, comes via God's covenant plan; if we are taught to love according to God's definition through faithfulness to covenant; if we are refined, grown, and transformed via this relationship, conducted faithfully as God intends, how important would a correct understanding of covenant be if the church is to fulfill the role God desires it to play in our world? Many people do display behaviors consistent with covenant within the body of Christ, but it would be fair to say that the principles and practices associated with covenant are not the rule in this community, to say the least. And I have never heard this reason given—"because we are brothers and sisters in the New Covenant"—to direct or encourage any behavior during my entire Christian life. Would it not be a powerful thing if we all understood the way we are actually joined in the New Covenant?

WHAT ARE OUR RESPONSIBILITIES IN OUR COVENANT WITH GOD?

We all want *amazing* from God, but what are *we offering Him* in the relationship? Covenant teaches us that the radical power, transformation, and gratification that we know *should characterize* a life in relationship with God can only occur if we build our relationship with God and our life according to God's plan, in partnership with Him. He desires that we have an intimate relationship with Him, under His direction and protection, fueled by His love, empowered by and provided for from His inexhaustible resources. On the other hand, God appears to be unwilling to create in our lives the wonders of which He is certainly capable if we are not willing to search out and implement His plan to build what He has told us to build. If we are to have the abundant life promised, we must realize what is required of us in the process.

WHY IS COVENANT NOT JUST A RELATIONSHIP, BUT A PLAN?

It was said earlier that covenant is not merely a relationship; it is also a plan. In order to implement the reality of covenant to full advantage, in order to build the relationship to the fullness of love, in order to develop most fully as people within this relationship, a series of steps must be followed. First, we must learn the nature of this relationship from its Author, and we must understand how the relationship is to be built. In this step, as in each other step in the process, we are going to need to decide what is true and what is not true about the relationship. Why? Because we are also presented with ideas about the relationship by our culture, our family, our own perceptions, and from within the Christian community that differ from God's revelation of the reality of this relationship. Thus, our first responsibility is to locate, identify, and embrace God's truth on these questions.

Our second responsibility is to align our sense of reality with these truths. We have been taught many things about what is best for us by our culture. For instance, we all come into a marriage convinced that it is important to be right—or at least to create the impression we are right—and to win arguments. In covenant, if we understand this relationship properly, the priority shifts from being right to making the best decisions and adopting the most constructive viewpoints. One must shift virtually every value, priority, and approach of single life, with goals and values informed by our culture, to a different approach. We are told many things to do and to be toward another. Many of these we will not want to do at the outset; we will not understand why we need to do them, or we may think there are many good reasons to do something different. We will examine God's system of motivation, adjustment, and revision of our thinking, our habits, and even our emotions in the rest of this series. For best results, we need to engage in God's system, but this remains a choice at every point. Our responsibility is to sort through our reasoning and to decide whether or not it is really in our long-term best interest to embrace God's way, even if we do not understand it at the outset. This is true for the overall process, as well as every detail.

Then, having made the decision to follow God, we must follow through. There will be many obstacles in our path if we are walking with God. Some of these come from within, and we will need to understand and overcome these obstacles. A large part of this series is aimed at providing the tools to do this. But there will be other challenges: we will be tempted to not be faithful to our covenant in myriad ways. Offers will come to follow other paths. Adversity will challenge our commitments. If we are to be faithful, we must develop the capacity to stay on the course to which we have committed ourselves. This will require, for most of us, developing new character qualities and strengths—willpower, resolve, perseverance, and others. God's plan can and will produce every needed thing to equip us—if we follow His plan. We should not envision this process as a gritted-teeth struggle against overwhelming forces, though. We are building an incredible relationship with the love of or lives, with the Lover of our souls. This is worth any effort and any price. But we must always keep this goal in view as we walk through life.

We must learn to deal with the distractions that will come. God's goal for us is faithfulness, growth, and learning to love. If we are to derive the most benefit from these relationships, we must adopt these goals and fulfill them. This will take everything we have as a human being, and more—for which we have God. When He told us that all things are possible through Him, this is one thing He had in mind. But none of the above will happen unless we have fully committed ourselves to believing in God, following His plan, and doing whatever it takes to succeed.

We also must learn to deal with deeper resistance and objections from within ourselves. Romans 12:2 speaks of being transformed by the renewing of our minds. We are new creatures who are charged with building our new lives in these new relationships. But there will predictably be things in our hearts and minds that oppose this building. Some are ideas we can just review and discard in favor of God's truth. But others are at deeper levels, at the level of character development and our sense of our identity. One of the most powerful, and wonderful, implications of covenant is that these real issues have already been dealt with by our change of identity and nature as we entered these relationships. The course of our lives, though, is guided not only by the reality of this transformation but by our perception of who and what we are. We must also review our understanding of ourselves. If our view of ourselves leads us to sabotage possible successes, or to refrain from trying or growing, we need to seek out the lie about ourselves we are continuing to embrace. We need to adjust our view of ourselves. We must acknowledge and embrace our true identity and nature and go through the process of learning to live this out.

WHAT IS, VERSUS WHAT WE BELIEVE TO BE TRUE

The things of God operate on many levels simultaneously. As we are learning who we are and learning to express who we are in covenant, as we experience the blessings of deeper love and deeper levels of commitment, as we begin to see real benefits from implementing God's truth about ourselves and other things—as opposed to what we originally thought about all of this—we are introduced to a very important reality. Jesus spoke of people who have eyes to see and ears to hear. (Luke 14:35, et. al.). Paul prayed that believers would be given a "Spirit of wisdom and revelation" (Ephesians 1:17). What we learn over time is that there are things that are real that we do not perceive or understand. This is also true of things within ourselves. We may be in a marriage covenant, or the New Covenant, yet not realize the nature of these relationships, or the transformation that has occurred within ourselves as we entered them. We may be misinformed about our identity. We may be misinformed about many things in life. Our misconceptions can play key roles, pivotal roles in directing our lives. Regardless of the joining that occurs in covenant, we can continue to act as if we are still separate beings. We can misunderstand our identity in Christ, and many other things that will misdirect the course of our lives. This comes down to the difference between perception and revelation. God tells us certain things are true. We may perceive things differently. We may be informed that the situation is not as God says. (Anyone who thinks back to the conversation between Eve and the serpent at this point is on the right track.) We are thus presented with a choice. Do we believe what God says, or our perceptions, or the perceptions of others? How does this impact covenant? Many things about this relationship cannot be felt or seen. Is what we feel or see, then, the truth of the matter? Or is what God says the truth of the matter? This is our first point of decision, but not our last if we are to follow God's plan.

What we believe ourselves to be is a remarkably powerful force determining an individual decision or the course of our lives. What we believe to be true is a more powerful force that most realize, in the same ways. What if I told you that a major part of God's plan involved a process whereby we first identify, affirm, and embrace each truth about these relationships? Then we go through a process of bringing our lives into conformity to what we now realize is true. The interesting twist that covenant introduces is that the reality of who we are changes. Each of us has spent our lives trying to figure out who we are and how to live. But now we are someone different, though we often perceive little of this change in the beginning. And we have often been grievously misinformed about life in many ways. Thus, our job in covenant is to learn who we now are, relying on God's revelation. And we are to review everything we thought we knew about life and love and be willing to cede our view if it differs from God's. But the job is not completed by simply recognizing truth for what it is. There is a process by which we adjust how we are living and bring our lives into accord with what is true. There are mechanisms God created within us that are brought into play in this process. This process of revision includes our mind, heart, will, and character. When God said to be "transformed by the renewing of our minds" (Romans 12:2), this is the process He is describing. God terms this overall process *renewing our minds* because the overall process begins with and relies upon embracing truth and rejecting things not true. The interesting thing is what else happens when we engage in this process. This is only a part of the overall plan of covenant, but it is perhaps the most important element in redirecting the course of our lives. Why? Because what we believe to be true is more powerful a thing in each of our lives that what is actually true. At least in the short run. In the long run—when God rewards us or recompenses us for what we have done during our lives—pure truth will at last determine the fate of each of us . . . as God compares His truth with the way we lived. Being in covenant with Him will place us with Him for eternity, or we can opt out of this covenant and remain separated from Him for all eternity. Even if we are with God, there will be rewards that are received, or lost forever (I Corinthians 3:12-15).

BEING INVITED INTO THE FAMILY BUSINESS

The picture offered so far is that we are invited to follow God very exactly and are rewarded for doing so in a number of ways—personal growth, the best relationship, and other things. But let's consider another picture. You are adopted by someone who owns the biggest and most profitable business in the world, and more than this, who is a person of outstanding character, a truly fine person. To your amazement, you are asked to begin meeting with this man, and he begins to orient you to the family business. He makes it clear that he wants you to play a significant role going forward. But, of course, you need to be prepared to do this. Your adopted father makes it very clear that, in addition to playing the role you earn through your preparation and performance, you will be rewarded in a way that reflects your effort and performance. How would you approach your meetings with this man? Would this opportunity—truly the opportunity of a lifetime—excite you? Would you listen to every word and pay attention to every nuance of this man's teaching; would you be determined to remember every word; would you want more than anything to get the most benefit from his wisdom, his experience, and do everything you could do to replicate his successful approach when given the opportunity? Would you be willing, eager in fact, to devote your life to this training process for as long as it took to become fully equipped? Would you stay up late and rise early to review your notes, to make sure that when you next met you were up to speed and ready for the next lesson? Would you do everything in your power to not let this man down when responsibilities were handed to you? Would you want more than anything to reward his confidence in you? Since more is caught than taught, aside from any other reward, what would it be like for you to simply be in the presence of this man, to labor together with him, to get to know him on a personal level, to be influenced by him at every level? Might your goal over time shift from learning to lead as he leads, to learning to live as he lives?

In covenant with God—adopted into His family—we have the opportunity to do all this and more. What is God's family business? Building the Kingdom of God. His rule is characterized by love, joy, peace, patience, kindness, goodness, faithfulness, gentleness, and self-control (Galatians 5:22-23, New American Standard Bible). Once He subtracts the influence of His enemies, His kingdom will be characterized by a lack of rebellion and the absence of evil in any form. His desire for each of us is simple: first that we would enter covenant with Him and join Him in His kingdom, now and for all eternity; second, that we would conform ourselves to His rule; and third that we would play a role in helping others enter His kingdom and conform to His rule.

All authority in heaven and on earth has been given to me.
Therefore, go and make disciples of all nations, baptizing
them in the name of the Father, and of the Son, and of the
Holy Spirit, and teaching them to obey everything I have
commanded you. And surely I am with you always, to the very
end of the age (Matthew 28:18-20).

In order to play the role God intends each of us to play, we must go through a vast and comprehensive preparation. This, of course, does not involve taking time off, going away somewhere, going through this process, and coming back ready to play our part. Instead, God has designed the ultimate on-the-job training process. We simply live our lives while meeting with Him on a very regular basis. We cultivate a deep relationship with Him and a deep love for Him. And we harness the potential of every relationship and every life situation—in conjunction with the truth of His Word applied to our lives via real-time interaction with Him. We learn what is real and true and continually engage in the process of conforming ourselves and our lives to what is real and true. As we do this, we will prove the reality and truth of what we have applied.

Taste and see that the Lord is good; blessed is the one
who takes refuge in Him (Psalm 34:8).

Do not conform to the pattern of this world, but be transformed
by the renewing of your mind. Then you will be able to test and
approve what God's will is—His good, pleasing, and perfect will
(Romans 12:2).

God is love. Whoever lives in love lives in God,
and God in them (1 John 4:16).

Covenant defines love. Covenant is the path to learning to love. Covenant is the path to personal transformation that allows us to

Covenant defines love. Covenant is the path to learning to love. Covenant is the path to personal transformation.

love more deeply and perfectly. Covenant defines the relationship between all of us in the body of Christ—it defines how we are to view each other and treat each other. Covenant is the reason for every ritual in which we engage, and it conveys the proper meaning of each, giving these rituals the power in our lives they are intended to have.

A more comprehensive understanding of God's plan for each of us in these relationships leads to a vision for what can be built by groups of people in God's family. Life in the Christian community is often challenged due to lack of love, lack of maturity, and lack of priorities in sync with God's. The maturity necessary to lead or to follow well in God's kingdom flows directly from the development process inherent in covenant.

The heart-cry of our world is for unity, brotherhood, peace—this from a world characterized by division, strife, and violence. The reality of the separation between people cannot be "well-intentioned" away. This separation, and the competing visions of self-interest that flow from it, are the foundations of all the things we would like to change about our world. Covenant addresses this at a personal level and at a global level by altering and uniting people in a real way, a way that could literally change the world—if people were in step with this reality. There is a problem of real separation among people not joined via covenant, and there is a problem of living out the perception of separation among people whose lives have actually been joined together in covenant. It is imperative that we understand God's plan for individuals and for our world.

GOD'S GRACE VS. RESPONSIBILITIES HE DELEGATES TO US IN COVENANT

One point of confusion merits special attention. We are told, correctly, that we bring nothing and add nothing to our conversion and salvation. God graciously offers us a new life via entry into the New Covenant. This new life becomes ours by accepting His offer of relationship on His terms. What we offer in this transaction is a life that merits being put to death; we offer this life up to God so that He may do precisely this, then raise us to new life (Romans 6:4). However, this reality is often blurred and confused with what God intends for the remainder of this relationship. Many believe and many teach that this same posture—grateful recipient who does nothing other than believe—carries over into the rest of our Christian life. "Jesus does it all," regarding our entry into covenant, becomes "Jesus does it all and we do nothing, now and forevermore." Anything we would propose to offer in the relationship—our effort, our sweat, our sacrifice, even our dedication and wholehearted commitment—would simply be insulting gestures to a God who has done it all and delights in having done so. All we can do is wait patiently for God to transform us into whatever He wants us to be. And we wait. And wait. Why? Because we are not being faithful to carry out the duties, responsibilities, and obligations of our covenant. Wholehearted devotion to God and wholeheartedly carrying out His plan for this relationship could not be further from the idea that we do nothing to build this relationship going forward. Once we have new life, we also offer all of this one back to its Author, in the form of obediently and faithfully building a relationship with Him, then doing as He instructs in all the rest of our new lives. One approach is "all in," the other is "sit, watch, and wait." God's grace is one of His attributes toward us for which we should be most thankful. And an attribute we should be careful to understand, not to extend and distort in a way that causes us to not obey God's plan for our lives in the name of His grace.

If we do not fulfill our delegated responsibilities, what happens to our growth and the growth of our relationship with God? Might this explain why our churches are full of people who are far less mature, powerful, and loving than they would be if these people were aware of their covenant obligations, responsibilities and duties and were faithful in these? For those who are in a deep and growing relationship with God, a comprehensive understanding of our role can only improve and strengthen this relationship. We see new opportunities for growth, new resources to draw from, and new dimensions of our life before God.

We will summarize the principles of a blood covenant. We will consider the common elements among all three covenants and consider how these principles are applied. What do these relationships look like, how are they built, and how are we built through them? In order to appreciate the importance of God's plan, as we go forward we will continue to contrast His plan with the alternative—the world's approach.

SUMMARY OF THE PRINCIPLES OF A COVENANT

- There is the **death of individuals** and **birth of new, joined individuals.**

- This conjoined identity **causes the two to prefer each other over all others** to the point of giving up one's life for the other if necessary.

- Covenant produces **a relationship that supersedes any family tie** except marriage.

- Covenant is not a relationship that can be revoked in any sense; it **is permanent and lifelong** because there is literally **no way to undo this merger of identity and nature.**

- **The highest priority in one's life** after entering it **is to honor one's covenant and honor the name and reputation of one's covenant partner** above all else.

- Covenant imposes **mutual obligations, responsibilities, and duties.** In no sense is this a giver-taker relationship; instead, it is **a mutual commitment of aid in any form required,** drawing from any resource possessed or any potential that might be developed.

- Each is to **defend, protect, and provide for one's covenant partner** as one would look to one's own protection, defense, and provision.

- **Family ties and responsibilities are now assumed by both.** One is to provide, protect, and defend the other's family as if it is their own, **which it has now become.**

- The resources of each are at the disposal of the other. **There is no limit on the claim one may make on the other's resources or efforts.**

- Friends of each become **friends of both**; enemies of each become **enemies of both.**

- Debts of each become **the liability of both; assets are shared.**

- Marriage between a male and female who are in blood covenant is viewed as incestuous and forbidden.

The basic concept of covenant is quite easy to understand. If this concept represents reality, the principles listed above are logical and common sense things. Beyond these obvious implications, it is amazing to me—and clear evidence in my mind of God's authorship—to consider the vast number of other consequences that flow from this simple reality, this joining. I have been avidly studying this topic for thirty-five years, observing firsthand these realities, but I am still seeing new implications and applications of these truths. There is far more here than one could understand in a lifetime, which once again suggests that God's fingerprints are on this form of relationship.

> There is far more here than one could understand in a lifetime, which once again suggests that God's fingerprints are on this form of relationship.

ACTION POINT: Take a few moments to consider what the underlying reality of covenant means in terms of your relationship with your spouse, and how this could impact your marriage. What areas of your relationship would this reality change? What difference would it make? Compare your thoughts with what follows.

FOUR OVERARCHING REALITIES OF COVENANT

Covenant has four central realities we must understand if we are to grasp its full impact. The full impact of covenant, faithfully lived out, is love. As you read the following, think of ways in which each of these elements is indispensable if we are to build a heart and life of love toward our covenant partner in the case of marriage; or partners in the case of the body of Christ (John 1:12; Hebrews 2:11).

NEW LIFE

First, covenant is about new life. In God's plan, this new life is not just another beneficial element added to our lives, not merely an incremental upgrade of our old self. In each covenant this new life offers opportunity, resources, and other things not present in the old life. This new life is *altogether different* from the old one. In a blood covenant one now has a partner whose resources are at your disposal, whose highest honor is to honor you, who will defend you to the death—and you are to reciprocate. At the time of marriage, people often have the (accurate) sense that their lives have really just begun, that everything up to this point was but a preamble. Now there is something larger than oneself to which one's life is devoted—spouse, children, family. It is now possible to build things greater than could be built as a single person, such as a legacy of people in future generations who are (ideally) trained to build excellent lives and impact their generations in turn.

With this in mind, new life via the New Covenant has vastly more importance, as this relationship does not cease at the time of bodily death; instead this new life is eternal, inextinguishable, and joins us to the life of the Creator of the universe. If one gains significantly by joining to another mortal, one gains *infinitely* by being joined to an infinite God, the Lord of

> God's plan is not to simply build onto the old. In each of these forms of covenant He fashions an entirely new creation as the old one ceases to exist.

all things. Note for now that God's plan is not to simply build onto the old. In each of these forms of covenant He fashions an entirely new creation as the old one ceases to exist.

ALTERATION AND MERGER OF IDENTITY AND NATURE

Second, flowing from the above reality, covenant is about an alteration of identity at the deepest level of our being. We enter covenant as a fully formed person who has been living out a particular identity our entire life. We are accustomed to our previous life in every way. And we do not, as noted, fully perceive the altering of our identity and nature that occurs in fullness at the time we enter covenant. In fact, we perceive these changes in the depths of our beings from our perspective only partially—if at all. One can think of the beginning of our new life much like the beginning of our initial one. Great potential, little of which is initially evident or discernible. This new life is something that is manifest over time, that grows in a way analogous to our initial life—a true identity that we become aware of only as we go through the experiences of living. We become aware of our new identity and nature experientially and progressively as we go through life. But the only way to fully apprehend this change, or to develop the fullness of our new potential, is to base our understanding of our new identity on God's revelation. God has a plan, and it begins with telling us who we now are. Or, we may never fully realize who we are. We may settle for lives that develop little of our true potential, that express little of the life actually within us.

We will cover God's plan in detail for the two covenants that are the topics of volumes two and three. Briefly, God instructs us point by point, step by step, how to grow our new identity to maturity. This path is synonymous with faithfulness to Him and His Lordship. It is also synonymous with faithfulness to these two covenant relationships. That is why we must be guided by God's revelation and His directions rather than our own perceptions, for our perceptions and beliefs previously embraced will not achieve what can be realized through carrying out the directions of our Maker step by step. Therefore, we must be guided by an ironclad commitment to faithfulness in either relationship if we are to build these relationships as God intends, for it is these relationships that build and grow us in the way God intends. We will be far into either of these relationships before our perceptions catch up with God's revelation about these realities—if they ever do. Thus, we are wholly dependent on God for guidance in these relationships from beginning to end.

If our identity changes in this way, what does this mean about our sense of who we are? This must change, and this change in understanding occurs at many levels. We must recognize and embrace this new reality as true. As we do, and begin to act in accord with this new reality, our hearts will follow—our emotions shift, our priorities change, our goals are altered, along with our values. Our remaining task is to learn how to live out this new identity faithfully. Inherent in this is identifying things that were part of our "old" identity but not our new one, and in refraining from living out things that are no longer real (such as continuing to live as if we are single if we are joined to another in marriage). The reason we must focus first on our identity as opposed to merely trying to live out some list of duties from a sense of obligation is that we will devote ourselves to being ourselves—to being authentic, to living from the core of our being—in a way that we will not devote ourselves to doing a list of things "because someone said so." (Even if that someone is God.) Obedience to things we do not understand may be grudging and partial, even resentful, while honest self-expression can be genuinely enthusiastic at the outset and grow into passion as this path is followed.

Covenant also offers fulfillment and gratification. How? What is our most gratifying and fulfilling experience? Is it not living authentically from the core of our being, and from this foundation building a life and relationships worth having? God's plan not only characterizes our new identity for us—merged with another—but He shows us how to live out this identity through loving the one to whom we are joined, whether to a spouse or to Him. This, in every way, in every sense, is the most gratifying and fulfilling life each of us can live. We are built to love and be loved. God shows us the path to this outcome. The dilemma faced in non-covenant love is that extending ourselves to the point of sacrifice may well collide with our view of our own self-interest, and at that point we must calculate how much we are willing to look after someone else at our expense, and how much expense we will subject others to for our benefit. There is nothing wholehearted about this calculation, no joy, for every sacrifice for the sake of love reduces, instead of builds, our lives. This may be offset by building our relationship, but our self-interest and our relationship remain competitors for limited resources. Neither can be fully satisfied.

> This may be offset by building our relationship, but our self-interest and our relationship remain competitors for limited resources. Neither can be fully satisfied.

JOINING AND RELATIONSHIP

Third, covenant is about joining and relationship. Every human has a wall in their lives, and they place people on one side of that wall or the other. Those on the inside are friends, people we trust, whether related by blood or not. Those on the outside are dangerous, suspicious, unknown, different, or merely irrelevant. This wall can never completely go away, for we are not to thoughtlessly expose ourselves to those who mean us harm—and those people do exist. On the other hand, God wants to reposition and redefine this wall in all of us, and He uses covenant to do so. We now have a new set of people on the inside—our covenant partner and those who are on the inside of our covenant partner's wall. But the most significant change is where our covenant partner permanently resides. In every previous relationship we have had the prerogative of moving people from the inside to the outside, and we were willing to do so in certain situations.

Our best friend, our parents, even our children can change from trusted ally to outside the circle if their agenda diverges enough from our own at a key point, or if they threaten our perception of our life to a certain degree. Remember what happened between Saul and Jonathan? Suddenly an enraged Saul is trying to pin Jonathan to the wall with his spear. But what happens in covenant? There is no more *my life* and *your life*. There is only *our life*. Remember what happened between Jonathan and David? This person with whom I am in covenant is always on the inside of my wall, for that is the only place they can be; otherwise I would be moving myself outside my own wall! The interest my covenant partner has in the lives of others now becomes my interest. This is true for a spouse or for one with whom we are in a blood covenant. The bricks that form our walls, as it turns out, are our perceptions of our self-interest. God's overall plan is to alter our perception of self-interest to correspond with His. His perception, by the way, is the only one based on reality. God is in the business of breaking down unnecessary walls.

> What happens in covenant? There is no more *my life* and *your life*. There is only *our life*.

Here, simply note that the most powerful divisive force in relationships between humans—divergent views of and competing self-interests—is completely transformed into the conjoined, synthesized interests of two people whose identities now coincide. This is not to say that people will not have different perceptions, even incorrect perceptions, of self-interest when they are in covenant. They certainly will. And initially they may contend sharply over competing priorities, at least as they perceive these things. But the next task of covenant is to recognize where one's deepest self-interest resides and to craft an approach to living that fully recognizes the needs, wants, imperatives, and agendas of the other, synthesizing these with one's own to form an agenda that is most mutually beneficial. What faithfulness to covenant prevents is one party, in the name of self-interest, getting one's own way, advancing one's own imperatives, while ignoring the realities of the other party and thoughtlessly harming them.

You can begin to see how this concept plays out when we are

in covenant with God. Everyone who is indwelled by the Spirit of God—a Christian—is also joined to other Christians by a covenant bond. Jesus described this in John 17, which I recommend reading at this time if you are not familiar with this passage. This reality was confirmed by behavior in the lives of the first Christian converts in typical abbreviated fashion in Acts 2:42-47. From this brief description it appears clear that these early Christians had the same understanding of the covenant they had just entered as the people listening to Jesus in John 6. To the extent that we do not see this reality lived out today, what has changed?

EXCHANGES BETWEEN THOSE IN COVENANT

Fourth, covenant is about exchanges. This reality is the logical, practical outworking of the first three realities. First identities and lives are exchanged. We have already detailed things now held jointly—family members, material things, debts, friends and enemies; and the obligation to use anything and everything to honor, bless, and provide for the needs of one's covenant partner. The sense of covenant, two becoming one, suggests something still larger. Rather than being obligated to any list of duties that could be compiled, the mutual obligation is completely open-ended. Covenant is the ultimate blank check. The correct answer always is: "Whatever I have to offer, and whatever it takes."

When we come to the New Covenant, the theme of exchanges becomes fascinating. The most amazing exchange of all is that Jesus, immortal God, came to earth to die, just as we are all destined to do under the curse of sin. Let that sink in for a moment. God did not come primarily to teach, to be an example, to make an offer, or to be able to empathize with us. In His coming He became fully human and fully helpless. He was an infant who needed His mother for survival. Everything from this point forward in His earthly life culminated in His hanging on a Roman tool of execution, literally holding His pierced hands out to all humanity, pouring out His blood for us, entering death for us, though soon to be resurrected to new life. When we look at why Jesus did all the other things He did, why He took on all the aspects of humanity that He did—born in a stable to a peasant, raised in a small town as the son of a craftsman, why He was cold, wet, hungry, and exhausted, why He submitted to the most degrading of executions, naked between two criminals in the most unjust killing in history—when we see the omnipotent God in human flesh being physically incapable of dragging His own cross to the place of His execution, thus requiring the Roman guards to press a bystander into service, and all the other human indignities He suffered, including betrayal to death by a friend—we can view all of this as God for some reason experiencing these things so He could sympathize with us in some vague way.

Or we can view Jesus taking part in one covenant exchange after another, first exchanging His divine and immortal life for the weakness of human flesh, signing up in the process for the death we earned via the fall. We can see Him taking on our debts (for sin and otherwise), our weakness, our shame, our pain, our grief, even our confusion about our lives as He sweated blood in the Garden of Gethsemane and begged His Father for another way than the path He was about to endure. All of this follows the pattern of covenant exchanges. What belongs to one life now belongs to both lives; lives that are joined in every way.

> All of this follows the pattern of covenant exchanges. What belongs to one life now belongs to both lives, lives that are joined in every way.

In return, what did Jesus offer of His life to those in His presence? He fed, He healed, He comforted and affirmed, He offered forgiveness and restoration, He laughed and celebrated, He respected those the world did not, those who were nevertheless made in His image, He defended in prayer and through speaking truth, His words were the Word of God, and His life was this Word in visible form. He offers us an inheritance, a family relationship with Himself and other members of the Trinity, and also with other people who are in covenant with Himself. Every aspect of His life on earth, every aspect of the offer He makes to us, including but not limited to eternal life and forgiveness of sins, and every aspect of what He requires from us in return—all of these are direct reflections of the covenant relationship that He ordained and offers to individuals as the specific and perfect remedy for the predicament in which we all find ourselves.

Without His life, the life He offers us via covenant, we live in a world largely crafted by Satan and under his dominion, containing within ourselves his nature and separated from relationship with God because we have joined in the rebellion even if we are unaware there is one! Therefore we are all under the penalty of death. The only path of redemption involves forgiveness of our sins, but it also involves much more. Most important, we are offered an entirely new life—death of the old, and new birth as a new creature, newly joined to our Creator in a relationship that reflects His original, loving intention for us. We are remade in His image because His identity—His Spirit—resides within us.

To actually manifest and live out this new reality we must turn—fully and completely—from the old and completely embrace and develop the new. We must understand our new identity and live out this identity faithfully. This is God's plan. What we must also realize is our role in developing the life God has graciously offered us and our responsibilities to God in covenant, which are considerable.

Do you remember the earlier multiple choice question about covenant?

Referring either to marriage or our relationship with God, what is a covenant relationship?

1. A declaration of love for our spouse-to-be, or for God.

2. A pledge of lifetime commitment to our spouse-to-be, or to God.

3. A promise that we will act in certain ways toward our spouse-to-be, or toward God, for the rest of our lives.

4. Giving ourselves to another person, or to God, just as we are.

5. Something different than any of these, and far more powerful.

As we can now see, the correct answer is number 5. One can make a variety of pledges and commitments to another person that would be consistent with the first four items. For instance, we may ask someone to marry us and pledge ourselves to them, but this does not create a covenant. We can even speak vows to another in a wedding ceremony, fully pledging ourselves to them for a lifetime, but until the marriage is consummated it is not yet a marriage.

Only God's covenant plan involves a transformation of identity, and it is this alteration of identity that distinguishes covenant from all other human commitments, agreements, and arrangements.

SEVEN

Aspects and Implications
of Covenant

ENTRY INTO A BLOOD COVENANT

Trumbull cites many examples of covenant ceremonies, all of which are variations on a theme. A blood covenant is entered during a celebration not unlike a wedding ceremony. Witnesses are present from the community. There are vows spoken between those entering covenant, and to deity. The two engage in ceremonial actions. Gifts are exchanged; the two often try to outdo each other with their offerings. One element is consistent and essential: the sharing of blood through various techniques. This sharing is witnessed by the community. Next, some permanent token of the covenant is designated. Often this consists of rubbing something into the incision from which blood was drawn to create visible scarring. Or a talisman of some sort is exchanged, to be worn from this point forward. Finally, there is a feast shared between those entering covenant, which is shared with the assembled witnesses.

One point bears mention about such relationships—blood covenant and the other two covenants we will examine. There is no ambiguity whatever about whether one is in, or is not in, a covenant. These are entered at a precise point in time, coincident with the merger and transformation of identity. This transformation defines one's entry into covenant.

ENTRY INTO THE OTHER TWO COVENANTS

One current point of confusion about marriage and about a relationship with God is whether one is in a covenant relationship or not. When, exactly, is one actually married? The Church of England, in which our son was recently married, has changed its official view of when "real marriage" occurs from the first act of intercourse—because this so commonly occurs prior to wedding ceremonies—to the point at which vows are exchanged. *This*, church officials have determined, is the point where actual joining occurs. Similarly, if one asks a sampling of Christian leaders exactly how and when one becomes a Christian, there will be a variety of answers. This ambiguity testifies to a lack of understanding of these relationships. One either is in, or is not in, a covenant. One is or is not a Christian. One is or is not joined by the Covenant of Marriage. There is no merge lane, no provisional status, no trial period.

> One either is in, or is not in, a covenant. There is no merge lane, no provisional status, no trial period.

In a world where we overvalue our own perceptions as the final litmus test for reality, where we cannot look at another, or at ourselves, and "see" this merger of nature and identity in the same way we can see hair color, we have one other source of information we can draw from to develop our understanding, and this is God's revelation to us of things we cannot perceive—His written Word. Since many in our world do not accept this source as authoritative, there is predictable confusion about entry into either relationship. Different churches teach different things about how one becomes a Christian, often seeking to merge the idea of entering a covenant with being baptized in a particular church building or joining a particular church body or holding one doctrinal viewpoint or another. If we understand what the Scriptures teach about entry into this relationship, particularly in light of a more clear understanding of covenant per se, such confusion does not occur. In the same way, marriage has been morphed, redefined, and blurred with other human agreements and arrangements in ways that confuse the nature of marriage and neuter its true power. If we really want to cut through this confusion we must carefully consider how and when a marriage covenant or a New Covenant relationship comes into existence.

How does one enter the Covenant of Marriage? There is a wedding, with one's friends and family in attendance. The wedding is generally conducted by a human spiritual authority, like a pastor or rabbi, or on occasion by a civil authority. There are vows spoken by the couple to each other—and to God in most cases. There is instruction about marriage, and there are blessings pronounced over the couple. Rings are placed on fingers. Then the couple is pronounced "husband and wife" by the one conducting the ceremony. The two kiss immediately after this pronouncement, and this prefigures the real joining, with the permission—and under the sanction of—church authority. Then there is a reception, which includes ceremonial actions that depict aspects of the covenant relationship like feeding each other cake and drink. Rice is thrown, and the full attention of the assembled is directed toward the couple as they ceremoniously leave the party.

When, then, does this covenant come into being? If we consider the analogy to Blood Covenant we end up with the historic view of the church as to when this occurs: marriage goes into effect only when the marriage is consummated, or when the first act of sexual intercourse occurs. It was fashionable in some historic settings to even display bloodstained sheets, as would be likely to occur if a virgin female has her first intercourse. In most denominations in years past a marriage can be annulled—or cancelled and deemed not to exist—if the marriage is not consummated by sexual intercourse. Why would this be the significant act as opposed to things that occur in the wedding ceremony like the exchanging of vows or rings? Because identity-containing body fluids are exchanged in sexual intercourse. Semen (which is obviously identity-containing, because along with an egg it can produce a new person who contains one's genetic information) passes from the man to the woman, and the woman's intimate fluids, plus or minus her blood, bathe the male. This exchange of physical substances institutes a marriage covenant in a way completely analogous to entry into a Blood Covenant. If we think about this reality in light of the radical change in sexual behavior over the last sixty years in our culture—the vast majority of people throughout the history of our country up until the 1960s, and most even in the 1970s, were virgins at the time they wed—this will obviously raise other questions. (We will address these in the second volume.) For the moment, simply note that sexual intercourse is the covenant-creating action.

At this point, identities undergo a transformation analogous to a Blood Covenant, and between the two a new entity is formed, which we call a family. Often the name of one person changes to reflect this change in identity. Though there are many similarities in these two relationships—Blood Covenants and marriage—there is at least one distinction: there is no limit to the number of people with whom one may enter a Blood Covenant. We are to enter only one marriage covenant, and maintain its exclusivity. To engage in sexual intercourse with another person once we are married does two things simultaneously: it breaks our first covenant at the same time it forms a new one. This exclusivity, one of the hallmarks of holy matrimony, explains why God allows divorce—public and legal dissolution of marriage—if adultery has occurred.

How about the New Covenant? How do we know we have entered this relationship? Romans 8:9 says, "But you are not in the flesh, but in the Spirit, if indeed the Spirit of God dwells in you. Now if anyone does not have the Spirit of Christ, he is not His." Again, this makes clear that the defining characteristic of a Christian is being indwelled by the Spirit of God. Does the analogy here between the New Covenant and the other covenants we are discussing—marriage and blood—seem obvious? See 2 Corinthians 5:17: "Therefore, if anyone is in Christ he is a new creation; old things have passed away; behold, all things have become new." In the model of covenant, it is reasonable to conclude that our becoming new creatures coincides with the entry of God's Spirit and that the initiation of our bond to Christ (becoming His) has something to do with His blood. What did He say about His blood in John 6? In the same way we have been discussing, there is also the death of the pre-covenant being as this new creature, this new life, comes into being indwelled by the Spirit of God (Romans 6:4).

There are some obvious distinctions between entering a Blood Covenant with another person and with God. The clearest one is that Jesus' physical blood is not available to us in the moment, yet it was offered to us and for us. God is not limited by time and space as we are, so our acceptance of His offer and the initiation of this relationship involves something that happens on a spiritual level between us and God, including our accepting of His vow to us and offering our vow to Him, both accompanied by the ceremony of baptism. There is also no role played by our own blood, which testifies to the fact that we bring nothing to the table—other than our willingness to die—trusting that we will be resurrected by God (Romans 6:4). One might view this in a slightly different light if one considers that in taking Christ's blood into ourselves (in type, via wine used in communion), what we ingest quickly ends up in our bloodstream. In this way there is, at least in the form of "substitute blood," such a physical mingling.

On the other hand, the communion ceremony is never described as initiating covenant. Baptism was modeled by Jesus, and in multiple Scriptures the act is associated with conversion, or entry into covenant. Whether God's Spirit enters us at the time of our wholehearted commitment to God, or at the time of baptism, is not precisely stated in Scripture, so I would offer respect to those who hold either position. God knows. If we are obedient to the Scriptural model of being baptized at the first opportunity in association with our conversion, this is not as much a practical distinction as a theological one. What baptism certainly does, analogous to a wedding or a Blood Covenant ceremony, is publicly serve notice of our New Covenant relationship as well as depict our cleansing, death, and resurrection. (We will discuss these issues in more detail in volume three.)

What we know with certainty, based upon a composite of the Scriptures, is that the initiation of our covenant with God involves *hearing* His offer, *believing* His offer, evidencing that we also *believe in Him* by entrusting and offering our lives to Him, *repenting* (acknowledging that, up until this point, we have been going in the wrong direction, basing our lives on something other than God's plan, led by voices other than God's, and therefore involved in rebellion against Him in ways large and small), then *receiving* Him as our Savior and Lord of our lives. We are then instructed to be baptized (John 1:12, 5:24; Acts 2:38).

COMPETITION BETWEEN THE PARTIES IS NO LONGER REASONABLE

In covenant, the strength of one party enhances the strength of the other. There is no place and no reason for competition between the parties. When one wins, the win is shared; when one is honored, the honor is shared; when one is favored or blessed these benefits belong to both parties. The destiny of these two individuals is now firmly linked. The purpose of this is to harness the joint resources and capabilities of the two, as well as the synergy of the potential of each, to better face the challenges of life.

COVENANT OFFERS NEW POSSIBILITIES AND OPPORTUNITIES

Covenants are thought to be *generative*, to give birth to things through the joining that would be beyond either life to produce independently. Faithfulness to every aspect of one's covenant duties, obligations, and responsibilities is thought to be one's most blessed course of action, while harming one's covenant partner, or refraining from offering every aid and help, is deemed a cursed course of action. Rather than some vague sense of betraying one's obligations leading to bad luck, in the covenanting ceremony a series of curses are enumerated for any breach, and divine enforcement is invited and as-

> Covenants are thought to be *generative*, to give birth to things through the joining that would be beyond either life to produce independently.

sumed. Beyond mechanical obedience to individual responsibilities, it is assumed that hearts will be wholeheartedly devoted to each other and to the relationship.

COVENANT PROMOTES INTEGRITY

In our culture we commonly say we will do things we have no intention of doing. Failing to follow through with our words or our commitments is thought to be of little consequence. Although deception and irresponsibility have never been uncommon in our world, in most cultures through history a vow and commitment of this type would lead to a massive effort to make good on one's word. In fact, the community's view of one's character, honor, and place in society would be dramatically affected if a person dishonored the kind of public vows that are made in a covenant ceremony or if a person dishonored an institution as ancient and honored as a Blood Covenant or marriage. Thus, people have paid careful attention to fulfilling every element of their commitments in this arrangement as a point of personal honor. We live in a day where dishonoring one's marriage vows is taken by most to be a reasonable exercise of personal prerogative, a do-over for someone who has fallen out of love, or become bored. This is diametrically opposed to God's view of good character and virtue, and extremely far from a path that will lead to any true satisfaction and gratification in a relationship. Can you identify the pattern of deception regarding the relative importance of our commitments and vows versus current views on personal freedom?

The sacrifices one is called to make in the name of covenant, if necessary, have been viewed through history as the most profound expression of love. There are many stories in ancient literature describing the lengths people would go to in order to honor their covenant vows. This was counted true heroism. It also kept before the human race an excellent functional definition of what it means to love another person. Perhaps this is what God had in mind when He turned this gift loose into a world that otherwise knew little of love thanks to the efforts of His enemy.

COVENANT BUILDS HEARTS AS WELL AS RELATIONSHIPS

Covenant is basically a two-pronged approach. There is a formal relationship with certain rules. Following these rules, however, impacts both the heart of one doing things to fulfill these rules and the heart of the one receiving from the other. If the specific things we are told to do are the very things that build loving hearts in a long-term relationship, we now build into the relationship the other dynamic—the feelings of our hearts—that will cause us to want to act in these very ways toward another person. Thus, rather than the perception of burden and sacrifice, the experience is of having the privilege and joy of giving.

> Thus, rather than the perception of burden and sacrifice, the experience is of having the privilege and joy of giving.

The only reason someone might take better care of another person than themselves—say, sacrificing one's life for their child—is their profound love for the other. In covenant, if both parties are faithfully supporting each other, treating each other well over time, we can see that two hearts will grow toward one another over time, though not in a romantic sense. Or, in the marriage covenant, two people start out with these intense, loving feelings toward each other. Being faithful to the duties, obligations, and responsibilities of covenant merely takes the relationship from this starting point and creates a more deep and beautiful relationship over time. Covenant, it appears, lines up perfectly with how our heart, mind, and will actually work. Which is what we would expect if God designed this plan.

COVENANT IS GOD'S PLAN TO CREATE UNITY

Do we not hear pop songs and other voices in our world yearning for us all to be one big happy family, to have peace on earth, to treat each other as brothers and sisters? Our deepest aspirations for unity, harmony, and peace line up with God's desire for us because He implanted this ideal in our hearts. Covenant is God's plan to unite the various selves in our world, a point which comes into focus more vividly if we consider the combination of marriage and blood covenants seeded throughout the world. Both of these covenants lay a foundation of understanding for God's ultimate plan to unite people to people, and people to Himself—the New Covenant.

Each of us has within our mind and heart a dividing line between us and them. Those outside the wall may not simply be viewed with disinterest. At times these people are viewed disrespectfully; they are mistreated, marginalized, shunned, ignored, oppressed, and even brutalized or cleansed. They may be viewed as if they are not a part of the world we want to inhabit.

True peace requires a connection with others and the mutual respect that flows from this connection. This sense must be based upon reality, though not a romantic notion that ignores reality. True peace requires trust. As fragmented human beings who start, and often remain, in rebellion against our Creator, we are not connected in healthy relationships. We often view people with suspicion, even as enemies, because they would damage or destroy us without a second thought. They are our enemies and should not be trusted. But much suspicion is unnecessary, more about a distorted sense of the nature of other people and a complete misunderstanding of their inherent value. We are all equally human, made in the image of God, with genuine interests equal in value.

People may have twisted and distorted perceived interests, and they may try to enforce their distortions on others in ways that should be opposed. Our lack of respect for others in some ways is a reaction to these distortions, and in some ways our disrespect reflects our own distortions. This lack of respect, lived out over time, has driven people further and further apart throughout history. We know this is not the ideal; there is something within each of us that wants to oppose these destructive divisions and bring unity to humanity. We sing about world peace and the brotherhood of man, and we build organizations to promote this ideal. But in reality our connection to those made in

God's image has been fractured in the same way this connection has been fractured with our Creator. Thus, the fundamental schisms between humans run deeper than our need to all be "a little nicer to each other." And the solution needed is more powerful than songs, romantic notions, and optimistic political slogans. God's plan involves more than a change of consciousness or understanding. His plan involves a changing of who we are, and thereby fundamentally changing the connection among us.

> The solution needed is more powerful than songs, romantic notions, and optimistic political slogans. God's plan involves more than a change of consciousness or understanding.

WHAT DOES COVENANT TEACH US?

In covenant, one's sense of responsibility expands. As mentioned, people's real interests and needs do not become identical by entering covenant. Thus, one is now committed to consider, and compelled to meet, the needs and interests of another equally with their own even if those needs are very different from one's own. Thus, one must learn what those needs are and learn to respect them equally with one's own. If the reader is familiar with Scripture, the concept that our needs are of equal importance resonates with numerous passages in the Bible. Then, if one is faithful to covenant vows, to respect and meet the needs of another, there is honor and joy when one enhances the life of someone to whom one is deeply committed. One learns that benefiting another elevates everyone. It is more blessed to give than to receive. Certainly such a refining influence will not in itself overcome human selfishness in a community, but it does produce virtuous character in individuals and rewards this virtue. In this it demonstrates an alternative way of living—a different set of choices everyone could make that contrasts sharply with the world—and demonstrates the benefits of this unselfish form of love.

Jesus taught His followers that the greatest among them would be the servant of all (Mark 9:35). Why would someone in this position be most exalted? Because the one who knows the most about the needs of others is the one who serves those needs—who is by definition a servant. Jesus came to serve, not to be served (Matthew 20:28). If we are to emulate Him, if we are to play the role He desires we play in the lives of others as He describes it here, does this not look remarkably like what it would mean to be faithful to serve the needs of our covenant partner? Or, in the case of the body of Christ, our partners? Covenant directs us to the connection between loving others and serving them; it directs us to the essential nature of the connection between us that makes such service our highest honor and duty; but faithfulness to covenant also includes many more aspects than simply serving one another. Jesus wants us to do as He said regarding serving, but this is the tip of the iceberg of the many facets of love He wants us to display toward one another. In covenant, the answer to another's needs is, "Whatever I have, and whatever it takes."

GROWTH WITHIN COVENANT

If one looks at the list of duties, obligations, and responsibilities noted above, this list touches every aspect of life. But this also is the tip of the iceberg. If one looks at the expanded list that emerges if one looks carefully into each item in the general outline cited earlier; if one looks at the entirety of what is vowed in a wedding; if one looks at the entirety of God's directives to us in Scripture—which correlated exactingly with the directives of covenant (reflecting, to me, that these two have the same Author, and are two sides of a coin regarding His overall plan)—the list touches every aspect of thought, emotion, and will, as well as every priority, value, goal, and aspiration. There is not an aspect of behavior not touched by these obligations, nor an aspect of ourselves. Though we all get some of this right, it is unlikely that any of us will get all of this right at the outset, or over the course of a lifetime. As we enter either of these covenants we are signing up for a lifetime of on-the-job training. Perfection resides in Jesus. Within us resides the need to grow, and the potential to do so.

Why have we not grown so that we do all of these things already? Because we have made peace with doing other things, and with being other things. We do not realize the importance of these elements of self and relationship. We may not see ourselves clearly, and think we are better than we are at love and relationship. Not to worry. God has just provided a clear picture of what we and our relationships are supposed to look like. And He has issued each of us a mirror—in the form of a husband or wife in marriage, or other members of the body of Christ in the New Covenant who will help us see ourselves more clearly than we do now. Circumstances also reveal what we are as opposed to what we hope we are. No one can see that discrepancy from a distance, but in close relationships it will become evident.

God has also provided vast motivation. We have committed ourselves to being and doing what is required in covenant. If we understand the nature of these relationships, we should be committed to authentically expressing who we have become. All of this, however, will test our capacity to do what we know we should do, as well as our ability to figure out what we should do in a given situation based on these principles. We will need to make decisions about whether we are going to be faithful to our covenant on a daily basis, and what this means in practice. As we attempt this, we will find that our personal resources to do even what we know we should do are lacking in many ways. Our character has been formed to make our lives work as a single person, or as a person completely out of sync with God. Our characters have all been misformed by our world, with habits and approaches that are antithetical to the intimacy of covenant. In the second and third volumes we will detail the processes of examining ideas, character qualities, and perceptions of identity that need to change if we are to properly build relationships, and properly build our new lives. Here, let us briefly outline a few of the parts of this process.

LIFE ISSUES AND CONFLICTS: DOORWAYS TO GROWTH

We do not feel the need to fix what we do not realize is broken. The way we realize something within us needs to change almost always involves a life issue or a conflict. When something in life is not working, or we are in conflict with someone, the default answer is that we are a victim. But covenant does not allow this easy answer. When any life issue arises, it is extremely helpful to ask two questions: 1) What is my role in this situation?; and 2) Lord, what are You trying to teach me? Anything in ourselves that is amiss will ultimately arise from an idea we have *embraced as true* at some point *that is not true.* This may be about ourselves, other people, God, or reality.

OUR THREE HUMAN POWERS: TOOLS FOR GROWTH AND TRANSFORMATION

We all realize that truth is a big deal, versus things not true. But do we understand why? Truth should be important to us because of a mechanism God created within us, as well as a responsibility He delegated to us. Each of us gets to make a determination about what we believe to be true and what we do not believe to be true. We make this determination every day about multiple issues, but we rarely understand the significance or power of this determination. I call this our power of *affirmation and dissent*. Once we determine that something is true (keep in mind that this has no bearing on whether or not something is *actually* true), this now becomes part of our sense of reality. We noted earlier that what we believe to be true has vast power to direct our lives. Here, we will briefly examine how this works. The other two powers involved in this process are our power of *attention* and our power of *intention*. In sum, with these powers we determine three things: what we think is true; what we decide is important; and what, if anything, we are going to do about it. These three powers are reserved solely to each individual. No one can make us render a particular decision about any of these things if we are willing to pay the price for refusing to do so. At the same time, these are our three influence points; in each of these three realms the power of our life is multiplied if we get things right, or dramatically weakened if we get things wrong. So, guess where Satan's deceptive efforts are targeted in our lives?

Once we embrace an idea as true, we more easily embrace related ideas. We also reflexively resist ideas that oppose an accepted idea. This mechanism has an important purpose: we do not need to continually ponder what is true in our world. We render decisions about an issue, then move on to the next one. Our minds do not like contradiction and conflict, so the rest of our ideas adjust to accommodate ideas we think are true and important. These impacts may seem obvious. But these embraced ideas also impact how we view other people, they impact our emotions, and they impact us on many other levels.

If we embrace an idea as true, and this becomes a fixed part of our sense of reality, what if someone embraces a different idea, or a contradictory idea? Such ideas are not merely different; we perceive them as wrong. If an idea violates our sense of reality, not only is this idea wrong, but the person holding this view is wrong. And if a person is out of sync with reality, as well as wrong about such an important thing, we now have grounds to disrespect this other person—who has simply embraced a different set of ideas from ours. Our idea, since it represents reality to us, can in our minds assume the role of a law of nature. People who differ deserve not only disrespect, but punishment or censure. If you are not clear about whether our minds work in this manner, listen to current political debates. People treat those with different ideas as something between enemies and sub-human. While most of us do not operate in these extremes, this dynamic in a more subtle form operates in all of our relationships.

Since our emotional responses come into play frequently in close relationships, at times in a way that is not constructive, it is helpful to realize the way our emotions are impacted by affirmed ideas. Once we embrace an idea, we develop an emotional attachment to it as well. We feel warmly toward what we believe to be true, and toward those who hold similar ideas. We feel cool toward those misguided ones who believe opposing ideas. These emotional reactions may be subtle, or not.

Once we believe something to be true, our behaviors, priorities, values, and goals come into line, and we form habits that support these views. In other words, our embraced ideas play a huge role in forming our character. For example, if we do not follow through with commitments—a character issue—we are basing our approach on reasons. Obviously not good reasons, but reasons nevertheless. We can simply feel bad about letting our partner down over and over. Or we can determine the idea or ideas that are the foundation of our approach and reexamine these ideas. Simply put, the process of growth and transformation is the process of discarding dysfunctional ideas and implementing new reasoning. Can you appreciate how important it would be for us to embrace ideas that are actually true in every area of life? To promote this process, and to provide a framework of truth, God offers us His Word and our covenant, with the intent that we be faithful to both.

The other two powers come into full play in this process as well. We have many more things clamoring for our attention than we can address. Some are more important than others. As an example, what priority do we assign to an opportunity which will delay or prevent following through on a covenant commitment? Is this an opportunity to do CPR to someone who might die without our help, or is this an opportunity to play a video game? We make such determinations every day, the sum of which could be called *our values*. Our values ideally accurately reflect who we are—our identity and nature, and key responsibilities, duties, and obligations we have assumed. But often they do a good job of reflecting neither. Covenant offers us an opportunity to grow this power to maturity.

The third power is our *intention*. This is our capacity to act, to impact, to change. Once we decide that we can and should act, this power carries that decision through to completion. Or not. Our willpower may be strong. Or, we may be very determined people based on prior development. But most in our culture have a notable lack of willpower to carry through with things they have purposed to do. Our lives are filled with distractions, and many do not have sufficient reason to push through such obstacles and diversions. In all three powers, our reasoning rules. We must have reasons to believe and idea or to disbelieve it. We must have reasons why something is important. And we must have reasons that are sufficient if we are to fight through obstacles to do what is truly important. Covenant is God's plan to exercise, refine, and grow each of these powers to maturity.

From the mature version of these powers comes a life based on truth, an authentic life, a life characterized by love, integrity, virtue, and correct priorities. Such a person will be faithful, determined, patient, and powerful. He or she will see important things through to completion, and do them as well as possible. This, in sum, is a highly responsible human being. This is a person one can trust and rely upon. Is this the type of person you would want as a covenant partner? Is this they type of person you would like to become for your covenant partner? God has a plan to produce this version of you.

THE COMMONLY UNDERSTOOD DEFINITION OF COVENANT IN JESUS' DAY

According to Trumbull's research this understanding of covenant, and all that flows from it, represented the common cultural view at the time of Jesus. This same view has been held, with minor variations, at most times and in most places throughout history. Trumbull notes that blood covenants were quite common in Palestine during Jesus' lifetime on earth, and were also present in a vast array of cultures throughout history. Thus Jesus' hearers, once they realized He was offering them a blood covenant with Himself, would have read into His simple statement everything they already knew about blood covenants. This obviously raised a number of questions for each of them. Their individual thought processes were not recorded for us, but their overall reactions were. Almost everyone turned and walked away. The idea of entering a blood covenant with God was incomprehensible. God was on the peak of a mountain clothed with fire; if people touched the mountain or saw the face of God, they died. They knew about following His rules and giving Him a fraction of their belongings . . . from a safe distance. But a blood covenant? A relationship known only among equals? A relationship that put everything about you right in the middle of the other's life? This could work to mutual advantage between two people, but how would this work with God? And why in the world would something like this be offered? Jesus answered this simply. "To enter the kingdom of God, you must be born again." This came up in a conversation with one of the Jewish religious leaders, Nicodemus, who sought Jesus out privately (John 3:3-14). Nicodemus posed another question in reply: "How can this be?" Jesus did not answer specifically; instead He chided Nicodemus for being a teacher and not understanding such a thing. It was only later—beginning in John 6, and ending with His resurrection, then Pentecost—when His Spirit began to enter people in a New Covenant relationship with Him, that the answer was clear: the new birth that occurs in covenant, which creates new creatures (2 Corinthians 5:17).

ENLARGING OUR UNDERSTANDING THROUGH EACH FORM OF COVENANT

Because there is so much common ground among these covenants, I believe it is logical and reasonable to use understanding that relates to one covenant to better understand the others, unless there is a specific reason not to do so (e.g., people can only be in one marriage covenant, but this restriction does not apply to the others). In doing this, we are following God's lead, for He draws analogies at multiple points between His relationship with Israel and marriage (Ezekiel 16:8 and numerous passages) and between a New Covenant relationship and marriage (e.g., "Husbands, love your wives as Christ loves the church"). The collection of believers through history is termed the bride of Christ (Ephesians 5:27 and other passages). The end of the earthly era and the formal beginning of eternal life with Jesus will be inaugurated by the "marriage supper of the Lamb" (Revelations 19:9).

COVENANT: THE MASTER PLAN OF GOD

All this would make perfect sense in only one situation: if covenant was God's master plan, the heart of His plan for each of us, and if these three were complementary parts of a master plan. This plan incorporates our creation as human beings, the family into which we are born, our upbringing and training, our finding the love of our lives and building a lifetime love affair/marriage, our procreation to create the next generation (which continues humankind), as well as continuing our societies via educational and spiritual training as we build our own families; and our rescue from the grip and domination of the enemy of God as we are adopted into God's family and indwelled by His Spirit, recreated, regenerated, and blessed eternally, joined to the body of believers as a brother or sister. Covenant is at the center of each of these, and these are intended to be at the very center of our lives and hearts.

Scripture does not address every element of life or every situation we will encounter in exhaustive detail. We have truth from God that touches every realm of life, but what we end with up as we try to apply God's Word in a given situation is akin to thirty pieces of a hundred-piece puzzle. Some things we know are true, but there are also gaps where God's Word is not explicit, or does not speak at all, or is subject to various interpretations. In these gaps and gray areas people draw in their own lines to complete their picture of life in a way they believe reflects God's intent, but which also reflects their own assumptions. This is the origin of many theological debates and most denominations, each person or group convinced they have a truer perspective on one matter or another than the folks down the street. The more our underlying assumptions and definitions of words are in line with those of the writers of Scripture, the closer our picture will be to what God intends. This is why good biblical scholarship matters, and why going back to the original languages for deeper meaning and looking for cultural context is essential if we are to truly understand God's Word.

Understanding covenant allows us to fill in numerous gaps with assumptions that are likely to be correct. Scripture does not mention that David and Jonathan actually shared blood. But if they did enter a blood covenant, and this relationship closely parallels the one we have entered with God and with other believers, we can do more than admire their mutual loyalty and devotion. We now have good reason to display similar loyalty today to those in the body of Christ, and certainly to display this same intense devotion to God. Their faithfulness in covenant can serve as an example and a guide for our lives in covenant. We can also reasonably infer that the responsibilities, duties, and obligations that are common in covenant relationships would also be a part of our New Covenant relationship with God. The Scriptures enumerating how we are supposed to act toward a spouse or toward God are widely scattered. To our modern minds some of these may be more than a little illogical. But once we view these Scriptures through the lens of covenant understanding, everything fits together into a seamless whole. Suddenly the whole package makes sense.

COVENANT TERMINOLOGY IN SCRIPTURE

When Jesus said (in John 17) that **He and the Father are one,** that **He and His followers are one,** and that **those in covenant with Him in the body of Christ are not only one with Him but also one with the Father and with each other,** can we now see that this refers to joined natures and identities that would occur as they entered covenant? It appears that the Trinity is the prototype of this relationship. Marriage and the New Covenant are offered to humanity to bring us into this heavenly order and teach us to inhabit it properly even as we enjoy the benefits of these relationships here and now. In the absence of understanding a covenant oneness of nature and identity, can we see how our understanding of "one" would likely be as a metaphor of our longing for unity, like a Beatles song or a bumper sticker urging world peace? A nice sentiment, but unrealistic and unattainable in a world guided by God's enemies. Armed with this misunderstanding, will we live out the power of God's plan?

"One flesh" is more than a metaphor. It is a description of shared identity which God intends to be indissoluble. When we look at the ways people in covenant are to treat each other, whether a Blood Covenant or a Marriage Covenant, can we now understand why we are to love the other person as we love ourselves? God has made this easy for us, in fact, and very real. Does it now make sense to define love as *the perfect bond of unity* among any people who are in covenant? This refers to what happens when covenants are faithfully lived out. This phrase describes not only a spiritual reality but the point of balance which can be achieved in covenant between living out our individual uniqueness and our covenant-based love for another.

> When we look at the ways people in covenant are to treat each other, whether a Blood Covenant or a Marriage Covenant, can we now understand why we are to love the other person as we love ourselves?

God wants us to understand covenant because, as we do, the Scriptures come to life. Humans draw lines between *me* and *not me*. We use the terms, "I can relate to," or "not relate to" one thing or another. When we read the Scriptures, do we usually have the perception that the people we are reading about are *us*, given that they lived a couple of thousand years ago in a very different culture? If we understand that we are in covenant with God, and also with these godly biblical characters—a relationship we will enjoy on a face-to-face basis at some point—would this understanding change what we are able to draw from Scripture for personal application?

These people are all very much alive at this moment, though out of our sight. But they are, in a real sense, in our hearts because we are in covenant with them if we are in covenant with Christ and they are in covenant with Christ. If our identity resides within Him, and His in us, what relationship would this create among all who are in covenant with Him? Would the godly example they have set for us be far more likely to come to life in us if we are aware of this reality? And if we read about one covenant behavior or another, would knowing *why* we are supposed to do this thing (beyond "because I said so, says God") help motivate us to actually follow these things? Would this understanding not completely overturn our understanding of obedience to God, which in God's plan is not fundamentally about keeping a list of rules but about building the best relationship with the Creator of the universe? Or, more precisely, living out with integrity the relationship God has graciously given us and the life God has already graciously placed within us?

COVENANT ALSO DEFINES GOD'S APPROACH TO US

> Rather than some hazy, diffuse, wishful-thinking, romantic idea about the true nature of God's love for us, we can reasonably infer that His love for us will take very definite forms and lead to very specific outcomes.

Covenants are not one-way relationships, but mutual: there are exchanges, responsibilities, and opportunities. If we are in covenant with God, He is also in covenant with us. If we understand how God directs us to display love and live out unity in covenant, we gain insight into how God conducts His end of our relationship. This is remarkably important. God loves us. What does this mean? Rather than some hazy, diffuse, wishful-thinking, romantic idea about the true nature of God's love for us, we can reasonably infer that His love for us will take very definite forms and lead to very specific outcomes. These are things we can rely on as we seek God's intervention in our lives.

WHAT IS FAITH?

The word *faith* then takes on a different meaning, moving away from "hoping very strongly that God does what we think is best in the situation." We now understand that **faith is more about *our faithfulness in the relationship,*** coupled with **confidence that God's love will be displayed toward us in ways that reflect the definition of love that He commits to display toward us in covenant.** We can trust, to the utmost, that God will act in our best interest—as He defines this—and will provide, protect, honor, and cherish us; and we can trust that it is our duty to display toward Him and others the elements that go together to make up His definition of love as revealed to us in covenant. God always leads by example. His involvement in our lives if we are in covenant with Him is, "I love you, therefore . . . " (see 1 John 4:19).

Our job is to actually mimic such love and attain such unity in these relationships in a practical and experiential sense, not just to think of loving others in some spiritualized, metaphorical sense. The next step, once we understand the foundation of these relationships, is to learn the path to living out and experiencing this unity of mind, heart, and spirit with our covenant partners. God has a plan for this, and it consists of showing us a large number of things to do and not do, to be and not be, in our relationships. None of us ever *do* all of these things or *are* all of these things—such perfection awaits us in eternity. In this life we are to simply start where we are and grow as God instructs us and enables us toward doing and being these things. God's plan includes commitment, growth, and transformation that can successfully develop these patterns in us and even create in us a passion for living out these patterns and designs, as we will see. Again, this is not about checking off items on a list of some type. This is about growing into the kind of people whose hearts, lives, and relationships are characterized by love.

WHAT IS A 'SIN NATURE'—AND WHERE DID OURS COME FROM?

Let us consider one other covenant term in Scripture and see if we can fill in the picture. What is a "sin nature"? This is the alteration of nature that occurred in Adam and Eve after choosing to disobey God and obey Satan. This describes the entry into all of humanity, via

Adam and Eve, of an element of the rebellious nature of Satan. Now, if an exchange of identity occurred, why would this exchange have occurred? Through obeying Satan, the parents of the human race apparently entered covenant with him. It is significant that Satan also engaged in a covenant exchange with Adam and Eve: the authority and dominion over the earth delegated by God to Adam and Eve was transferred to Satan, and the sentence of death that rested upon Satan for his rebellion now extended to Adam and Eve—and to their progeny.

Covenant is not a relationship reserved exclusively for humans and God. Covenant can also be entered with other celestial beings—fallen angels—who are God's enemies. It speaks in the book of Enoch, a para-biblical history book quoted several times in the New Testament, of fallen angels covenanting among themselves. Because the human race is in this covenant with Satan, everyone begins life literally under his dominion, manifesting portions of his nature even as we also manifest elements of God's nature, made as we are in His image (Genesis 1:27). From this beginning point we are offered a choice to enter the New Covenant with God. On the other hand, we can further bond and bind ourselves to God's enemies. We will cover this in the third volume, as it explains many things we see in our world.

MATURITY AND FAITHFULNESS DO NOT INSULATE US FROM REALITY

One thing to be clear about: a well-built marriage does not insulate us from the problems of living. A deep and powerful relationship with God does not shield us from the effect of darkness in the world around us. Misunderstanding at this point is the source of much consternation and disillusionment with God. Why does He not protect us and our families? He says that even these things—hard, difficult things—are for our good (Romans 8:28), to teach us deeper lessons, to grow us to maturity, to strengthen our relationship with Him. God offers us the resources in covenant to walk through literally any trial with Him, or with our spouse, and grow deeper and stronger, becoming more wise and more loving. The question is whether we know these resources are available to us and how to access them. It is impossible to imagine any trials more severe, threatening, and painful than the ones endured by Jesus. It is said that He learned obedience through the things He suffered. It is frankly difficult to imagine that Jesus was benefited by going through these things. But He was. This is good to keep in mind as we walk through our own trials.

There are three sources of problems that will continue to impact us for the rest of our lives. **First, our own growth and maturity will never be completed in this life**—we will struggle with our own stuff for the rest of our time here. But if we are following God's plan we will put away one issue after another. Over time we will create vastly fewer problems in this equation.

The second source of problems will be **our marriage partner or our covenant partners in the body of Christ.** See above: there will always be issues from these sources; but in the same way, if people are following God's plan, these problems will become less and less over time.

Last, **we will always be impacted by the cumulative effects of sin and rebellion of everyone around us.** An individual act of rebellion, any violation of God's moral law, is like a rock thrown in a pond. These acts do not just impact the ones who commit

> The impact of these things flows outward like ripples, in circle after circle, which proceed from the place where the rock landed.

them. The impact of these things flows outward like ripples, in circle after circle, which proceed from the place where the rock landed. These ripples impact an ever-widening circle of people. Now imagine the pond surrounded by people, all throwing rocks into the water again and again. The waves produced by all of these impacts resonate and grow into a surf that washes over everyone. This is the world we inhabit. We cannot escape the effects of other people's behavior on our lives.

EIGHT

What Are God's Goals for Us?

Like a wild animal born and raised in captivity, we have literally no idea what it would be like to live in the world we were created to inhabit, for which our bodies, minds, and hearts were fashioned. If we were to enter our natural habitat it would be so unfamiliar, perhaps frightening in its unfamiliarity. Until we grew accustomed to living there—and found that this was the life we were created to live.

WHAT WAS IT LIKE WHEN EVERYTHING WAS AS IT IS SUPPOSED TO BE?

" . . . and we've got to get ourselves back to the Garden!"
WOODSTOCK, JONI MITCHELL, RELEASED 1970 [1]

If we want to get a vision for life as it could be if we follow God's plan, we can simply look at what God initially created. What did He intend for us from the beginning? What did that world look like? What did we look like? What did relationships look like? As we look at the overall plan of God, it becomes clear that God is merely trying to return us to where we began—in our relationship with Him and with each other, but also in every aspect of life. This most massive of all do-overs requires dealing comprehensively and totally with the mess that has been created in our minds, hearts, and lives. As we consider His plan to deal with what is wrong in ourselves and our world, we want to be sure to look at the endpoint of His plan. What is God trying to accomplish in the end? What does He want for us? What was it really like to live in the Garden of Eden?

We are immersed in a world that is shades of gray. Some things look brighter, some look darker. We often do not grasp that gray—our perception of our world—is not a color. It is the combination of two completely opposite things: white and black. The variations of gray we see are simply varying proportions of these two colors. We assume that gray is the natural color of our world, that things have always been as they are now; that the confusion and uncertainty and pain—as well as the joy, love, and exaltation we experience in this world—are as they have always been. But this is not true. There was a time when black was added. Before this, there was only white, only the pure glory of God and a creation made in His image, with all things functioning as intended. This is how our eternity will be if we are in a covenant relationship with God. But what about *now*, if we are in a covenant relationship with God?

I have always been fascinated by the reflexive answer of many to the question of eternity. Being with God would be "boring," some say; they want to follow the fun to hell, where all their friends will be. Lies and manipulation, being a victim of theft or violence, or any other of the wonders birthed in our world as humanity joined in rebellion against God . . . these things are interesting? Betrayal is an experience worth having? Standing in line to be oppressed and abused makes sense? Perhaps to these people. It is true that many are attached to the idea of self-expression at the expense of others, and many think this is the way to get to the top. However, given the big picture outlined earlier, any attraction people feel to all of this is a deceptive sales pitch, a promised *somewhere-out-there* benefit which will never materialize.

This is a party everyone will regret attending.

This rebellious influence is part of our world; its impact will be here as long as the world is colored gray. We can, however, deal with these things and their influence in an entirely different way via God's plan than we could on our own. If God is in covenant with us, His faithfulness is unquestionable and His resources are always available. God can even use unpleasant and destructive things to our benefit—redeeming these situations—if we are in the close relationship with Him that He wants us to build.

What if evil had never appeared in this world, or appeared within us? What if we had never heard the other voice, or if we refused to listen to it? What if the voice offering and urging destructive ideas, wrong beliefs, distorted values, twisted priorities, and useless goals for living fell on deaf ears? What if there was only good in the world? While this eternity awaits us if we are in covenant with Jesus, what does God want to see in our lives, hearts, and relationships now, *in this gray world*? If we simply look at how He has instructed us to act and to be toward each other, and look at the things He instructs us to remove from ourselves; if we look at the new life He places within us via entering covenant and how He instructs us to build this new life, it's clear He wants us to crush the influence and effect of His enemy. His instructions, if followed, result in removing this influence from ourselves to the fullest extent possible here and now, not just in eternity. He wants us to inhabit His kingdom and to learn how to live in it now. He does not intend that we buy a ticket now to travel there later.

God wants pure white. This is what remains when blackness is erased. From our vantage point we think gray and black are different. Gray is OK, especially light gray. And even lighter gray—off-white—is really good. We think it is only pure black that we need to avoid. But this is not true. Light gray is white influenced and impacted by pure black. In our way of thinking, it has perhaps been impacted to an acceptable degree, perhaps even a degree that is attractive to us. We have all made peace with the presence of black—at least to a point—because we experience its presence as an unalterable reality. Here God differs most sharply from us. This is why Jesus presented people with the option of *all of Him* or *none of Him*, and would push people to a point where each had to make this decision. There is no blending of God with His enemies and their ways. This will never work. This is analogous to blending a cancer in with the rest of our bodies, a cancer that must be effectively treated to the point that it disappears completely. Even a little remaining cancer is a problem; this will become evident over time. Perhaps not right away, but in the long run such things grow, damage, and ultimately kill.

> This is why Jesus presented people with the option of *all of Him* or *none of Him,* and would push people to a point where each had to make this decision.

Therefore, God does not want to see us compromise with the world, make peace with His enemy, or continue to advance His enemy's agenda. Why? Because this blending approach separates us from God and from the blessings He intends for us. With this mind-set we literally cannot follow God's path because the introduction of black is the plan of His enemy. God's path first and foremost is about wholehearted love for Him, wholehearted devotion to Him, and wholehearted faithfulness to His covenant and His plan (all of which are synonymous). Any departure from this path simply means we are not on this path. Satan's most potent weapons in this realm are the beliefs that black is inevitable—unstoppable—and that much of it is beneficial.

We cannot be at peace with black in the world. There are things so black, so devastating, so painful, so mindlessly destructive, or such an unwarranted assault on white—the death of a small child, a random drive-by shooting, a young mother taken from her family by cancer, a student killing classmates. There is a point where almost everyone questions the presence of black. But usually in this way: "Why did God cause/allow . . . ?" "Why didn't He stop . . . ?" "Why didn't He answer our prayers?" "Why did He allow this to happen to me?"

People try to assign to God responsibility for the presence of black, and they blame Him for its effect. They shake their fists. They proclaim they could never believe in a God who would allow such things to happen. But they miss the essential reality. God did not invite black into our world. *We did.* God created a plan to deal with black now and for eternity, a plan that involved the greatest personal sacrifice on His part. While not responsible for black, He nevertheless offers to bear the full brunt of its impact for us. He offers us this plan from a heart of pure, perfect, glowing white love. He wants us to join Him in His heart, and He wants to join us within ours. His plan for this is covenant.

OUR LIVES WITH SATAN'S INFLUENCE SUBTRACTED WOULD LOOK LIKE . . .

For the sake of our discussion, let us pick one relationship and paint a picture of this relationship without evil—without destructive things, without people hurting each other, without hidden agendas, misplaced priorities, and wrong goals. How about marriage—yours and mine? What would a marriage look like if two people are deeply committed to treating each other in the best and most loving ways possible over the course of a lifetime? And, discovering that this commitment is beyond the reach of either at the outset—which everyone will discover if they actually try this—each commits to growing and changing into a person who can love the other in the fullness of God's definition, as each has committed to do.

What kind of relationship, and what kind of people, would be produced by this approach? What things would be required *to make* these commitments, and what would be required *to keep* these commitments?

CHARACTERISTICS OF A MARRIAGE BUILT ON COVENANT PRINCIPLES

A marriage built as God intends is synonymous with a marriage without the influence of evil. This is achieved by systematically stripping away those things that are destructive, while wholeheartedly building lives in the way God instructs. This process is never 100 percent effective during earthly life. But perfection is not the point; progress is the goal, moving toward this life, moving toward becoming these people. We are, after all, in a training process for life in the kingdom of God, now and for eternity. We are not only building God's love, joy, peace, patience, kindness, gentleness, goodness, and self-control, along with other virtues, into our lives; we are emulating Him—building His character progressively into our character—in a way that improves our quality of life here and now, as well as impacting our eternity.

We often find, to our surprise, that following God in every detail of life is what we have always wanted to do; we just did not realize it. What seems at the outset like some kind of struggle with ourselves—involving a sacrifice we are not sure we want to make—in the end feels like the most authentic and satisfying life we could live. We are like a captivity-raised lion, who for the first time experiences the thrill of catching a gazelle and enjoying, for the first time, the food he or she was created to enjoy. In a curious counterpoint, following Satan's agenda initially feels like something we really want, but in the end it is *anything* but what we want. In the Greek paradigm, one does not do a particular thing until one understands it. In the Jewish paradigm, one cannot understand a particular thing until one does it. In the end, we find that the only thing we want to understand is the righteousness of God, not the rebellion of His enemy. Unfortunately, we all have the opportunity to experience both.

What are the specific qualities of a relationship built on covenant principles? Here we will look briefly at qualities of a mature, godly marriage, a picture we will paint in much more detail in volume two. As we take this quick look, I do not want you to be thinking of what it would take for you to create this type of relationship. You will see the answer to this question as we go forward, and the answer is likely not want you think at this moment. The thing I want to focus on here is what it would be like for you to have someone relate to you in these ways.

These relationships are reciprocal. Both people completely, whole-heartedly invested and totally committed. The highest purpose of each in these relationships is to honor the other party. There is complete openness, honesty, and transparency. There are no secrets, nor is there any reason there would be. There is safety; the relationship is a refuge from the rest of the world, a place of rest, peace, support, healing, and communion. There is security, which speaks of safety not only today but forever; to provision, to protection, to defense if necessary—and it will be necessary for all of us at some point. And there is the ultimate security: permanence. There is no concern about waking up one day to find the other gone, of looking into eyes that no longer care. And although one of the partners will one day leave, entering eternity, with the other following, even in *this* God's intimacy is sufficient, though the loss and pain of this separation will at first be real and painful. There is a curiously out-of-time quality of the kind of deep love built by faithfully living in covenant. Soon it seems as if the two have always known each other—and always will. Which is correct if both inhabit the same eternal home.

> There is a curiously out-of-time quality of the kind of deep love built by faithfully living in covenant. Soon it seems as if the two have always known each other—and always will.

These relationships are defined by intimacy. This is the sum of all of the above. It is two people knowing each other to the depths of each other's soul, mind, and heart, and entering into every part of each other's lives—supporting, helping, encouraging, enabling, equipping, healing, building, growing, maturing, and much more! The two become one at the outset. Over time, they begin to experience this oneness. Intimacy is the authentic experience and expression of this conjoined identity. It is the polar opposite of loneliness; it is the fullness of heart that flows from loving well and being loved well. This is a love God intends to grow and spread—to children, family, church family, and community in God's plan.

The words *intimacy* and *love* are thrown around in our culture to describe sexual activity with multiple partners, devoid of commitment or meaning. This experience in no way resembles true intimacy. Intimacy is about transparency, fully knowing each other, fully embracing and supporting each other in the context of a rock-solid, lifetime commitment. Intimacy is about receiving each other and embracing each other in our imperfection and immaturity. Intimacy is about creating the ground—safety, security, and support—from which maturity grows, about spurring each other on toward perfection, about developing our potential, about growing up into the man or woman God created us to become. Many things in our minds and hearts cannot be and should not be revealed to someone if we are unsure of their commitment to us or their love for us. This level of trust must be earned and confirmed; we must trust not only the words and intentions of the other person, we must also trust that their character is capable of following through with such commitments. Many things go into entering, building, and confirming such a relationship, and each of these elements is built through faithfulness to covenant.

Covenant involves two building processes: the one that occurs before we enter covenant and the one that occurs after we enter this relationship. In our pre-covenant relationships we get to know the character of the other. We learn whether we enjoy each other and we note things that will be issues to overcome. At a point we determine whether (or not) this person would be a good covenant partner. Given the nature of covenant, this obviously involves something beyond physical attraction, and beyond the things we think this person might add to our lives. Can we learn together? Can we continue to grow together? Does the other person have the necessary integrity and the necessary foundational understanding of marriage? God intends the end point of this building process to be entering covenant through intercourse, accompanied by an appropriate public commitment that acknowledges the nature and gravity of this commitment. Through intercourse we are giving our most precious thing to each other—our very lives. And from this we receive back new lives, joined lives, totally committed lives. And through this same act is the possibility of creating yet more new lives. God's plan builds a foundation of trust, respect, integrity, and reality. Upon this foundation an experience of oneness can be built that is worth anything we have been called to do, or ever will be called to do in faithfulness to covenant.

> Consider instead what it would be like if every message we heard was true, supportive, encouraging, helpful, collaborative for the rest of our lives?

Upon this foundation we can build true passion for another person and for life. In many lives distorted messages about self, relationship, and life hold people back from being what they could otherwise become. Consider instead what it would be like if every message we heard was true, supportive, encouraging, helpful, and collaborative for the rest of our lives? We are created to have passionate love for our wives and husbands. We are created to have passion about the things we are created to create. We are created to have passion about the world God created for us, and most of all passion for the One who created all of this and offers it to us—because He passionately loves us. Created in His image, we are created for passion. Passion and love are the two greatest driving forces in the human heart; at their end points they are synonymous. From these two driving forces we build the big things worth building in our lives.

Covenant relationships are also places of forgiveness, grace, mercy, healing, and growth. If the environment detailed above is present in a relationship, the two can play many roles in each other's lives that promote growth, transformation, and maturity, which are God's primary goals for these relationships. In covenant we are to focus mainly upon building the relationship and building up the other person. As we devote ourselves to these things over time, we are in turn built *into* something. Covenant, in fact, is designed with every element necessary to produce the greatest possible growth and transformation as we go about our daily lives.

None of us, even those who are good with people and who have strong character, can step up and live out all of our covenant responsibilities flawlessly. Even the best of us cannot even get close at the outset. Why? We cannot love someone well until we know them well; it takes time to know someone well. And this assumes that we are capable of loving them perfectly once we know them, which is not the case. We must learn another person from top to bottom. We must learn about our new selves, the one that came into being as we entered covenant. We must learn all the possible applications in daily life of each of the things called for in covenant. So what does God want to see in this relationship? Perfection from beginning to end? No. It is these very shortfalls which provide our personal agenda for growth. And it is covenant itself, as we will see, that provides not only the *what*—the things called for, as well as the new identity that is the foundation for this new life—but the *why*: sufficient reasons for us to do all the things called for by covenant. And in addition to this is the how, the means by which we *grow into* this new being we have become. What we will see is that *everything we are called on to do in covenant is completely consistent with who we now are and with who our covenant partner now is.*

We are not asked, at any point, to do something that is not in our ultimate best interest, or something that is out of sync with our true identity and nature. What must change once we enter covenant for us to be completely faithful to that covenant is our perception—of ourselves, of our covenant partner, of our relationship, and of our true best interests. Once we get all of this, we will do what God calls on us to do naturally because these are the things we will want to do. Why? Because *this is who we are.* And because these are the only things that align with truth and reality.

This shift of perception and being is a lifelong project. We never quite get there, but it is so much fun trying! What God wants to see is that we are committed to His plan of covenant. This means we are committed to love our covenant partner, to learning what this means, and, to the extent that we are not capable of any part of love, to show up for His training process of growth and transformation. In response, God will do things in us and in our relationship, and in life overall, that we could not possibly do; things, as He says, "immeasurably more than all we ask or imagine, according to His power that is at work within us" (Ephesians 3:20).

If a marriage is built well upon this foundation, it will be the path to the greatest joys, delights, gratifications, and satisfactions we can know in this life. God, who built our hearts, might also understand how to best reward us in the depth of those hearts.

> *Anyone who comes to Him must believe that He exists,*
> *and that He rewards those who earnestly seek Him.*
> HEBREWS 11:6

COVENANT UTILIZES MECHANISMS FOR GROWTH, TRANSFORMATION, AND REWARD THAT GOD HAS CREATED WITHIN US

Let me step away from the author voice for a few moments and speak to each person reading this, one on one. I am deeply excited as I write all of these things, but especially on this topic. I believe this aspect of God's plan is the most exciting of all. The way God's plan integrates every factor—our needs; our hearts, minds, and wills; the nature of love—how love is built, expressed, and received; and the needs of our world—for continuity, virtue, love, and living examples of the love of God—all of these and more clearly establish His authorship of this grand scheme. God has a plan. This plan is intended to impact everyone, to lead each of us to the life He created us to live. This plan is intended to undo the remarkably destructive influence of His enemies that is present in all of our lives. In short, this plan is adequate to the task of building in every detail the lives each of us will be most glad we lived. And this plan is adequate to the task of addressing every problem of our existence in this world while preparing us for the next.

What I invite the reader to see as we go through the rest of this series is that God created the very mechanisms within us that are needed for each of us to accomplish His plan and purposes. He placed the necessary key for all of this, the essential ingredient, within these rela-

---

tionships themselves. Then He fashioned a plan around all of this that can accomplish His purposes for all of us. This plan simultaneously is building something intended to impact our community and our world, and building things within which will make us better husbands, wives, and parents—while building within us the capacity to enjoy these relationships and life overall. Every move of obedience we make, every truth we implement, every deception we identify and eject from our lives impacts us in positive ways at many levels, in the moment and for the rest of our lives. And, of course, the converse is also true: anything we neglect, any truth we deny in favor of a lie, any unfaithfulness at any point—regardless of any benefit we think we will enjoy through these choices—predictably sets in motion negative consequences that will show up in many ways and at many points going forward.

We are going to study true love. We are going to see that love-for-a-lifetime is not something one falls into but something two people build over time. We are going to see that love is built by many elements—beliefs, habits, character qualities, emotions, priorities, values, and more—all of which translate at some point into actions. We will consider the ways our hearts respond to the accumulation of actions of another; that this accumulation creates our heart response to the other person. And our experience of the other person is also created by our own beliefs, values, priorities, expectations, and other things. Thus, our best experience involves more than the other person learning to love us more perfectly; we must also learn to love more perfectly. We are going to explore some surprisingly strong links between our minds and our hearts. How we feel is not necessarily an intrinsic expression of our very nature. How we feel is often determined by what we believe, and what we believe may not always be what is real and true. Thus, our emotional reactions in an intimate relationship, if dysfunctional, can become functional, healthy, and constructive by a process that is part of God's plan.

In order to understand this plan we will consider the way our mind and heart are structured and how these two are related. We will see how this connection forms emotional responses, and how it may be harnessed to change those responses. This will impact our own experience of another person, and the experience we create for another in relationship. We are going to see how our character is formed, as well as our habits, for it is these three—our emotions, our habits, and our character—which determine the vast majority of the ways we treat another person, which in turn determines the quality of the relationship. We are going to see how our true nature and identity impact the ways we behave, and how our perceptions of ourselves—which may be correct or incorrect—also drive our behaviors. All of these impact the quality of our experience—how we give and receive love. We are going to examine the impact of covenant on all of these things, and how God's plan of covenant can address issues and direct growth at every level.

Covenant calls upon us to love another wholeheartedly and comprehensively. But we are not good at doing this at the outset for several reasons: 1) because our perceptions of what is best for us and our lives argue against making certain correct choices; 2) because our habits of viewing and treating each other are distorted—we do many counterproductive things without thinking; 3) because our character has not developed in ways that would allow us, for instance, to always tell the truth or always follow through to complete necessary tasks; 4) because the way we view ourselves is distorted. As it turns out, each of these—our perceptions of our best interest, our habits, our ways of viewing others, our character, any misunderstanding of our true identity and nature, and essentially every other thing that would keep us from faithfully carrying out everything called for by covenant—each and every one of these is controlled by our choices, and our choices are governed by what we *choose to accept as true*. This reality offers us vast opportunity to change our lives for the better if we understand how to employ this reality. We note what is not working, or what is out of accord with what is true. We realize that what we think or feel is true does not define truth. God reveals truth. We simply embrace it and implement what is actually true in our lives.

There are two things not impacted by our choices and beliefs: our true nature and identity. On the other hand, we are deeply impacted by *what we believe* our identity and nature to be. If we come to correctly understand *how our beliefs and choices have formed us and grown us* into what we are, we can then play the role God assigns us in His plan. If we do play this role, we will grow and change into a person capable of being faithful to the rest of God's plan, and a person who enjoys being faithful.

In other words, God has created this huge, interlocking system: our world and its cause-and-effect moral system; our heart, mind, and character, which are formed in certain ways; our relationships, which if properly conducted require that certain ideas be embraced and lived out; and covenant, which offers us truth about ourselves, other people, love, and relationship. These are truths that, when embraced and lived out, produce the very growth, development, and transformation needed to build not only the best relationships but the best lives we could live in every realm. Only God could come up with such a plan.

> His plan is there, perfect, powerful, effective, waiting for us. To do what? To implement, starting now and continuing for eternity.

I can only imagine how it will feel at one point to look up . . . and there is no more gray. How much will we then appreciate its absence? God's plan stretches across the entirety of our experience on earth, into the depth of our being, from the beginning of time into eternity. His plan is there, perfect, powerful, effective, waiting for us. To do what? To implement, starting now and continuing for eternity.

His plan? Keep in mind, *truth* and *reality* are synonyms. In this plan, if we say one term, we mean both terms. To learn the truth. To embrace actual truth as *our truth.* For our emotions to be grounded upon truth. To conform our actions to the truth. For our relationships to be built on love and truth, or upon reality and covenant, all of which are synonyms. For our potential to be grown into capabilities. For our character to be *re-formed* according to truth and virtue. For our integrity to become spotless. For our word to become good and true. For our willpower and resolve to become strong enough to overcome any obstacles so we have the strength to fulfill our commitments. For our commitments to be binding and trustworthy, our obligations to be met in full, our responsibilities to be carried out enthusiastically and joyfully, our duties to be our priority, and fulfilling our duties to become our joy. For our love to be strong and true. For our priorities to be formed after God's priorities and His truth. For our values to be in line with God's. For our covenants to become the first priority in our lives, cultivating wholehearted love for our partner and community of partners in the Body of Christ. For faithfulness to our covenant(s) to be non-negotiable. For our covenant relationships to be formed according to God's plan, building each element carefully and lovingly so hearts remain on fire for those who have also given their lives to us. For us to grow according to God's plan into people capable of doing all that God requires and desires. For His desires and delights to become our desires and delights. For our hearts and minds to be refined to the point that we can delight in what is good and pure, to enjoy the rich rewards and massive blessings that God pours into the lives of those whose hearts are completely His.

NINE

What Does God See When He Looks at Our World?

ON AN INDIVIDUAL LEVEL

As humans, we have been separated from God since the parents of our race handed themselves over to God's enemy. We are under a sentence of death because, expressing the nature of the angel whose rebellious nature became part of our nature, we all play our role in that rebellion. Remember, when one enters covenant the old self dies. If we enter covenant with God, He raises us to new life. If simply choose to maintain our original connection with Satan, the lord of this world, we join him in his destiny; our current separation from God will become an eternal separation. Our rebellion is manifested in two forms: what we do, and what we are. This is why simply following rules and refraining from one rebellious act or another is not sufficient to remedy our problem. Our separation from God is not just an issue of rules, but of nature—from which proceeds rebellious thoughts, feelings, attitudes, words, and deeds. We cannot feel, sense, or hear God in this state of separation, and we can do nothing to reinstitute a relationship with Him.

However, created for this relationship, we all experience an emptiness. We all desire to rejoin our God in relationship, but this longing and drive can be sublimated and misdirected in many ways. It can lead to one kind of existential crisis or another, but there is only one way to fill this emptiness, which the noted physicist and theologian Blaise Pascal called "a God-shaped vacuum." And until this void is filled, while people may be amused, or anesthetized, or distracted with the trinkets or lusts of this world, there is in the depths of each being a genuine existential crisis. *Who am I? Why am I here? What meaning does life have, if any?* Why must I suffer and endure what life brings? What is the point of any of this? Jesus described this state in very simple terms: people are like sheep without a shepherd. We are all headed into harm's way with no hope of rescue. Jesus came to earth in person to deliver God's plan to deal with all of these issues of death and life—His plan of covenant, which His shed blood, death, and resurrection would usher into existence. He desires to be our shepherd, our Redeemer, our Lord and our God and reaches out to us with His offer of redemption.

> There is only one way to fill this emptiness, which the noted physicist and theologian Blaise Pascal called "a God-shaped vacuum."

We have considered what God wants to see and have glimpsed how His plan can bring each thing He wants to see into reality. But, while we consider the plan of God, we also benefit by considering the world's plan. Why? First, we need to become capable of clearly distinguishing between God's plan and that of the world; we need to clearly distinguish the elements of white and black that swirl together to form the gray around us. Second, we have all been immersed in the world's training process; thus, we have been persuaded that many elements of this plan are good and good for us. We have all developed an attraction and affection for certain elements of this plan. This is based on groundless optimism, to be sure, but this optimism is a deep-seated and powerful force welding people to some parts of this plan, even if they find fault with other parts.

Thus, we need to consider the outcome of the world's plan—stripped of deceptive optimism. This is not an academic exercise.

Each of us must make countless decisions for the rest of our lives, to follow God's plan or an alternative—a plan we will call "not-God." The more clear-eyed we are about the real nature of these choices, the better chance we have of not being taken in by a cleverly packaged, very attractive, but ultimately destructive alternative. This alternative has been successfully offered to humanity since the very beginning. *That we all keep falling for this stuff is the reason for the sum of the problems in our world.*

HOW THE WORLD DOES RELATIONSHIP

THE FOUNDATION OF THE WORLD'S APPROACH

We have grown up in an environment filled with ideas about living that are authored not by God but by His enemy, who is also our enemy. All of these ideas are offered to us seemingly for our benefit, all appear on the surface to be beneficial in some way—see the definition of the word *deception* for details—and all have a hidden cost that corresponds to their hidden agenda. All of us have embraced at least some of these ideas and incorporated them into our views of ourselves, other people, and the path to our best life. But these ideas will in fact hamper, diminish, or destroy the relationships God is offering us the opportunity to build. This explains the mixed results we've all had with relationships to this point, and it explains why relationships that actually continue to grow and flourish are so rare. At the same time, made in God's image, we get parts of this right, and are capable of building some degree of relationship with others.

> All of us have embraced at least some of these ideas and incorporated them into our views of ourselves, other people, and the path to our best life.

God wants us to see that even at our best, His ideas are better. And we do better by embracing His ideas when ours are not in synchrony with His. We also have a nature and identity that incorporate elements of His enemy's nature if we are not already in a covenant relationship with God. (How this changes if we are in such a relationship will be covered in the third volume.) Without any input or guidance, simply "doing what comes naturally," we will express this aspect of our nature in ways that damage relationships and damage other people. Further, our coherence as a being has been turned into incoherence. Parts of ourselves oppose each other, and other parts that never come to the surface to be developed. Why? Because we now house two competing natures: one made in God's image, another diametrically opposed to our Creator. The phrase "that person is his or her own worst enemy" comes to mind. Does this explain some of the incomprehensible choices people make?

And beyond the real confusion created by our opposing parts, there is confusion generated by a massive history-long misinformation campaign about living. Who we really are, our true worth, the true worth of other people, the things in life truly worth valuing, the best way to provide for our own needs, what things actually represent our true needs, and many other ideas—along with the emotions that follow the ideas we embrace and choose to live by—all of these and many more have been distorted, twisted, and turned inside out in our world by . . .

Remember, the most effective deceptions all contain a kernel of truth.

. whom? Remember, the most effective deceptions all contain a kernel of truth. Most of the world's advice about living contains at best only a kernel. But this deception gains credibility when we see everyone around us embracing and living out the same ideas, and we hear people express boundless optimism even as they follow a Satan-inspired path toward the edge of a cliff.

None of the ways of living authored by the alternate god, in the end, produce the promised results. People are caught in a trap; they pursue the same strategies to deal with current challenges that created these challenges in the first place, strategies which will only produce additional challenges. But people are eternal optimists. They continue to pursue counterproductive strategies because they expect them to be successful at some point. We all think we are investing in our best future, even as we offer our most precious resources to the consummate scam artist.

HOW ARE RELATIONSHIPS FARING IN OUR WORLD?

Not only is the path to a happy and rewarding marriage less clear than ever, but do relationships in general not seem progressively challenged? Our world is a wonderful mixture of optimism and problems. We cling to the hope that the new unholy trinity—science, education, and technology—are going to ultimately solve the big problems of humanity, but in the meantime things are, shall we say, a bit messy. And messier than we would expect, given how scientific, technological, and educated we are. How long must we wait to see the promised benefits of these approaches? Is antidepressant use decreasing or increasing? Suicide decreasing or increasing? Hope for our collective future increasing or decreasing? Do our rising generations look forward to a better life than those who have gone before?

What, though, are the problems we most need to solve? We can look around our world and view this question from a broad-strokes perspective of cultural statistics, or we can simply look around our own lives and see what is most apt to ruin our day or make our future needlessly challenging. Fingers point in many directions, and people are pulling at us from all sides to alert us to one threat after another that is about to wreck our lives, or to destroy humanity altogether. What's my nomination for the one thing that would change almost everything in terms of our experience of daily living, for each of us and our society as a whole? We have relationship issues.

IS *CHANGE* THE SOLUTION?

As we experience the changes in our world that people are so excited about, changes that we are so hopeful will lead to a better future, one change we are not experiencing is people relating better and more successfully. We want to be progressive. But are we progressing toward better marriages, closer families, more supportive and successful workplace environments, more harmony, more respect, more understanding, and more collaboration among ethnic groups? Are we progressing toward more informative, respectful, and collaborative civic discourse? Are we less lonely, isolated, and alienated? Are we progressively safer from the dark impulses of those among us—emotionally and physically? Is our quality of life really improving? Are we becoming a more enlightened, gratified, and satisfied society? Or does the progression of the social media environment toward a more harsh, dangerous, and predatory neighborhood reflect what it feels like to live in every other part of our current world?

A recent study found nearly 30 percent of teens have sent or received a sexually explicit text or picture.[1] One in eight of those communications were forwarded to other parties without the knowledge or consent of the sender. What part of this sounds like a good idea? Might this curious permissiveness and profound lack of respect form the foundation for more extreme patterns of disrespect, and even sexual abuse, in later years? At the very least, such behavior reflects judgment that is light-years from God's plan for sexuality. God's desire is not just to keep us from making a complete mess of our lives. He wants us to build genuinely good and rewarding lives.

CHANGING OUR NATION'S RELATIONSHIP WITH GOD

While much has changed across our culture in the last few decades, what has happened that specifically impacted the quality of relationships? My nomination for the chief reason may surprise you. Rather than being committed to traditional (mostly Scriptural) morality, virtue, and character development, we are now committed to *change* of . . . apparently everything. The timing of this particular society-wide shift is interesting; it began in the late 1950s and accelerated in the '60s and beyond. This coincided with our nation officially declaring, via a series of Supreme Court decisions extending from the late 1950s into the early 1970s, that for the first time in history the United States is not a Christian nation. We are not a people living "under God"—under His protection and also accountable to Him, as prior government proclamations declared, from the first public act of the newly installed legislative, judicial, and executive branches of the United States in 1789[2] to a reiteration of this reality by President Eisenhower in multiple public statements in the 1950s.

Despite the rich heritage of our national relationship with God, His Word, His laws, and conversations with Him were removed from public schools and the public square. Favorable mention of Him, displays of honor toward Him, and celebrations of Him were removed from public life. This truly radical change in the relationship of our society with God also represented an equally radical shift in the publicly proclaimed values upon which our society was founded. As President Eisenhower said, "Without God, there could be no American form of government, nor an American way of life. Recognition of the Supreme Being is the first—the most basic—expression of Americanism. Thus the Founding Fathers saw it, and thus with God's help it will continue to be" (*US News and World Report,* May 7, 2009, J. Randy Forbes).[3] Eisenhower was right. The consensus views on many issues in our culture bear little resemblance to commonly held views prior to 1960. The American way of life has radically changed. Some of these changes are good—such as stripping away legally sanctioned segregation—but most have inflicted far more damage on our citizenry than our upcoming generations can imagine. This is most graphically seen in the realm of morality. As our country ceased to teach upcoming generations God's moral law, we see results extending from family disintegration to students who are willing to massacre classmates. Such things were simply never a part of our nation when our national character was heavily formed by a sense of accountability to God, and a far greater measure of respect for those made in His image.

Once our national relationship with God changed in this way in the 1950s—opposing rather than supporting and honoring God's Word and His ways—other changes in our culture are simply predictable consequences. Until this point, even among those who did not have a personal relationship with God, an underlying respect for God and His ways heavily infused our culture, including His words about how we are to regard and treat each other. The respect that our nation formerly showed God and the things our citizens were taught in schools and the public square about right and wrong mirrored moral teaching in homes and churches. This produced a society founded on a strong sense of right and wrong, and a respect for virtue. As a society we understood that dealing with each other truthfully, fairly, and respectfully was appropriate and would be rewarded, while converse behaviors were entirely inappropriate and would result in negative outcomes. People did not believe that they could do whatever they wanted and expect no negative consequences. And people certainly did not believe that each was free to determine what was right for himself or herself regardless of God's stated opinion. In other words, as noted earlier in our discussion about truth, reality, and consequences, our populace was taught a realistic view of morality, and its importance for each life. This set of concepts, again, radically shifted beginning in the 1960s as philosophies for personal conduct taught in schools ceased to include God or His objective moral standards. The standard shifted to the importance of pursuing individual desires, whatever those might be, and in whatever direction those desires might be cultivated.

Furthermore, just as they did not think it worthwhile to retain the knowledge of God, so God gave them over to a depraved mind, so that they do what ought not to be done. They have become filled with every kind of wickedness, evil, greed, and depravity. They are full of envy, murder, strife, deceit, and malice. They are gossips, slanderers, God-haters, insolent, arrogant, and boastful; they invent ways of doing evil; they disobey their parents; they have no understanding, no fidelity, no love, no mercy. Although they know God's righteous decrees that those who do such things deserve death, they not only continue to do these very things, but also approve of those who practice them.
ROMANS 1:28-32

For men will be lovers of themselves, lovers of money, boastful, arrogant, abusive, disobedient to their parents, ungrateful, unholy, unloving, unforgiving, slanderous, without self-control, brutal, not lovers of the good, treacherous, rash, conceited, lovers of pleasure rather than lovers of God, having a form of godliness but denying its power. Have nothing to do with such people.

2 TIMOTHY 3:2-5

SINCE WE DIVORCED GOD, THE CHARACTER OF OUR PEOPLE HAS SHIFTED

Did people follow these historic cultural standards perfectly? Of course not. Public statements and proclamations do not determine personal behavior and choices. But there has been a progressive, radical shift in personal behavior and choices over the last sixty years that reflects a corresponding personal rejection of God's plan for personal and public behavior. What standards of conduct are replacing God's?

Many of the values taught in our homes, schools, media, and society, such as respect, viewing others and their interests as of importance, integrity, honesty, consideration, kindness, and many other values derived from Scripture—things we could term our civic duties and responsibilities—have largely evaporated. These have been replaced by a concept of personal rights. Our civic life does not consist of what we are supposed to do for others, but about what we have a right to expect from them, even if we offer nothing in return.

The Scriptures teach that we are all fundamentally equal and equally accountable to God for our behaviors. No one is rich enough, powerful enough, strong enough, or smart enough to avoid accountability to God—thus we are all on equal footing before the laws of God, though in many other ways we may be unequal. This equality before God was reflected in the idea of a society where people are equal before the law and where people are to be offered equal opportunities. While there were several glaring areas where this ideal was not achieved—racial segregation comes to mind—it was this very ideal that was the basis for attempts to legally eradicate segregation and move toward color-blind legal and educational systems. Do you know where the concept of the equality of men, women, slaves, free, and all others made in the image of God was first articulated in history? By Jesus and the writers of the New Testament. These were some of the most radical ideas, the most countercultural ideas, that were set forth by Christianity in light of everything else in the world until that point. The only reason the idea of the fundamental equality of all people could possibly reflect reality is because we are all made in God's image and precious in His sight. Otherwise, we are not at all equal.

Based upon any other foundational understanding of humanity there is merely the survival of the strongest, the prosperity of the most cunning, and domination and oppression of everyone else. "There is no God" is the seedbed for everything from prejudice to genocide, as well as cheating, lying, stealing, and any other behavior by which people feel their causes can and should be advanced despite the impact on others. This was the rallying cry for the philosophers of the 1700s and 1800s, who spawned the philosophies taught in our schools since the 1960s; these same philosophers laid the foundation for Nazism and Communism and for the eugenics philosophy of Margaret Sanger, founder of Planned Parenthood. These same philosophies were the foundation of many other atheistic progressive movements that wreaked havoc on the world in the twentieth century. This century was the most violent century in history when we add deaths due to wars to death due to government efforts to crush dissent (123 million deaths by Matthew White's estimate). The highest death toll among the categories was totalitarian government crusades against their own citizenry—41 million, versus 37 million military deaths and 27 million collateral citizen war deaths. Some have estimated the death toll for just two of these campaigns—

The most fundamental of these problems is that there is now no socially agreed goal and standard for how we are to live with each other. We are all free to do as we want.

Stalin's against Ukraine and Mao's against resistant Chinese—to exceed 55 million people.[4]

We have problems in our culture that are more profound and significant than the remaining vestiges of racism. The most fundamental of these problems is that there is now no socially agreed goal and standard for how we are to live with each other. We are all free to do as we want, to implement our individual standards and agendas. None of which agree. Thus we are descending into a form of tribalism, where smaller groups joined by interests or identity square off with the rest of the population asserting their rights, demanding that they be respected or appeased in one way or another. Yet, what basis is there for anyone else to care what these people feel or think if everyone is devoted only to their own self-interests? Why should anyone care when we have been trained to make judgments based solely on our own inclinations? As a nation, we used to all be *Americans*. There was an *us*, for which we fought and built. Now we see protesters on every side who reject our country as a whole. Are we as a nation moving toward divorcing each other? Does *us* no longer exist?

In what other directions have we progressed? Now many are firmly committed to a lack of long-term commitment in personal relationships. Rather than being disciplined to respect and take into account the interests of others, we are taught that we are each the center of our own little universe. Other people are either value-added to our universe or the reason "things are not working for us." We are victors or victims. Again, there is no *us*. Each makes his or her own rules. We are ultimately accountable to nothing beyond our desire to do something and a sense that this is the best way to get what we want. We used to hope in a righteous, just, and merciful God for the ultimate solution to life's problems. Now we fix our hope on something different: change. If there is a problem, the solution is obvious: change. The newest . . . most educated . . . latest scientific development

> We are victors or victims. Again, there is no us. Each makes his or her own rules.

. . . or awesome technologic advance, trending and fashionable, will take on the problems of humanity, and we are fully confident that we will succeed where others have failed. Why are we so sure? Looking around at our changing culture, what possible reason is there for such optimism?

OVERVALUING CHANGE, UNDERVALUING EVERYTHING ELSE

When everything is new, when everything can change, when nothing is fixed or permanent, what can we count on? What meaning can something have if it might be gone tomorrow, and certainly will be gone by next year? Best not to get overly attached to anything in our lives, including other people. Losing something we value hurts. Best not to hold to anything too tightly—family, viewpoints, old ways of doing things. We must embrace change. The future is our future. Thus, what can we value beyond ourselves? This is all that matters, if anything matters at all.

Obviously, we should also be changing . . . while we continue to hope that these changes bring us something we do not yet have: the life we really want to be living. In fact, the end point of the philosophy of change is that our current frustrations are the result of *what is;* therefore, whatever is . . . *should not be.* If change is the answer, there is no end point, because people's ways of living will not cease creating the very frustrations which produce the motivation to upend everything. If lives were producing an experience worth having, would people not defend their way of living rather than being eager to discard present ways in favor of unproven sales pitches?

CHANGING CHARACTER LEADS TO CHANGING OUTCOMES

The sum of these changes has had a dramatic impact on one of the most enduring, meaningful, and useful cultural institutions on the planet throughout history: marriage. Male-female roles changed. Then the value/sanctity/importance of marriage changed, and a new "sort-of married" state—living together—became common, often replacing marriage as a life goal. Then marriage changed, from a male-female relationship to other combinations. Then people began changing from being male or female to being whatever they designate themselves to be, which also can apparently change from time to time. Now we may be facing our greatest crisis ever regarding marriage. What is that? When it comes to marriage, if we fix our hope for improving life on change, we are running out of things to change.

THE CHANGING RELATIONSHIP BETWEEN INDIVIDUALS AND REALITY

Perhaps the biggest—and least recognized—change over the last few decades is that we used to realize things are what they are. There is something called *reality*. We built our lives around the *realities of life*. The big quest in life was figuring out what was real—about ourselves, other people, and the rest of the world. In a few short years our society has come to believe that things are whatever we want them to be. Also, we can become whatever we want to be—at least, that is what many think. Have we gained some wonderful new power in just the last few decades? Can we actually fashion the universe and ourselves after our own desires and inclinations? In cyberspace we can be whatever image we want to create. But a marriage is not cyberspace; it happens in real time in the real world. Two humans interact with each other with real consequences in hearts and lives. We are building something real, for better or worse.

We see this idea—that we are sup-

> Was God correct in His prediction of what would happen if Adam and Eve tried this maneuver: in turning from Him they would lose everything that mattered of the life God was trying to give them, and ultimately even life itself.

posed to choose what we want ourselves to be, and by so choosing, we then become—most clearly illustrated by the movement toward gender reassignment. Is this idea, that we can take charge of altering something as fundamental as our gender, real? More importantly, is this the path to a better, more satisfying life? Or have we recently been carried away by some group delusion, losing touch with the realities of life and of ourselves? Have we finally achieved the offer that was made to Eve by Satan in the Garden of Eden—"You shall be as God"—and actually become the gods of our own lives by turning away from the real one? Or was God correct in His prediction of what would happen if Adam and Eve tried this maneuver: in turning from Him they would lose everything that mattered of the life God was trying to give them, and ultimately even life itself.

Examining this question scientifically, a long-term Swedish follow-up study of gender reassignment patients treated between 1973 and 2003 (Dhejne, et. al.)[5], noted a rate of suicide among those whose "transformation" was complete as nineteen times greater than an age-matched population. There was an almost equal increase in unsuccessful suicide attempts. In the author's opinion, the evidence suggests that medically addressing "gender dysphoria" did not have the positive impact on these patients' lives that was anticipated (though this was the premise upon which massive medical and surgical treatment strategies were offered, performed, and government-funded). Change—yet again—does not appear to be the answer.

MEASURABLE OUTCOMES RELATED TO THESE CHANGES

While we have been launching a new-and-improved *us* to face the problems of life, such as building better marriages and families, how is it all working out? In 1960 the divorce rate was around 0.8 percent (8/1000 people).[6] In the Sixties and Seventies the divorce rate skyrocketed. By 1980 it stabilized, with roughly 40 percent of marriages ending in divorce. While the divorce rate has slowly declined since, this decline actually mirrors a downturn in the number of people getting married. We are getting married significantly less frequently, per capita, than at any time in our nation's history, and that number continues to trend strongly downward. Why?

HAVE HUMAN NEEDS REALLY CHANGED? A PERSONAL QUESTION . . .

Have we correctly determined, after millennia, that an enduring and happy marriage is really not that important after all? Have we determined that children raised by never-married or divorced singles provide an even better childhood experience, one leading to better, happier, more functional adults? Over 25 percent of children today are being raised with no involvement of their fathers.[7] At this time, about 30 percent of Caucasian births are to single mothers; in the African-American community the figure is about 70 percent.[8] Are these changes for the better? Have we reasonably concluded that marriage is at best optional, if needed at all, for best personal and social outcomes?

Or does everyone still want and expect their happily-ever-after, but for some reason marriage itself is not working nearly as well as it used to? We seem inclined to try to change marriage so this institution will remain in sync with current thought—philosophies, priorities, viewpoints, and ways of relating to each other. As people continue trying to change the definition of marriage, marriage *is* changing: it is ending or not being formed in unprecedented numbers. Have we not yet changed our thinking about marriage enough? Or, are we dealing with a form of relationship that only works well when conducted in specific ways, guided by ideas based on the reality of this relationship? Is the character of our people simply moving from a set of qualities that favor the success of marriage toward qualities that are more likely to implode a marriage, or qualities which make even the weakened concept of marriage too daunting a commitment? So, will we be able to refashion marriage successfully, or must we refashion ourselves and our ideas in order to find our happily-ever-after? Might the key to this question be to pull out the original, millennia-old blueprint?

DO WE STILL KNOW HOW TO HAVE SUCCESSFUL MARRIAGES?

How do we build a loving and durable marriage? A majority of current marriages still succeed, or at least endure. Many families are thriving and are busy raising the next generation of children who are learning to develop their character and potential. How is this done? While creating a great marriage over the coming decades is certainly possible, as it always has been possible, how confident can any of us be that we have not been influenced in our viewpoints and priorities in the very ways that will cause our own marriages to struggle or even fail?

Our culture of change has profoundly altered viewpoints, making marriage and family less successful. Beyond the statistics is a much more important issue. We don't just want a marriage that survives; we want a truly rewarding, deeply meaningful lifelong love affair with another person.

There are no statistics about the number of people that have the kind of marriage that, somewhere in the depths of our souls, we know is possible. Is this not what we really want? How do we have this marriage? Let's look at a few basics and practical matters about relationships in general in our culture.

THE HEART OF THE ISSUE: TRUSTING, LIKING, AND RESPECTING OTHERS

The relationship issues we face in our society go far beyond marriage and family. If intact, functional families have always been an integral part of God's plan to teach people how to successfully live alongside one another, what could we predict would happen in our society if families ceased to build such capacities in people?

How can we best describe the heart of the relationship problem? As we listen to public conversations, people do not appear to respect each other or even like each other. Many profoundly distrust the direction that other people want to lead them. For people in their teens, twenties, and thirties, having not lived in any other world, it seems as though things have always been this way. But the way we view each other and relate to each other really has changed across the last six decades. This is not just an older generation throwing rocks at Millennials. There are solid sociological statistics, cited in many recent articles, backing this observation. For instance, a USA Today poll published in 2013 noted that only about one-third of people believe we can "basically trust other people."[9] In 1972, roughly half believed we could. As we go backward each decade before that, more and more people generally trusted the people around them. Why do we much more frequently and profoundly distrust the people around us? According to some social scientists, this is the trend that most threatens the very fabric of our society. We are at increasing risk of simply divorcing everyone around us, of having the very fabric of society—what sociologists refer to as "the social contract," which binds us together as a society—completely disintegrate.

> We are at increasing risk of simply divorcing everyone around us, of having the very fabric of society—what sociologists refer to as "the social contract," which binds us together as a society—completely disintegrate.

CAN WE TRUST PEOPLE WHO TRUST IN CHANGE?

I suspect this society-wide shift in people's trust of other people is a reasonable, even necessary, change. Trust has to be earned. How many people around you have earned your trust? Though some people cannot find it within themselves to trust anyone, most of us learn to trust people who show us they are worthy of trust by their actions, character, integrity, and consideration for others. Here is a crucial question: *Are the people who are so eagerly promoting and urging soci-*

etal change acting in ways that reasonably inspire trust? If one's view of the world is based on rejecting everything of the past, this necessarily involves God and the view of humanity He commends to us. If one digs up the foundation of good character—integrity, consideration, honesty, and other qualities God commands—from beneath people's lives and replaces it with a foundation of "whatever we feel like in the moment," what confidence may we have that any of us will be shown respect and consideration? Or dealt with honestly? This is not to say that many individuals do not still display rock-solid character and integrity. But one cannot overlook the culture-wide shift in the ways people view each other and deal with each other and the trust issues which flow from this shift. These societal changes cannot help but have a dramatic effect on the capacity to develop good relationships across the whole of our society.

If you do not trust someone, are you apt to respect them? Are you likely to *like* them? Do you trust their agenda for your life? Do you expect them to act in ways centered around the good of others, or do you expect them to seek their own rewards at the expense of others, possibly at your expense?

THESE EMERGING RELATIONSHIP ISSUES ARE REALLY CHARACTER ISSUES

Thus it appears the relationship issues in our world run deeper than simply learning to be a little nicer to each other and more accepting of each other (though that would help). Those superficial things do not address the core issues. There has been a dramatic shift in our society during my six decades of life away from recognizing the fundamental importance of other people and balancing other's needs with our own. This has been replaced with the view that self and our own perception of self-interest are the only things

Other people's interests are collateral damage worth incurring if our interests are advanced.

worthy of consideration. Other people's interests are collateral damage worth incurring if our interests are advanced. There has been a shift from valuing honesty and integrity toward valuing dishonesty, cheating, and manipulation if they achieve one's goals. Statistics on school cheating and workplace cheating are remarkably different in the new millennium than they were in the mid-twentieth century.

As mentioned, there has been a dramatic shift in how we value commitment, but the full impact of this change is often not appreciated. One reason commitment was highly valued is that we used to realize the best things in life flowed from faithfully living out our commitments in ways small and large. Part of the benefit came from our own character development, from growing and expressing our integrity and the satisfaction of doing so, and part came from the blessings that integrity brings in relationship. In stark contrast, current thinking is that a commitment made today might stand in the way of something better that is just around the corner. Thus, we are like shifting sand, easily blown here and there by promises of the next great thing, even as we neglect to build the character which would enable us to build something worth having if presented the opportunity.

IF IT ISN'T WORKING, IT MUST BE YOUR FAULT

Even if someone is living out these new philosophies and values, they still have the ever-present human need to love and be loved. However, this thinking leads to behaviors which make true intimacy challenging if not impossible. Many people have redirected their drive to find love toward serial sexual encounters, grievously misnaming promiscuous intercourse "making love." These people believe they are still searching for love, and they hope to fall into it. But the love they seek does not exist in the real world, and certainly will not be found amidst seduction, manipulation, selfish indulgence, and the pursuit of self-interest at another's expense. The version of perfect, true, unconditional love these people believe in means that a person should be loved just as he or she is. Period. Certainly no change (and no reciprocal imperative of unconditional love) must be required. This person's job is simply to find a soul mate, then to expect, against all odds, that this one will continue in their assigned role indefinitely. If this person's candidate for "right person" ceases to meet expectations, their faux love quickly evaporates.

The flip side of this belief is that we have not been loved well thus far because we are inherently unlovable. Our world points at our shortcomings and flaws and tries to make this point in every commercial and social media post. Love is reserved for those who have no such flaws, who are perfect. We see the air-brushed, photoshopped images of this faux elite staring vacantly at us every time we pay for groceries. Following this lead, people go to great lengths to create a pleasing image, to conceal imperfections. Social media assures us we will win the love lottery if we can just get the right posts. By creating the perfect image we will win love. How is this plan working?

GOOD CHARACTER STILL LEADS TO GOOD OUTCOMES

Granted, these are general social trends, and there are people today, as there always have been, who are of excellent character, people who build and sustain quality relationships. Most of the people who will choose to read this book likely fall into this category since this is a book about building better relationships. But these exceptions actually prove the point, because we must explain why these people are different. These people consciously, or even unconsciously by virtue of their nature or upbringing, live out certain principles. Which principles? Here it should be pointed out why science, technology, and education are not only not solving our relationship issues, they are perhaps compounding them. These issues are not about knowledge per se. These are character issues and spiritual issues.

ISSUES OF CHARACTER ARE ACTUALLY SPIRITUAL ISSUES

Science can study broad trends in ideas and behaviors in populations. To some degree science can sort out things that are pathologic from what is deemed normal, such as depression or bipolar tendencies (though concepts of what is normal and abnormal within the scientific community also have shifted in recent decades). But science has no reach whatever into the realm of values, personal priorities, the meaning of life, or the purpose of an individual's life. Nor can science, beyond the most superficial questions, delve into whether a person perceives that he or she is living life to the fullest or wasting that life. Science is even more poorly equipped to determine whether a choice based on an idea or value will have beneficial or harmful effects over the course of a lifetime. Yet, it is the accumulation of the consequences of our choices which will most determine our experience of living. And it is our ideas—those we have embraced and affirmed—which will guide our choices.

The ideas which populate our personal guidance system—which form, among other things, our values, priorities, aspirations, and goals—are spiritual matters. What is right, and right for us? What is wrong, and wrong for us? What matters, and what does not? What would be good for us to do, or not to do? All of these reside in the realm of moral reasoning. There are two sources that speak to these matters: religion and philosophy. Religion presumes a supernatural source of information, and there are several to choose from. Each purports to explain the reality of our existence. Then there is philosophy. Currently, this body of thought guides our educational system, our culture, and our government. Philosophers—though that word means "lover of truth"—gave up over a century ago in their quest to arrive at truth by combining logic with their own misconceptions. As mentioned, the fruit of their cumulative labor can be measured over the last century by the astronomical body count. The people who think "religion has done terrible things" should take an honest look at the outcome of these philosophies, and they should take an honest look at the direction of a culture that continues to be transformed and guided by these same thoughts.

God, in contrast, has offered truth to humanity for thousands of years. Truth that is unchanging and eternal.

SPIRITUAL ISSUES: A LARGER PICTURE OF GOOD AND BAD, RIGHT AND WRONG

There is a cause-and-effect system in the universe. Decisions and actions unleash a variety of consequences, some long delayed. Science has no way of understanding the impact of this highly complex cause-and-effect system. How would one design a study that would track all of the consequences of even a single decision over a lifetime, much less the impact of this decision on every other person it impacts? This falls in the realm of moral law and moral reasoning, which is an understanding of why some things are right and others wrong. God's revealed moral law is not, as many believe, simply an arbitrary assignment fundamentally designed to shame our impulses and ruin our good times. These laws accurately reflect the entirety of the system of cause and effect God designed for us to inhabit. We may get away with lying or stealing for a period of time, but only for a time. There will be an accumulation of bad consequences that become evident over time for any action that violates God's moral law. Once the fullness of those consequences plays out, everyone will be able to see why something was designated as right of wrong.

However, we view this cause-and-effect universe from an interesting vantage point. We exist in something called "now," which is a time after previous consequences have been set in motion, but before all of them are evident. This vantage point creates an insurmountable problem if we want to only learn "what is right for me" from experience. There is no point when we can be assured that all pending consequences have come to light. Even when consequences have occurred we may not realize that a particular consequence is related to a certain act. Therefore, we can "reasonably" believe that certain actions have no bad consequences—because they have not yet occurred or were misinterpreted. We see this kind of moral confusion all around us. We generally have only the vaguest idea of the extent to which our choices have created problems in our relationships. In fact, there are only two options for the source of problems in relationships: the other person, or me.

The good news is that almost every problem in our lives results from the actions of others. We must simply be patient and wait for others to get their act together, then our lives will be exactly what we want them to be . . . right? Or, instead of waiting for something that has not happened in the entire history of humanity and blaming others for things for which we bear huge responsibility, far more than we realize, we could perhaps seek information about this cause-and-effect system from the One who designed it. And we could then begin living in ways that produce a growing harvest of good consequences and outcomes in our own lives.

WISDOM: MAKING CHOICES WITH THE BEST LONG-TERM OUTCOMES

Over the centuries people have sought for wisdom. Wisdom takes this cause-and-effect system and these deeper spiritual realities into account and charts a course for living that leads to best long-term results. Such insight can come through the writings of wise and perceptive people, including the "great literature" of Western Civilization, as well as from Scripture. These writings were a part of general education until as recently as the 1960s, for education was thought to be about both knowledge and wisdom. Not only has Scripture been stripped from our educational system, but also the lessons found in great literature from past centuries. Why would we need Augustine or Aristotle in our head when we have the Internet in our purses or pockets? Since our hope is the future, why look back at all? Why, indeed?

THE WORLD'S PLAN FOR RELATIONSHIP

THE CONTRACTUAL MODEL

In order to fully appreciate the radical nature of God's plan for human relationships, we need to contrast that plan with a plan we are all familiar with: a contract. A contract is an agreement between two or more parties that defines what the parties will do and not do. It specifies what acts will be done and what goods supplied, generally in an exchange of some sort. There are formal written contracts, legally binding documents that describe behaviors to be engaged in or avoided, which also limit the scope of expectations and liability.

But there is also an informal version that governs virtually every human relationship and interaction. This fashions our general understanding of what we can reasonably expect people to do and not do. If someone accepts a dinner invitation at our home, we expect that they will arrive at our address, reasonably hungry, and at more or less the appointed time. We do not expect that they will bring fifteen other people to dinner without, at a minimum, alerting us beforehand. Many similar things form our overall sense of social expectations. This same format governs individual relationships. Things in every relationship that are the result of an informal negotiation between the parties that defines what each person can expect from the other. Who pays for dinner? Is it a welcomed act of courtesy for the guy to open a door for the girl, or would he never dare offend her in this way?

In a contract, both parties bring something to the table. The ideal is a situation where both parties feel what was received is of more value to each than what was offered. This is referred to as a "win-win" situation. Then there are all manner of scenarios where people misrepresent the value of what is offered or otherwise manipulate the situation to take advantage of the other party.

When two people are building a close relationship, such as a romance that may move toward marriage, a much more detailed negotiation occurs. Both parties are seeing if they enjoy each other's company, find each other attractive, have a strong heart response toward one another, and like being seen in each other's company. This heart response is first termed having "a crush," or being infatuated. As feelings grow, it is called "falling in love." But, at the same time, both parties are doing calculations. How much is this relationship going to cost me, and how much am I going to get out of it? If the overall package looks like a good deal to both, they move forward in the relationship. In the past this meant getting married in one's very late teens or twenties, while today it may mean either moving in together and/or possibly getting married at some point before the biological clock runs down.

The thing to note is the essence of a contract, particularly one that is not formal and legally binding but binding in the sense of agreed-upon expectations—or at least expectations we thought we had agreed upon. "What do you mean, 'You want us to move to Colorado'? My job and my family and all my friends are here!" Entering and continuing the relationship is a function of how we see that relationship affecting our self-interest at every point. If it is working for us, we stay in it. If it is not, other decisions follow.

THE WORLD'S CONTRACTUAL VIEW OF MARRIAGE

I want to pose a few questions for your consideration. Based on this description of the principles of contract, would you agree that virtually all the marriages and romantic relationships you are aware of are conducted on this foundation? Is this a fair description of the way our world does relationship? "The best marriages are fifty-fifty kinds of things," people will say. Further, it seems to be commonly assumed that if we have feelings for another person that are strong enough, if it is *true love,* then this benefit to our existence will make everything else fall into place. It is assumed that someone else's love for us, if it is true love, will be sufficient motivation to ensure that the other party will continue to offer us a good deal for as long as we both are alive. Feelings of love for another person certainly do bring out the best in us—in fact they seem to transport us to an altogether new and delightful experience of living—and they motivate us to extremes of good behavior toward each other. But if the things we most value from a relationship are our own loving feelings toward the other person, and the blessings they offer us are motivated by their own new, deep feelings for us, how stable and enduring a foundation are we basing our happily-ever-after upon? Why might we want to take a closer look at this approach?

Why, if marriage is a covenant, are we talking about an entirely different format for conducting most marriages? One of the themes of this book series is that one can be in a relationship that is actually one thing but conduct the relationship as if it is something else altogether. And we can actually *be* one thing but persist in acting as if we are something else. Everyone who is married is in a covenant. One does not need to understand this relationship to actually be in one. However, one does need to understand this relationship and all it involves to conduct the relationship in a way that realizes its true potential. Let's look more closely at the relationship produced by superimposing the world's mind-set on top of a marriage covenant.

THE CONTRACTUAL MODEL CREATES THE "COMPETING KINGDOMS" MODEL

If marriage is based on a contractual model, a contract is made between two separate and distinct entities. People never make contracts with themselves. If we are going to have a contractual model of marriage, this necessarily means we will have two separate lives held together only by a bond of agreement. I call this the Competing Kingdoms Model of Marriage. If one is not consciously living out a covenant model of marriage, this is literally the only other option.

If we are not aware of our identity change as we enter marriage, how do we view ourselves? In the same way we always have. We have spent our lives building what? Our own lives. We want marriage to be what? Value-added to our lives. How do we build the life we want according to our culture? By getting our way: having things the way we want them, pursuing our preferences, satisfying our needs, gratifying our desires. Our life is a kingdom, and we are the monarch. As the head of our lives, we deeply desire to be in charge of as much as possible; enlarging our influence, after all, equates with having a better life. Thanks to many cultural influences, we so easily come to believe that this is our path to true happiness. Whether this is actually true is another question. But this is the starting point in marriage for almost everyone, even if they are head over heels in love.

Even if we love the other person, they are still the *other person*. So now we have the dilemma of balancing our good intentions toward this other person with our perception of our best interests—and this has to be played out at every point in our lives together. In practice, this leads to two often sharply competing sets of priorities within each party as they try to juggle good intentions and personal interests. It also results in sharply competing priorities *between* the parties. Why? Because the other person is doing the same juggling act, calculating how much they want to give, or are willing to give up, to get what they ultimately want, which will always reflect their perception of self-interest.

The root of the conflict in this model is between two things that are often completely opposite in practice: perceived self-interest, with a willingness to sacrifice relationship to get the "win"; versus goodwill and the desire to build the relationship, which will involve some degree of self-sacrifice if one genuinely cares about the other party. The rest of this dance is the two figuring out who is going to do the sacrificing and who gets their way in each scenario. To the extent that people pursue self-interest at the expense of the relationship, what happens to the relationship? Will it inevitably sustain damage? The quality of these kinds of relationships are determined by the way the parties strike the balance between these imperatives. Kind, considerate, and good-natured people often do a pretty good job of building more relationship and inflicting less damage, which is why marriages founded upon this model can "work." But if our relationship is ultimately at the mercy of what each of us feel like doing, and if our sense of self-interest diverges enough from the interests of the other party or the relationship, what happens? "No, I will not move. You must understand how much my career means to me!"

> The rest of this dance is the two figuring out who is going to do the sacrificing and who gets their way in each scenario.

So as this plays forward we have two people negotiating and jousting, and at points going at each other as hard as possible, all for the sake of protecting and promoting self-interest. Even if these people genuinely like each other and have warm feelings toward each other, you still see people undercutting each other, trying to neuter each other to alter the balance of power. Why? Because the more power the other person has, the less apt one is to get one's own way. After all, isn't this really the path to our own happiness?

> *But I am afraid that just as Eve was deceived by the serpent's cunning, your minds may somehow be led astray from your sincere and pure devotion to Christ.*
> 2 CORINTHIANS 11:3

THE COMPETING KINGDOMS MODEL WITH A CHRISTIAN VENEER

Even when we overlay Christian principles and beliefs on this model, we still see this jousting match with the same results—ongoing relationship damage. Because of the precepts taught in Scripture about how we are to treat each other, Christians may have additional relationship skills that help build marriages, and they may pursue their own interests somewhat less aggressively, at least outwardly. There are principles in marriage-help books that dampen some of the conflict. And there is a train of thought in the Christian community that we are supposed to be sacrificial, to lay down our own desires, feelings, agenda, and will for the sake of God and each other. But all this only partially mitigates the relationship damage inflicted over time by two people who still fundamentally view themselves as separate and distinct individuals, who are agreeing to pursue their separate and distinct lives side by side. Whenever Jesus commented on marriage, He always pointed directly to the original intent and plan: a one-flesh relationship. Taking the world's plan and softly overlaying a veneer of Christian "niceness" does not yield the results produced by God's actual plan.

OTHER MISUNDERSTANDINGS FLOW FROM MISUNDERSTANDING COVENANT

Covenant obviously creates scenarios that call for personal sacrifice. But what is this sacrifice to look like? We will examine this concept in more detail later; briefly, there is a correct sense in which this should occur. However, it is a very different thing to lay upon God's altar of sacrifice our misperception of our true interests, which is part of God's plan to revamp our perception of our true best interest, versus completely ignoring our own needs and priorities, acting as if our own needs do not exist or are unimportant. Two competing concepts are often discussed in Christian circles: being selfless and being selfish. Being selfless is commended; being selfish is condemned. We must be very careful how we define these terms, however, to ensure that being selfless does not mean that we view only other people's needs and desires as legitimate while believing that God wants us to act as if our needs and desires exist only to be ignored.

Selfishness is correctly defined as believing, and acting, as if our interests are inherently more important than the interests of others. Somehow, though, selfishness has been redefined by some to mean any recognition of our own needs and desires, as if God does not want us to have these. God wants us to equate the importance of our needs and desires with those of other people (note Philippians 2:4 [NASB, suggested] in light of the rest of the passage). To the extent that real sacrifice is called for, there is another reality in play as well. Christ sacrificed something real by emptying and humbling Himself, but He offered up these things to obtain something of greater importance. True, godly sacrifice always offers up something of lesser importance to gain something of greater importance. The rub comes in our frequent misunderstanding of what is truly important. Thus, God's call to us to sacrifice certain things often involves reeducating ourselves about the actual importance of things. In a similar way, God at times will allow life to strip away valuable things from us to prompt us to fix our affections on things of greater importance.

In covenant, God completely redirects our sense of true self-interest and invites us to rid ourselves of inadequate and incorrect views.

At no time does a loving God tell us that our real needs are unimportant. The only questions are: 1) how we will get those needs met; 2) how to balance our needs with those of others; 3) what source will meet our needs (this may be God, instead of the person we are relying upon in a given situation); and 4) which of our needs are real and truly important. In light of all of this, if we do not understand the realities of covenant, we will never be able to chart the course God desires to meet our true needs, nor the true needs of others. One of the greatest powers of covenant resides in altering our identities, and therefore our deepest needs; then providing the training process that allows these new needs to be met for ourselves and our covenant partner. While in this redirecting process, we may feel that we are having to sacrifice one thing or another that we have come to value in our lives. But there will be no net loss at any point, only gain as we move toward reality and authenticity.

At times in the Christian community teaching on sacrifice and submission can lead to an outcome God clearly does not intend: devoting ourselves to fulfilling someone else's selfish desires for them, while tolerating or even enabling abuse or misconduct. This common distortion of the meaning of love, and of God's plan, can lead to codependency, to continuing to pour our lives into the lives of people who are simply using us—even as we continue to hope that our love will change them. Which it will not. We need to think through this pattern extremely carefully and look at the example of Jesus, who was sacrificial at many points but also confrontational when people were taking advantage of others, abusing them, misrepresenting themselves, or lying to Him.

It should be noted that all of the above misunderstandings and missteps, and most of the others seen in marriages, have as their foundation a misunderstanding of the fundamental relationship between people in a marriage covenant. If this relationship is misunderstood there will be inevitable confusion at every level in a marriage. God's gift to us, the model of a working relationship, is a model of interdependence and mutual support. It represents a merging and synthesis of interests between the parties, which is in keeping with the reality that the two formerly separate individuals have identities and natures that are now altered and merged. The true shift in a covenant relationship is the shift in what represents our actual best interests, and this is based on an alteration in our identity. The path to the best relationship is found in recognizing and applying this new value system. Any plan that retains and defends the old value system and view of self will ultimately pit one's perception of their own best interests against the perceived competing interests of a spouse. This is a recipe for ongoing discord, discontent, and disappointment, and possibly divorce.

Since becoming a Christian certainly can, and should (but often does not, for reasons we have been discussing) result in a person shifting their primary focus in life from their perception of self-interest toward faithfulness to their covenant, it is no surprise that Christian marriages would be troubled with a frequency that mirrors non-Christian marriages. In fact, it can only be through learning and embracing and living out the covenant model of marriage that we can term a marriage a truly "Christian marriage."

CHRISTIAN COMMENTATORS MISUNDERSTAND COVENANT

It is also worth noting that modern academicians, even biblical scholars, if they are not aware of an accurate understanding of the nature of covenant, will analyze these relationships through their own lens of current cultural expectations and practices. Trumbull's book was widely known in its day, but it is definitely not widely circulated today. There have been virtually no follow-up works building on the foundational understanding laid by Trumbull. Therefore, people offering commentary on aspects of our covenant relationships—marriage, or a relationship with God—will inevitably attempt to overlay these relationships with the principles governing contracts. This has a number of unfortunate effects. This model, misapplied to the New Covenant, results in the view that God simply offers us something that we cannot pay for; thus, we offer nothing in return. Our sole role in the relationship is to become a recipients of God's grace. There is little acknowledgement of the offer of our lives to God, or of our responsibilities in this relationship. There is only one responsibility recognized, which is our obligation to stop sinning. But the meaning of sin is reduced. Sin does not represent an entire course of life and way of being, which we properly recognize as flawed and agree to lay down. We offer this self up to God to be put to death in a true covenant understanding, trusting in Him that He will raise us to new life as new creatures who are now able to follow God's plan for our lives under His lordship. Instead, sin becomes a list of activities and perhaps attitudes from which we believe we need to refrain. This is not about love; this is about checking off boxes on a list "because God said so."

If we hold up our end of this contract, we believe, God blesses us. If we do not, we invoke the penalty clause of the contract. Is this not in fact the same view the Jews had in Jesus' day concerning their relationship with God? Is this not the same concept Jesus began to confront as He pointed to the nature of the relationship—of our believing in Him and following Him—as the truly important things?

> There has been no contract ever written that can fully define love much less successfully require it.

In the same way, the contractual view of marriage reduces the Scriptural injunctions on marriage to a list of "thou shall nots." There is no recognition that God is offering expert advice on how to build the marriage and love affair we all most deeply desire. I would suggest that the picture we will see when we overlay, not principles of contract, but principles of covenant to these covenant relationships, will be a much more rich, deep, coherent, and powerful one than the "contract version." There has been no contract ever written that can fully define love, much less successfully require it. Only covenant can do this.

We are to repent, which literally means to turn 180 degrees from our initial path of life; we turn and walk an entirely different path in a different direction toward a different destination, building the new life that is already within us in the process as we enact God's plan in our lives on a daily basis. The image evoked by the Greek word we translate "repent" draws to mind not a specific list of actions but an entirely new direction of life.

Thus, the obedient life is not about a list but about a *direction*, which means following God, walking with Him, and fulfilling our assigned roles according to His plan. In the process, our relationship with our Creator grows; our hearts will grow to burn with passion for the true lover of our souls, the source of our lives, the source of all good things. We are not trying to obey God to satisfy some abstract construct of the "obedient life," but to build into our lives and relationships necessary elements of success that are revealed to us by a trusted and wise mentor, one who is a loving Father as well as the Lord of all Creation. Though the individual things we do with either mind-set may overlap quite a bit, the reasons we do these things are vastly different in the covenant model versus the contractual model. One model commits us to "not sinning"; the other is about building a loving relationship while being careful not to offend because we value our relationship. And, even more, we value the other being with whom we are in relationship.

Which model would you prefer?

THE WORLD'S IMPACT ON GOD'S PLAN AMONG CHRISTIANS

The Spirit clearly says that in latter times some will abandon the faith and follow deceiving spirits and things taught by demons.
1 TIMOTHY 4:1

As we glance around we see that everyone has an opinion on everything, including marriage and a relationship with God. On the surface, all of this appears to be an exercise in human diversity. But as we look deeper, we see these ideas sorting themselves into ideas that are on one side of a line or the other. Ideas on one side pull in one direction, and on the other in a completely opposite direction. As we look at the direction in which these two sides are pulling, they correspond to the two sides of a history-long spiritual war. From these two sides we are offered contradictory and conflicting guidance for living. We have looked at the identity of the authors of these ideas and their respective agendas. These two voices speak to how marriage is to be conducted—or whether it should even exist. These two voices weigh in on whether we should have a relationship with our Creator and, if so, what it might consist of. We have looked at some of the outcomes achieved by following one or the other of these voices.

As we look more closely we see that the enemies of God attempt to hinder His plan at every level. This includes voices in our culture but also includes these same messages within the Christian community. There are, as the Scriptures note, wolves in sheep's clothing who intentionally lead the people of God astray. And there are those who have concluded that the Word of God should properly be amended (distorted) to pay homage to the counsel of God's enemies, who have informed most of the viewpoints in our culture. This effect is widespread within the Christian community even among those who appear to be sincere in their desire to follow God and teach about Him. We see this same corrupting influence in the first century Christian community, an influence which was identified and opposed by several New Testament writers. We must be as vigilant today as these first century writers were if we are to follow God's plan for our lives.

One of Satan's greatest victories, his first win, is obscuring the reality that there is a plan for these relationships. His second victory, if one realizes there is such a plan, is to confuse the nature of this plan, to portray it as simply a bunch of unkeepable rules proffered by a God who is waiting for us to step over the line so He can shame and punish us. The same God who is so out of step with modern society that obedience to Him will make fools of us. Thus we must shift His plan to polish His image before a watching world so He can be liked by our society, and so we can be liked as we follow this new and improved offering, this one-off plan offered to us straight from Hell.

The reality, though, is there is a God who is the same yesterday, today, and forever (Hebrews 13:8). There has been a plan for marriage for as long as marriage has been in existence (currently dated in the scientific community as far back as the Sumerian culture). In other words, since there has been human society resembling our own—roughly six thousand years—there has been marriage. God says in His Word that He conveyed marriage to the first humans made in His image, likely shortly before the Sumerian civilization began. God's plan for this relationship has not changed.

THE VARIABLE IS OUR COMMITMENT AND DEVOTION TO GOD'S PLAN

To commit ourselves to God's plan with the devotion required to actually carry it out, we must connect a number of dots. First, God's plan is not just about meeting a number of arbitrary standards; His plan is about conducting ourselves to reap the best real-world outcomes in our relationships. Thus, God's plan, in addition to being about His love for us—which can seem fairly abstract if we are in the midst of painful and difficult places—is ultimately synonymous with our best interests in every way. We must realize this if we are to reap the benefits of challenging circumstances.

These very painful scenarios, reversals, failures, conflict, discord—these are the things that point us toward necessary growth and transformation in God's plan. These things are not the enemies of our happiness or our future; these very things provide the pathway to our best future—if we view them correctly and respond to them in ways that allow God to use them for our growth and transformation. These things are the foundation upon which future success is based, the foundation upon which happiness and gratification will stand. God also uses good times and blessings to form and shape us. Pain, unfortunately, is an inevitable consequence of living in a world in rebellion against God. Divorcing ourselves as far from this rebellion as possible will not, unfortunately, shield us from pain. But this pain can be used by God to reveal to us ways in which we still need to grow, ideas we still need to discard to follow Him properly, and to love as He desires. If we are in this process before God, or if two are in this process together in marriage, God will sustain them through the most challenging and difficult circumstances. Even if everything we have is taken away, we will find that we still have one thing the world can never take away—our relationship with our Maker and the Lover of our souls. And we will find that, if this is all we have, we have everything we really need. This is the most profound and most important lesson of all.

Endure hardship as discipline; God is treating you as His children. For what children are not disciplined by their father? If you are not disciplined—and everyone undergoes discipline—then you are not legitimate, not true sons and daughters at all. Moreover, we have all had human fathers who disciplined us and we respected them for it. How much more should we submit to the Father of spirits and live! They disciplined us for a little while as they thought best; but God disciplines us for our good, in order that we may share in His holiness. No discipline seems pleasant at the time, but painful. Later on, however, it produces a harvest of righteousness and peace for those who have been trained by it. Therefore, strengthen your feeble arms and weak knees. Make level paths for your feet so that the lame may not be disabled, but rather healed.
HEBREWS 12:7-13

TEN

Summary of the Concepts Surrounding Covenant

When we view our lives as mostly about our desires, needs, freedom to choose, and agreements, we do not build a world worth inhabiting; instead, we render our world progressively uninhabitable.

What is covenant? Is it, as asserted by modern theologians, simply a contract, one authored by God? In the case of marriage, is it merely an agreement between two individuals, one that for some unknown reason is unusually binding? Or is a covenant a true union of souls?

Let us ask this question another way: Why did God not simply forgive us through the penalty paid for our sins by Christ, and move on? Why, instead of just forgiveness, did He offer us the death of our old selves and a new birth and new life? If we focus only on forgiveness of sins and a ticket to Heaven, are we missing something vital in this picture? When Jesus shifted the focus in John 6 from righteous acts to the nature of the relationship with Himself, what was He trying to say to each of us?

Is a marriage a vaguely defined arrangement we enter, then figure out as we go, making it what we want it to be? Or is a marriage a definite thing—with a definite structure, function, and purpose, and a definite set of guiding principles? Is God's plan for marriage a constraining and unrealistic thing that inevitably collides with our hearts, or is His plan the path to the best relationship, the deepest love, and the most profound satisfaction and gratification?

What is a relationship with God supposed to look like? Do we just pray a prayer, start going to church, and try to stop sinning? Are we moved occasionally to make small changes while we focus on looking the part? Or is there actually a way to live the abundant, alive, transformed, high-impact life that common sense suggests should be possible if we are not only in a special relationship with the God of the universe, but He has come to live inside us?

The central premise of this series of books is that God has a master plan for our lives that consists of two fundamental parts. Both of these parts are covenant relationships—marriage and the New Covenant relationship with God. These relationships have distinct but complementary functions: through marriage the human race is literally perpetuated, and if God's plan is followed rising generations are loved and trained to create a better world; through the New Covenant God recreates the relationship with individuals that was originally intended, in the process reversing our sentence of death (or in one sense carrying it out, since by entering covenant we die and are reborn as new creatures).

Yet this recreated being has not achieved perfection, even though he or she is inhabited by God's Spirit. Instead, this new creature consists of potential, placed in a life that consists of opportunity. To properly develop this potential and make the most of these opportunities, this individual must cultivate a deep and intimate relationship with God and carry out His plan for living. This plan will shift the life of this individual from good citizenship in the kingdom in which they have lived to this point—the kingdom of God's enemy, the prince of this world—to good citizenship in the Kingdom of God, now and for eternity. But God's plan must still be chosen, as a whole and in each individual part. It must be carried out faithfully, consistently, with perseverance. The only sufficient motivation for a lifetime of such devotion is love for God, which God's plan also cultivates. But each individual must choose the path that leads to all of this, first by choosing to enter covenant with God—accepting God's gracious and magnificent offer—then choosing to be faithful to this covenant and its Author.

I stated at the beginning that covenant is the core—the very heart—

Even the most basic definition of a covenant relationship, the exchange and merger of identities, is not commonly understood in our Christian culture.

of God's plan for humanity. As we have seen, the grand scheme of the plan of God (and any of its particulars) may not be clearly and immediately evident. If we are to understand God's plan in the largest sense, and in all its particulars, we must understand the heart of His plan, the engine that drives the plan. This understanding is crucial if we are to live out God's plan in fullness, yet even the most basic definition of a covenant relationship, the exchange and merger of identities, is not commonly understood in our Christian culture.

If one of the strongest forces building and directing our lives is our understanding of our own identity—for better or worse—would it not be crucial to understand the change that occurs in our identity as we enter covenant? If everything we are told to do, everything we are and are told to become—everything we feel and value, every priority, every goal, everything about our sense of self-interest, and every bit of the deepest satisfaction and gratification we will find in this life—is defined by and flows directly from the core reality of covenant, should we not make every effort to understand this relationship?

If the growth, maturity, and transformation we experience is directly related to our active participation in God's plan for these relationships, should we not make every effort to understand how such personal change occurs and what is required of us to accomplish these things? If the love of God is shown to us through covenant, and if our proper response is defined through covenant, should we not make every effort to understand this relationship and our role in it?

God's first and most important commandment is that we love Him with our heart, mind, soul, and strength. If covenant is the development process which renders us actually capable of fulfilling this most important of all commands, should we not understand and engage in this process as if our lives depend upon it? If love in marriages is defined by covenant and displayed in fullness by faithfulness to covenant, should we not make every effort to learn the lessons of love that covenant has to offer?

We have all been told that the ultimate reality of God toward us is love. We know that we are called on to love God in return and with our entire heart. We know that the core of a marriage—the central reality that forms it and the force that drives its development—is love. But we are rarely if ever taught that love and covenant are synonyms. Every element of covenant is an expression of love, and as we express ourselves to our covenant partner faithfully in accord with the principles, duties, obligations, and responsibilities of covenant, we not only express love in the largest and most comprehensive sense, our hearts grow in their capacity to display and experience love.

One might be tempted to sound-bite God's plan into something like this: "Fine, we will be the nicest and best toward each other we can possibly be." This is the general view about how to do well in a marriage and how we are supposed to live with each other in the body of Christ, the church. If we do not correctly understand covenant, this is the best we have to offer. But God's plan has more to offer—much more. The problem with the sound-bite reduction is that it simply does not work. It produces no transformation or growth; it has no power. Of course, being nice is better than not being nice, but in order to go through the rigors of life in an intimate relationship we need a plan that is a bit more powerful than "I will be as nice to you as I can, for as long as I can, as long as I feel like it and you do not get in my way beyond a certain point."

Instead of something superficial, trite, and ineffective, God's plan is massive, immensely powerful, and highly effective if applied. In both covenants God's plan defines love in all its complexity and fullness. It calls on us to love Him and each other, not only in a general sense but in the ways that truly mean the most and please the most across the spectrum of life. Doing all of this is impossible for anyone at the outset; we are not mature, wise, understanding, disciplined, or faithful enough to get all of this right consistently. Thus, God's plan is lifelong;

it uses the mundane, everyday things, and it uses our mountaintop encounters with Him; it uses the successes as well as the disasters and epic fails, the pains and joys, the delights and sorrows, to lay out an agenda for growth, maturity, and transformation. God's plan equips us to harness the potential of the life and relationships He has given us—to learn to do the right things, to grow and change as necessary.

Of course, the other problem we all face as we consider living out the plan of God is that at some level we do not want to follow and obey. At a deeper level, our own nature argues against doing so if we are not already in covenant with God. We must always be aware that the plan of God is *always implemented in our lives through our choices, through our agreement on a moment by moment basis to obey Him and follow Him.* Therefore, one of our most important duties is to identify and always keep in mind reasons why we would want to make the choice to be obedient at each and every point, for our world will offer us no shortage of reasons to make other choices. In fact, it is at precisely this point that we find ourselves in the crossfire of the unremitting, history-long battle between God and Satan, played out in each human life through ideas offered and choices made. Even though we are in covenant with God, even if we harbor His Spirit within, we are still subject to deception; still subject to following Satan's directives instead of God's; still subject to knowingly or unknowingly rebelling against the true lover and redeemer of our souls. We do this to our shame and our harm; but even in this God provides a way of repentance and restoration.

If we are to walk in God's plan as His child, understanding our change of identity as we entered covenant is vital. He does not offer us just an obedient life, a life in which we follow rules for some vague future benefit that runs cross-grain with our very nature. He offers us a new life in covenant with Him. Our new nature, if properly understood, leads naturally and logically to a life in accord with God's plan. In marriage He bonds two together with a new, joined identity. If properly understood, this will naturally and logically lead to developing a relationship in accord with His plan. Problem solved, right? New nature, new life, great lives together, great marriages. Except that this is demonstrably not what usually happens. It is crucial that we understand why the lives that are now *present within people in fullness* are not expressed by these people in a way that leads to the abundant lives and the head-over-heels-in-love-for-a-lifetime marriages that, on paper, should be the norm instead of the exception.

Several realities are important to understand: our new lives are initially present only in potential, in a way similar to a newborn. New life must grow, and growth takes time. Growth must be shepherded and properly directed. This new life is surrounded by perceptions, habits, ideas, and character built prior to entering these relationships, elements which are now out of sync with this new self. These holdovers must be identified and consciously rejected, or they will continue to direct attitude, emotion, and behavior. The more a marriage relationship grows according to God's plan, the better the environment for this growth and transformation, and the more help our spouse will be in this process. Supporting our spouses in their growth and transformation is a gift that gives back many times over; this is one key function of love. The relationship, in turn, becomes a place to field-test our growth; a place where we can try out and prove our growing capacity to love.

People's lives may be less than God's plan can produce due to the mismatch between people's perceptions of their identity and nature versus an accurate understanding of their identity and nature. We noted that our identity is not something we can look into a mirror and see, nor can it be discerned by peering within our heart and mind. So how can one know who one is? We have many people, many voices, many experiences informing us about who we are. To live out God's plan we must develop one key piece of understanding: some things we have come to believe about ourselves are a lie, while others are true.

Despite what is true, what we will build our lives upon are our decisions about what is true—what we *come to believe is true*. This is especially true about whom we think we are. We will fashion our life after our vision of ourselves, shaping our hearts and determining the quality of our relationships and life experiences in the process. In the same way we have been misinformed about our original identity, we can embrace incorrect views of our new one, the most common being the belief that we are who we have always been, even though in covenant. This is one particularly serious negative impact of teaching that covenant is a form of contract. In covenant, and in Scripture, we are offered clarity about much of our identity. The remainder—our individual potential, capabilities, and wiring system—come to light as we go through the experiences of life and take advantage of the opportunities God offers to us. One of our highest priorities should be to become clear about who we are, in marriage and in Christ, for we will live up to, or live down to, our vision of who we are.

Whether about our identity, or about other issues, various sources of information in our world purport to be the source of truth, *the revealer of reality*—family, friends, the media, the educational establishment, scientists, the Scriptures, and other religions. Beneath the surface, once the content of the messages from these sources is distilled, there appear to be only two distinct sources for the content of these messages: God and not-God.

Not-God is actually a being who is leading a rebellion against the real God; we have identified and described this being and his agenda in detail. We also discussed the challenges his influence poses, because he does not just peddle things that are not true; instead, he packages his lies alongside things we can become persuaded we really want, even desperately need—because these things, we are told, hold the promise of a better and more fulfilling life than the life God offers us. These promised benefits never occur; the price of embracing these lies always includes consequences we do not see coming, or we choose to ignore due to the depth and urgency of our desires. But these consequences will come if we choose to follow this course, and will teach us, if only in retrospect, why following this voice is a mistake—always.

As we look for truth, we must be aware of Satan's game and the way we can be drawn away even from a desire to find truth. Even this most basic desire can be set aside in favor of something we may come to believe is more important than truth: personal benefit. If we recognize this pattern as this game begins to unfold, and realize who is engineering the attempt to draw us away from God and His plan, we will be armed to resist such con jobs. This is important even for the little things in life. How much more important it is to avoid deception about the bigger things in life—who we are, what is real, and the things that actually comprise the best life.

We noted that what is true, right, and good are not simply labels arbitrarily assigned. What is true is also a statement of reality—what will ultimately prove to be the case in the end. What is good and right is so because of the consequences of these things—once all of these consequences have occurred. Things that are right and good have good consequences, for thoughts, attitudes, emotions, priorities, motives, and actions occur in the context of a moral universe that was created by God for us to inhabit. This universe perfectly reflects God's moral framework.

But, as we also noted, this overarching moral framework cannot be entirely seen by us in a given moment. It must be revealed to us, and it has been if we care to read about it and embrace its reality. In contrast, other voices offering other things, from recreational drugs, to an opportunity to steal, to any other moral temptation that people pursue for purported personal gain, inevitably provide less than the promised benefit, and a much higher price tag that was initially apparent. One source of information offers truth and reality, the other offers deception leading to bondage. The first voice is the source of life, the second source brought death to the human race. Yet we continue to have the prerogative of deciding for ourselves what, among the many messages, is true, for better or worse. We get to choose what—actually, whom—to believe. The ultimate reality is that what we choose as our truth or want to be true in no way influences what is actually true. Two things will become apparent: the fixed, immutable nature of God's moral law, and the irrelevance of our opinions about these matters. The only thing that will matter to us is whether we have recognized actual truth and founded our beliefs and our lives upon it, or not. This is true not just in the end, in some eternal sense, but also in terms of our relationships and the course of our lives.

God invites us to "live by faith and not by sight" (2 Corinthians 5:7). We need to be clear about how we best decide which individual ideas are true, and which sources offer truth. We spoke earlier of seeing the big picture in relation to Adam and Eve while they were in the Garden of Eden deciding whether to believe in Satan or God. One fascinating aspect of this question is that there is no source of information that is so clearly, self-evidently true that everyone on earth with a working brain has full confidence in this one source. This is because we all have been given the prerogative of deciding what we think is true, and because there are many sources of information which offer some truth, partial truth, or a grain of truth along with deception. And, since we live in a world full of people whose nature contains an element of the nature of God's enemy, that enemy's lies find a welcoming home in the hearts and minds of his subjects. This is why following the herd—or our culture's newest, latest, greatest ideas—may not be our strongest move.

All sources are not equally true, truth is not relative (in the eye of the beholder only), and one's belief about what is and is not true plays no role in determining what is actually true. There is one source of truth that is synonymous with all of reality. This truth—God's revelation—and the reality we inhabit both come from the same Author. God does not ask us to simply decide to accept His Word based on no corroborating data, engaging in some kind of "leap of faith." True faith, instead, is found by entrusting ourselves to a source which has proven itself credible. If I tell you something forty-nine times, and each time things occur precisely as I have said, what if I tell you a fiftieth thing? Is it reasonable to believe that this next thing will also be true? This is extrapolating the known to the unknown. If, on the other hand, as soon as you meet me for the first time I tell you something, and you have no basis whatever to assess my credibility, your decision would truly represent a "leap of faith." You would be deciding based upon . . . well, in truth, nothing.

Think back to the story of Eve conversing with Satan in the garden. Her experience with God involved more than forty-nine previous correct statements and revelations. God never said anything to Eve or Adam that was not completely true. To simply continue to believe in God would have been no stretch at all; it would have been common sense. But how about Satan? He had established no credibility at all. Keep in mind, as we listen to voices throughout our culture, many are asserting something that Satan also asserted strongly in the Garden—God is a liar and His Word is not true. But God's Word was proven true, as it will continue to be proven true. Belief in God and His Word is not a leap; instead, it is a rational and logical conclusion based on overwhelming evidence. But we are still offered the opportunity to make this same choice many times each day. God has warned us of this situation. He prepared us to see it clearly as we are being approached by this enemy in person, or by his emissaries, just as Eve was approached and engaged with these same ideas, and this same sales pitch. One of the many things that argues strongly for the divine Authorship of the Scriptures is that in the third chapter of the first book of the Bible we see a very clear account of the same approach that is made to each person in our world multiple times per day—the offer to morally compromise for promised gain. It is from the acceptance of this offer myriad times a day across the globe that the cumulative misery of humanity flows. For those who value science and scientific data, the results of this experiment—following the advice of the enemies of God—are already clear. In billions of human lives through history. And the results of following God's actual plan (not the caricature proffered by Satan and his friends to discredit God and those who truly love Him) has also been demonstrated in countless human lives through history. The problem that remains is not of history, or of the reality of the consequences of these two courses; the problem is one of ongoing confusion and deception about the virtues of Satan's commended approach versus its cost. Yet as we look at the addictions, brutality, oppression, enslavement, and less dramatic things like the degree of untrustworthiness of the people around us, how can we not see the fruit of Satan's approach with crystal clarity?

OUR ROLE IN COVENANT

Our primary job in covenant is to shift our life-directing beliefs from these not-true, not-God things to truth and reality. We will discuss how this is done in detail in each of the next two volumes. How do these life-directing lies come to our attention? This happens as we find ourselves unwilling to be faithful to God's plan, or to our covenant(s), which are one and the same. To the extent that we believe it is in our best interest to do otherwise, why is this so? Because we have previously embraced other guiding ideas—incorrect ones. And it is our responsibility, as God says in Romans 12:2, to renew our minds. How? By embracing and living out truth. (We will also go over the ways this is done, step by step, in the next two books.)

The job of living out our covenants faithfully in every respect is obviously more challenging than simply sifting through and amending our beliefs, though this is a vital part of the process. The other thing required to live in the way God directs is that our character must be built in certain ways. Much of the way we approach life, and much of how we approach others in relationship, is determined by our habits, by things we do without thinking. These are things that "feel like us" because they are so familiar to us, like our oldest and most comfortable pair of jeans. However, these things are not "us" in the sense of flowing out of our identity and nature. Like jeans, these are things we have simply put on at a point in time. At several points in the New Testament we are told by God to *take off* such things that were associated with our old life and identity and *put on* the things consistent with our new life and identity.

> This is the definition of transformation: dismantling what is there that should not be there, and replacing it with new behaviors and attitudes.

To do this, we need to know how these things got "on us" in the first place. These things came to be through decisions, then by repeating behaviors until patterns are established. The sum of these habits could be called our character, or what people expect of us and what we expect from ourselves in terms of behavior, attitude, and viewpoint. It is from these habits that problems occur in close relationships. This is the

257

definition of transformation: dismantling what is there that should not be there, and replacing it with new behaviors and attitudes. This is where the world's plan runs into a dead end, for the very things that most need to change are celebrated as valid forms of self-expression. These things damage or destroy relationships if left in place.

Why do people "fall out of love"? Why do relationships shift from *the answer,* to *the problem,* to *"see you later"*? It is most often due to character issues and destructive ways of treating each other. The other major relationship-killer is the competing perceived self-interest of two parties due to an incorrect understanding of the actual nature of their relationship, and this flows from an incorrect understanding of their own identities and natures while in covenant. If one misunderstands covenant, thinking it is just another agreement between people, one's perception of self-interest always, at some point, in some way, at some level will wage war against our devotion to this agreement, whether between two people or between a person and God. If this dilemma of self-interest is real, as Satan has gone to great lengths to persuade us is the case in our relationships with God and in our marriages, these relationships will be more characterized by division and competing agendas than unity and cohesion. In contrast, the Scriptures picture God's intent in this way:

> " . . . *being of the same mind, having the same love,*
> *united in spirit, intent on one purpose.*"
> PHILIPPIANS 2:2 (NASB)

What we are going to see in the coming two books is that God created the mechanism within us by which we can grow into the truth of who we are, whether in a covenant with Him or in marriage. We have three human powers God has planted within us which are solely at our discretion: the **power of assent and dissent**, the **power of attention**, and the **power of intention**. While we can be influenced in each of these areas, no one can compel us to make a decision in these areas that we choose not to make. No one can force us to believe something. We may be influenced, even coerced, but the choice to believe is ultimately a choice each of us alone makes. It is the same with priorities and values. No one can make us choose one priority or value over another. We select our own view of what is important. In the same way, no one can make us act in a certain way if we are willing to suffer the consequences of not doing so.

These three powers appear to be simple, commonplace things we utilize without thinking. But they are remarkably powerful. It is from these powers that we decide what is truth and what we will follow, and it is from this same power that we determine whom we believe in and whom we will follow; we determine what, among all the contenders, is important enough to merit our attention. And we decide what, if anything, we are going to do about one matter or another. It is by using these powers that we can grow and mature into people whose beliefs are coherent and in accord with truth and reality; that we can become wholehearted, focused, and passionate; that we can set our lives on a course and stay on course, overcome adversity, and accomplish what we were put on earth to accomplish. It is through learning to use these powers that we develop the potential God has placed within us. This is the way we become who we were created to be. These powers were placed within us so we might become people capable of being faithful to our covenants; and, by becoming increasingly faithful to our covenants, to become people capable of loving more perfectly. Or, like any power or capability that remains undeveloped, these three powers can lie dormant. We can be weak, easily deceived, easily distracted, and pushed around here and there by the smallest coercion. We may have no willpower and thus fail to develop much of who we were created to be.

This is a basic overview of God's plan for us as individuals. There are other layers and levels at which this plan operates. One thing you might have noticed when we were talking about marriage being part of God's plan for everyone is that everyone is not married—so how can this be part of God's plan for everyone? As we will see, since intercourse forms a covenant, everyone who is conceived is brought about through a covenant. In our society, where the common perception of sexual activity has become completely untethered from marriage, our concept of childbearing has also become unhinged from the reality of a two-parent household. This is absolutely not God's plan nor His intent. If you have sex with someone, you are in covenant with them. The only question is, will you be faithful to the covenant relationship you created?

In this, as in every area of life, God has offered us the opportunity to follow Him or not follow Him. As in other areas of life, there are many people following the plan of not-God, who are therefore producing outcomes that look nothing like the blessings of God's plan. At the same time, fortunately, the fact that a child is not born into a loving, functioning two-parent household does not determine the outcome of that child's life. God has been dealing redemptively with sin-induced disasters and unfortunate life situations throughout history. His is a plan of redemption and an offer of new life. But following God's plan from the beginning produces much better results than having to continually engage in damage control.

> God has been dealing redemptively with sin-induced disasters and unfortunate life situations throughout history. His is a plan of redemption and an offer of new life.

His plan is a loving, functioning two-parent household comprised of mature, wise, loving parents and the children that come from this relationship. This is what His plan is designed to produce, and this is the way children have the best opportunity to build into their young lives a way of life that works—one in accord with God's plan. This is God's design for perpetuating families, and through these families to grow working communities and societies. The family has been the primary social unit in every human society throughout history.

The only asterisk to this statement would be totalitarian societies, in which the State has tried to usurp the primary child-training function of the family. These societies never endure long, for they are unstable and profoundly unsatisfying. Our society's educational system since the 1960s has tried to assert more of a fundamental role in this way. There has been a corresponding deterioration in our society's emphasis on the importance of the family, and thus fewer and less successful families than at any point in our nation's history. And statistics on teen pathology—from suicide rates to addictions to homicidal acting-out—has dramatically increased, as has the percentage of young adults who do not have the social skills or inclination to form new families. These realities not only represent personal disasters, they impact God's plan for society in remarkably powerful ways. Strong and functioning families are the bedrock upon which functioning cultures are built. As our families go, so goes the destiny of our nation. The question is simple: will we be guided as a society by God, as we have been for two centuries, or by not-God, as we have been for the last sixty?

The second institution heavily impacted by ideas foreign to God's covenant plan is the Christian community. There has been a corresponding weakness and lack of impact of the Christian community as our society veers away from functioning values and behaviors, and as many in the Christian community embrace these false values. Again, God's plan of covenant is primarily designed to impact those who have come into covenant with Him and are therefore in covenant with each other. This is, and is supposed to function like, a family of covenantally-related people. From this joining should spring not only a particular set of behaviors, but also growth and maturity. God intends that this growth and development flow not only from our relationships with Him but from our relationships with each other. This overall plan is compromised, though, when few in our Christian community are wholly committed to following God's plan; few even realize that He has a coherent plan for living, thanks to decades of leadership that attempts to synthesize the leadership of the world with the leadership of God. We spoke of Jesus' view of this approach earlier, and in our current Christian community we graphically see why He made this point so clearly.

Even at best, Christian teaching has shifted emphasis over the last

> Do you see the connection between this distortion of God's plan and the anemia of the body of Christ?

150 years from growth and transformation—personal and corporate holiness—to simply teaching the great truths in a classroom-like format and assuming the job is done. Pray a prayer of commitment to God, attend church, listen to truth, and await transformation by God. Do you see the connection between this distortion of God's plan and the anemia of the body of Christ? It creates people who have not actually engaged with the truths of God across the spectrum of life, who are not faithfully living out their covenant commitments, and who are not grappling with the forces within themselves that are preventing them from doing this. The result? People remain weak and immature. Nice people, perhaps, but not powerful and effective people in God's hands who are capable of impacting society.

On the other hand, in many other countries—mostly in the southern hemisphere—the body of Christ is functioning much more as a covenant body and the influence of Christianity is exploding. It is imperative, for our sake as well as for the sake of our children and the future of society, to gain a much clearer view of God's overall plan and how our personal response to God's requirements in relationship fit the overall plan. First, God needs mature, loving people, people refined by increasingly successful attempts to carry out the commands of God—to love other people, first in covenant, then in general. For us to become such people we must show up for God's growth and transformation process. This is not a burdensome, sacrificial, arduous, and painful process wielded by an ogre-God. This is the path to our best lives and our greatest reward and satisfaction. What is not to like? The only thing to rid ourselves of are lies. What *is* to like about those?

The biggest questions we will face on a daily basis have to do with truth and our ability to recognize it, with our personal commitment to God and truth, and our strength of character to make good on this commitment. God's plan is covenant, and the heart of His plan is love.

> He invites us to join Him in this most wonderful of all journeys of life. His intent is to bring purity and light to a dark world. Starting with one life at a time.

Covenant is the only mechanism by which we actually learn to love. God says we love because He first loved us (1 John 4:19), and He displayed His love for us in and through covenant. He invites us to join Him in this most wonderful of all journeys of life. His intent is to bring purity and light to a dark world. Starting with one life at a time.

The purpose of this book series is not only to paint a picture of what these relationships are to look like, but also to learn how to build them. Not only to note that many do not build these relationships to their potential, but to understand the reasons why this is so and to learn how to overcome these obstacles so we can build these relationships in the way God designed. Therefore, we will look at God's plan as the integrated whole that it is. We will look at our heart, our longings; we will look at how these relationships address our greatest and deepest needs; we will look at the way these relationships form and grow our heart, mind, character, and will if God's plan is followed. We will in turn look at the things we must draw from within ourselves to successfully carry out our end of these relationships.

We will also look at the roles God plays in these steps. Much is made of God, His grace, and His gifts. At times the focus seems to be wholly on God and what He has done. This is appropriate if we are considering what God has done for us, put in place for us, and offered to us. But if we do not understand covenant, we can fall into the incorrect belief that little if any is required from us in these relationships, especially in our relationship with God. Even in marriage, what is required of us is often quite unclear. Covenant, however, clearly defines our role in both relationships. Covenant is "whatever I have, whatever it takes, and whatever I need to grow into to do what is necessary." God can do

Covenant, however, clearly defines our role in both relationships. Covenant is "whatever I have, whatever it takes, and whatever I need to grow into to do what is necessary."

much in our lives, but He appears not to do what He certainly could if we are refraining from doing what He has told us to do, if we are not playing our assigned role in His plan. We may be thinking that His grace will "make up the difference." We also may think that we can continue to behave in our marriage in any way we desire, and it is up to our unconditionally loving partner to make up the difference by tolerating, embracing, and even celebrating us as we ignore our proper role in the relationship. Neither path of neglect will lead to the best relationship. God holds us responsible for what He has told us to do, and He blesses us accordingly.

It is true, and vital to grasp, that God has done many, many things we cannot do. God offers us a covenant relationship with Himself. We do not deserve this offer; we bring nothing to the table beyond offering our lives up to Him—to death—in anticipation that He will raise us to life as a new person with a new nature. The only role we play at this point is to believe in God and to accept His offer on His terms.

The deep inner workings of how we come to believe in Him are similar to the way we come to the decision to give our lives to another in marriage and receive their lives into our own. It takes a long time to recognize our love for someone, and to acknowledge that love to them—and it should. We must get to know the other person—their character, their heart toward us, where we fit into their lives, and many other things—before we can offer our heart to another.

There is theological debate about the role God plays in our decision to believe in Him versus the role played by our own decision processes. Whatever theological position one might choose in this matter, from the vantage point of one contemplating giving their heart and life to God, precisely the same kind of consideration is in progress that would occur if one was about to offer or accept a proposal of marriage. In both, we must believe in the One, or one. We must decide to enter covenant, then do so. There clearly is a role played by God in opening our eyes to His true identity, His love for us, and the reality of His offer to us. It is recognizing Him for who He is, and seizing the reality of His love for us, that drives us to open our arms to embrace and receive Him and all the gifts He offers in covenant.

When God opens our eyes to Himself and His love, our next move is to accept the offer of covenant relationship He has extended. The way we do this is virtually identical to the way we would enter into marriage—we vow to God that we are giving our lives to Him so He can raise us to a new life. Inherent in this is acknowledging that our lives up to this point have been under the wrong guidance and going in the wrong direction; that is, we confess that we have been wrong, and have done wrong by turning from God and His directives. We want not just God's forgiveness and blessings, we want a new life that goes in a new direction under His guidance and lordship.

As the Scriptures depict this process, we are to:

- Hear—understand God's offer of covenant, and the heart and nature of God

- Believe—the offer itself, and believe in the One making the offer

- Repent—renounce and turn from life under the lordship of the king of this world; confess our sin—our rebellious acts and heart toward God

- Receive—God as our Lord, along with His offer of new life, forgiveness, and all things inherent in covenant; this involves our personal prayer of acceptance, committing ourselves to God (our vow to Him, in reply to His vow to us—the Gospel), as well as a public profession of our commitment, and the prescribed public ceremony (Baptism).

*Very truly I tell you, whoever **hears** my words and
believes Him who sent me has eternal life and will
not be judged, but has crossed over from death to life.*
JOHN 5:24

*Peter replied, "**Repent** and be **baptized**, every one of you, in the
name of Jesus Christ for the forgiveness of your sins. And you will
receive the gift of the Holy Spirit."*
ACTS 2:38

*If you **declare with your mouth**, "Jesus is Lord," and **believe** in
your heart that God raised Him from the dead, you will be saved.*
ROMANS 10:9

*Yet to all who did **receive Him**, to those who **believed in His name**,
He gave the right to become children of God.*
JOHN 1:12

There is an outward and visible ceremony that accompanies our conversion, again akin to a wedding ceremony: baptism. While there is some debate among believers as to when, exactly, we become a Christian, covenant tells us the answer, as do the Scriptures: when the Holy Spirit enters us (Romans 8:9-11). At which point, though, does this occur? In the Christian community there are differing opinions, which we will not discuss at the moment. Some believe this occurs at the point of baptism while others believe this occurs as we commit our lives to God in prayer. The main thing is to be obedient to God's picture of this entire process, which includes baptism as soon as possible following a prayer of commitment. We want to commit ourselves to God in a face-to-face conversation, proclaim to the world that we are His, and celebrate and illustrate this via baptism as God instructs, following the example of Jesus. Then, we want to join God in proving why this matters.

What is your response to God's offer?

_____

_____

_____

_____

_____

_____

_____

_____

_____

_____

_____

_____

_____

_____

_____

_____

_____

_____

_____

_____

_____

_____

_____

_____

_____

_____

_____

_____

THE BOTTOM LINE: THERE IS A LINE

One reality sums up a major part of the message of this book. There is a line. Some things are on one side of this line, other things are on the other side. Also, there is a cloud of confusion that often obscures the location of this line, or even its existence. We have talked about many things on one side of this line or the other. In God's plan of covenant, it is intended that we learn to select things that are only on one side of that line. The second reality? We get to choose whether an item on either list ends up in our mind, heart, and life. And, just as we chose once, we can move in a different direction if we choose to do so; we can choose a different set of elements in our life, a different path under different leadership.

But there is more to this process than simply saying to oneself, "I am now going to choose only things on this side of this line," isn't there? In fact, saying in essence, "could and should," puts us right back where I found myself during the first year I was a Christian. OK, I see the goal, but how do I get there from here? What this involves are processes that occur as we consistently choose and implement a path. None of us know how to do this as we look at this path, standing in place, trying to decide if we want to walk this path. Nor do I even want you to make that decision at this moment. First, let me show you this path and where it leads. I will spend the next two volumes of this series showing you these decisions, this path, and the processes which lead us toward the life God intends for us. Which requires that we build the relationships that He intends that we build, and do it His way. In the next two volumes we will see how this is done.

For added clarity, let us review, in a visual format, a few of the items we have discussed that are on either side of this line. Allow me to begin this list. It will greatly benefit each of us to go through the process of finishing this list, of learning to see this distinction in every area of life. This effort will give us far greater clarity as to what our lives can, should, and will look like if we commit ourselves to God and His plan for our life.

God and His Kingdom	Satan and his Dominion
Pure White	Pure Black
Enter Covenant with God	Remain in Subjection to Satan
Spirit of Truth	Father of Lies
Reality	Misrepresentation of Reality
Truth	Lies and Deception
Love	Hatred, Abuse, Indifference
Union and Unity	Domination and Subjugation
Wisdom and Understanding	Confusion and Chaos
Faithfulness, Devotion	Manipulation, Betrayal
Marriage Covenant	Sexual Activity, Deny Covenant
Self-Developing and Giving	Self-Centered and Selfish
Duties, Responsibilities, Obligations	Rights
Discipline Leads to Freedom	Lack of Discipline Leads to Bondage
Build Relationships	Damage Relationships
Plan for Growth and Development	Plan for Slow or Rapid Destruction
Transformation	Bondage and Powerlessness
Fully Developed Life and Opportunities	Failure to Develop Self or Opportunities
Authentic	Image Without Substance
Good Character, Virtues	Destructive Character, Vices
Overcomer	Victim
Communion, Relationship, and Intimacy	Isolation and Loneliness
Joy, Peace, Satisfaction	Frustration, Emptiness, Futility
Issues Lead to Growth	Issues Lead to Resentment
Adversity Leads to Growth	Adversity Leads to Bitterness
Gratitude for One's Life	Resentment Over One's Life
Learn to Love as God Loves	Learn to Hate as Satan Hates
Follow God Because of Love and Truth	Follow Satan Because of Lies and Fear
Eternity in Communion with God	Eternally Separated from God
Life	Death

Endnotes

CHAPTER THREE

1. *Twelfth Planet: Book 1 of the Earth Chronicles,* Zechariah Sitchin, Harper, 2007.
2. "Sympathy for the Devil," Mick Jagger and Keith Richards, Decca Records, 1968.
3. *Reversing Hermon*, Dr. Michael Heiser, Defender Publishing, 2017.

CHAPTER FOUR

1. *Hitch*, Columbia Pictures, 2005.
2. *The Mask of Zorro,* Sony Pictures, 1998.
3. *The Blood Covenant: A Primitive Rite and Its Bearing on Scripture,* H. Clay Trumbull, original publication date 1885; Republished by Impact Christian Books, Inc., 1975.

CHAPTER FIVE

1. *Eternity in Their Hearts,* Don Richardson, Bethany House Publishers, 2006.

CHAPTER EIGHT

1. *Woodstock*, Joni Mitchell, A and M Studios, 1970.

CHAPTER NINE

1. *Time Magazine,* article by Alexandra Sifferlin, quoting *JAMA Pediatrics* meta analysis of thirty-nine studies, February 6, 2018.
2. allianceforreligiousfreedom.com\educate-yourself\america-dedicat-ed-to-God-in-1789
3. *U.S. News and World Reports*, article by J. Randy Forbes, May 7, 2009.
4. *Twentieth Century Atlas—Historical Body Count,* Matthew White, copyrights 1999–2010.
5. Celia Dhejne, et. al., "Long Term Follow-up of Transsexual Persons Undergoing Sex Reassignment Surgery: Cohort Study in Sweden." PLOS One; 2011; 6(2): e16885.
6. *The Washington Post Online,* "144 Years of Marriage and Divorce in the United States," Anna Swanson, June 23, 2015.
7. *USA Today Online,* "Fatherlessness Is Harder on Father's Day," Jayne O'Donnell and Sierra Lewter, June 15, 2018.
8. *The Washington Examiner,* "77% Black Births to Single Moms, 49% for Hispanic Immigrants," Paul Bedard, May 5, 2017.
9. *USA Today*, "Poll: Americans Don't Trust One Another," Connie Cass, November 30, 2013.